For my darling Granny

First published in Great Britain in 2005 by
PAVILION BOOKS

An imprint of **Chrysalis** Books Group plc

The Chrysalis Building
Bramley Road, London W10 6SP
www.chrysalisbooks.co.uk

Design and Layout © Pavilion Books, 2005
Text © Jenny Chandler, 2005
Photography © Jean Cazals, 2005
Map © Michael Maslan Historic Photographs/Corbis

Associate Editor: Kate Oldfield
Senior Editor: Lizzy Gray
Copy-editor: Kathy Steer
Designer: Gemma Wilson
Cover Design: Smith and Gilmore
Photographer: Jean Cazals
Home Economist: Jane Suthering
Stylist: Sue Rowlands

ISBN 1 86205 679 X

A CIP catalogue record for this book is available from the British Library.

10 9 8 7 6 5 4 3 2 1

Printed and bound by SNP Leefung, China.
Reproduction by Classicscan Singapore

Contents

Introduction

The Northern third of Spain, from Galicia's rocky Atlantic shores to the Mediterranean coast of Catalonia, is a glorious place to eat. This is the gastronomic heartland where more elegant sauces, elaborate braised dishes and flavoursome stews replace the rustic frying and roasting of the South.

The Basques and the Catalans have earned themselves reputations as the kings of the Iberian kitchen and there's a veritable Milky Way of Michelin stars to confirm the fact. The *Nueva Cocina*, literally new cuisine, is a lighter, more contemporary approach to local ingredients and dishes, and it's taken the North by storm. While many restaurant masterpieces are out of the reach of most home cooks, there are certain ideas and combinations that are perfectly possible and very delicious too. But, while hip cities such as Bilbao and Barcelona buzz with creativity and cutting-edge style, you need only to hop into your car, drive for an hour or two and you could be on another planet. Cowbells, cider, no-frills home cooking and a menu that's barely changed in the last millennium. Innovation and deep tradition live side by side.

Northern Spain is a land of astoundingly different cultures and landscapes and so the variety of regional cooking styles come as no surprise. Misty Galicia and Asturias with their legendary seafood and lush grazing for cattle could not seem further from the arid vineyards of Castille. A mushroom collector in the mountains of Navarre seems a world away from his Catalan brother wading through the river-delta rice paddies. The Celts, Greeks, Romans, Moors, French, Italians and even the modern tourists have all had a finger in the pie too. It's a melting pot if ever there was one. Add to this the inexhaustible Spanish passion for eating, drinking and socializing and you have a recipe for simply fabulous food.

In a country obsessed with all things edible, an interest in food is like a passport into the unknown. An excited discussion about tuna in a San Sebastián bar led to an impromptu cooking class in the steamy kitchen of an all men's *txoko* (private cooking society). I was welcomed with open arms at an annual mushroom "cook off" and given the dubious honour of sitting on a judging panel tasting over 50 dishes. On one occasion I drove for hours along tortuous mountain roads through the Pyrenees to a *butifarra* (sausage) competition, only to discover that *butifarra* was the name of a card game too. It's been a tremendous adventure gathering the recipes for this book. My car is invariably packed with oranges, nuts, cakes and bottles; it seems impossible to ever leave empty-handed. You're not even immune on a bicycle, as I discovered after some ill-timed praise for a certain, giant cauliflower that I had to balance my way home with.

I hope this book will give you a picture of Northern Spain with its wonderfully passionate people, and an understanding of the key ingredients that give the food its distinctive flavour. This is by no means a definitive collection of recipes. I've included some traditional classics and other less familiar dishes of the *Nueva Cocina.* There will be those who call out for pig's trotters (feet) and others who bemoan the lack of snail dishes. I've simply chosen the recipes that I love to cook, and that best reflect the way my Spanish friends eat today. I want to lure you into the kitchen with food for celebratory feasts and simple one-pot dishes to add to your everyday repertoire.

Author's Notes

Names of dishes and ingredients have been given in Spanish (Castellano) except in cases where they are better known by their local Basque or Catalan names.

Ingredients featured in the store-cupboard section are by no means the only stars of the Northern Spanish larder. Where are the tomatoes, aubergines (eggplants), saffron and almonds? I hear you cry. I have chosen to explore the ingredients that are often baffling to the outsider but vital to the understanding of Spanish cooking. Many of these are increasingly available at your local deli or store and will really give your food the true flavour of Spain.

The recipes are divided into different courses to make your life easier when putting together a menu. However, many of these are interchangeable and you shouldn't feel bound in any way by convention. A Spaniard may eat a hefty bean or pasta dish as a starter (appetizer) and follow this with a plate of meat, I certainly couldn't. Salads and vegetables will usually be served before a main course and not alongside it, but there's nothing to stop you doing otherwise. In short, enjoy the recipes and use them as you will.

I have taken the Duero and the Ebro Rivers as the southern boundary for my book rather than following political borders. It seemed more logical and the river banks are home to some of Spain's finest wines, fruits and vegetables.

The restaurants, bars and guesthouses featured are a very subjective and eclectic collection of places that have inspired or contributed many of the recipes in this book.

The Background

1

Galicia

Spain at its greenest and wettest; land of the Celts and the setting sun. For centuries Galicia was considered the end of the earth, Europe's most westerly tip where the Atlantic horizon just dropped off into space. The countryside is littered with dolmen, the traditional instrument is the *gaita* or bagpipe, and the local language Gallego owes more to neighbouring Portugal than it does to Castille. This is about as far from the Spanish stereotype of Flamenco and sangría that one could possibly stray.

Galicia is historically one of the poorest regions of Spain. Celtic tradition and inheritance laws have led to property being continually divided among heirs, leaving a landscape chopped into minute, almost unworkable parcels. It is said that a Galician does not use his handkerchief, he farms it. The countryside is highly populated and every inch of land is farmed; hillsides are terraced for vines, low granite walls surround vegetable patches striped with cabbages and turnips, and every blade of grass has a hungry cow's name on it. There are few commercial crops, one exception being the *pimiento de Padrón*, the lively little *tapas* pepper, which has found an enthusiastic following and is eaten all over Spain.

Curiosity found me peering over a Galician garden gate one day. Three hours later I was enjoying a plate of freshly fried piquant peppers while recording over 40 different types of produce that Luis and Maria Fuentes Garcia grow on their smallholding (small farm). The lack of frosts and consistent rainfall make Galicia a Garden of Eden for a grower with enough land; citrus fruits grow alongside potatoes, watermelons next to garlic. Maria introduced me to the family: three goats, two sheep, dozens of hens, rabbits and more rabbits and a motley selection of guard dogs. This year's pig lived down the hill; last year's was hanging in newspaper bundles from hooks on the kitchen ceiling. This is the old way of life, but even most town dwellers still tend their own small vegetable patch.

The Galicians have left their homeland in droves over the centuries, many unable to eke out a living from their tiny plot of land in this isolated corner of Spain. They were among Columbus's intrepid explorers, making their mark as fearless *conquistadores* then emigrating in great waves to the new promised land of Latin America. Some returned home, prodigal sons with fortunes and new high- yielding crops such as potatoes and maize (corn) to replace the rye and barley of their forefathers. Today the region is sliced by remarkable highways linking long lost Galicia with the rest of Spain. Many of the traditional granite houses have been rendered in lurid pastel shades or replaced with modern bungalows, but the old stone grain stores or *hórreos* still stand proudly alongside them, like Wendy houses on stilts, a constant reminder of the harsher times. Most lie empty but in times gone by corn cobs stacked up in the *hórreo* were used for vital bread supplies throughout the winter. Nowadays most of the corn goes straight to the cattle, producing highly prized meat and some really delicious cheeses, while bread is made with wheat and bought from the bakery.

We must look to the sea for Galicia's lifeblood. With a rugged coastline pierced by great estuaries, this is Spain's chief producer of shellfish and home to Vigo, one of the biggest fishing ports in Europe. Vigo's wholesale fish market is a mind-blowing affair: fleets of white vans (trucks) descend on the port in a 5 a.m. rush hour, by now the boats are on their way but the excited screams of seagulls announce the catch. Inside the cavernous sale rooms you must keep your wits about you, wading along the slippery floor, not a moment for flip-flops I discovered, dodging porter's trolleys and avoiding any sudden movements that might signal a sale to the bellowing auctioneers. The adrenaline and fizz is palpable even as a bystander: distorted shouts on screeching megaphones, big dealers bidding for prize lots to export or rush to the capital in time for lunch, market ladies snapping up the remains. Literally tons of fish are shifted every day. The surrounding Rías Baixas, or estuaries, are famous beauty spots, surrounded by vineyards but more importantly home to huge beds of shellfish for which Galicia is famed. Mussels, clams, cockles, oysters, scallops, shrimp, prawns, crab and so it goes on, the markets are brimming with succulent seafood. The north coast, the Costa de la Muerte, or Coast of Death, can look pretty uninviting and perilous even in mid-June (the bikini certainly never got a look in). Shabby fishing towns cling to the coastline, lonely ladies make lace, while faces lined like walnut shells tell of tough times on the trawlers. An air of hardship and melancholy pervades until you reach the vibrant port of La Coruña, with its glassed balconies and bustling fish bars. On midsummer night the huge beach is ablaze with bonfires, everyone is cooking sardines and baked potatoes then, at midnight, the scene takes on a distinctly pagan air as revellers hurdle the flames.

In the misty chestnut valleys of the inland provinces of Lugo and Orense, where *caldo* soup warms winter bellies, tales of sorcery and superstition live on. Sharing a bowl of blue flaming *queimada*, the locally distilled rocket-fuel liquor, is an eerie experience; faces glow in the darkness while ancient rhymes are chanted to ward off evil spirits. Who would believe you were just a stone's throw from one of the greatest shrines in Christendom, Santiago de Compostela? The jewel in Galicia's crown, the monumental city of Santiago is famed throughout Catholic Europe as Saint James the Apostle's final resting place. This Holy City, on equal footing with Rome and Jerusalem, has drawn thousands of pilgrims across northern Spain for the last millennium. Even a heretic would be hard pressed to resist the spirituality of the great cathedral.

Religion aside, Galician cuisine warrants a pilgrimage of its own. It is famed for its simplicity with local dishes such as octopus and paprika, freshly steamed seafood and flat *empanada* pies. But now, that cutting-edge chefs are creating exciting renditions of classic dishes, you can expect to see some Celtic magic in the kitchen too.

Asturias and Cantabria

Blue cheese, cider, salmon and kiwi fruit are not the first ingredients that spring to mind when you think of the Spanish kitchen, but this is Atlantic Spain, land of thick sea mists, snow-capped peaks and even the odd wild bear. The area is dominated by the Cantabrian mountain range in the south that hems in a narrow coastal strip along the Bay of Biscay. Although the regions of Asturias and Cantabria have little in common when it comes to social history and politics, both share the humid climate, similar terrain and thus the same local larder.

Cantabria prides herself on being the cradle of Iberian civilization with dozens of caves packed with Spain's most ancient art from the Paleolithic Period. The caves of Altamira are the icing (frosting) on the cake, decorated with bison, stags, boar and horses painted in the 12th century BC. Meanwhile, Asturias has a similarly impressive claim to fame, as the founding kingdom of today's Spain. When the Arabs raced across the Straits of Gibraltar in 711 (that's an easy date to remember, just think of the corner stores) they gradually conquered the entire peninsula bar Asturias, a seemingly insignificant region tucked over the rugged Cantabrian Mountains in the north. This last Christian enclave proved to be the Achilles heel of Muslim Spain, the launch pad for the *Reconquista* (the Christian crusade to retake Spain), a struggle that would last over 700 years, shaping both the Spanish psyche and diet.

Pork had always featured heavily on the northern Spanish menu, the pig being a relatively easy animal to keep, snaffling up anything and everything edible in its path. The pig became a symbol of Christian independence and a tool for unearthing unfortunate Jewish or Muslim "infidels" forbidden by religion to eat its meat. The *matanza*, or pig kill, became a rallying point celebrated throughout the newly conquered land. In the humid north curing hams was nigh impossible so the local means of meat preservation was the sausage. Today Asturias in particular, is renowned for its smoked *morcilla*, or black pudding (blood sausage) and spiced *chorizo* sausage, two of the key ingredients in the region's legendary dish the *Fabada* stew.

Traditionally the lifestyle was a harsh one, herding livestock down mountainsides, battling the Atlantic swell or, more recently, backbreaking mining in the coal and iron ore rich valleys. Such an energetic existence led to a local dish packed with protein, fat and carbohydrate, in the form of cured meat and beans, perfect to keep the body fuelled. Nowadays with our more sedentary lifestyles a plate of *Fabada*, commonly eaten as a starter (appetizer) in these parts, can lay you out for the rest of the day, as I discovered. The beans, the celebrated *fabes de la Granja*, fetch astounding prices, the only down side on the bean front so charmingly put by a local politician being that "they talk behind our backs!" Cantabria also has its fair share of one-pot wonders, the hefty *Cocido Montañés* with its selection of pig bits (nearly everything but the squeak), turnips, potatoes and of course more beans. A trip to the butcher's, the grocer's, the weekly market, even the supermarket will never be bean-free, the locals are bean crazy.

The great wall of the Cantabrian range that acted as a fortress against the Moors, also forms a natural barrier, trapping the Atlantic rain and resulting in plenty of lush, green pastureland. This is the dairy of Spain, one of the few regions where butter plays a role in the kitchen: there are milky puddings, creamy pastries and as for the cheeses, there are just dozens of delicious varieties. The star of the show is the internationally acclaimed *Cabrales* cheese, a mixture of cow, sheep and goat's milk with its web of pungent green mould, matured in the limestone caves of the Picos de Europa mountains. Visit the Monday market in the Cantabrian town of Potes and you'll find dozens of artisan *quesucos*, or small truckle cheeses, made by local farmers. In the Asturian capital, Oviedo, I sat down to the most gargantuan cheese feast in history, a wooden slab of about a dozen cheeses chosen from a possible 40 local varieties. I needed hungry friends and fast, I certainly found them among the gregarious cider drinkers. The street known as Calle Gascona in Oviedo, quite literally runs with cider. The Asturians consider themselves the world's greatest cider makers and there's no doubting that they are accomplished drinkers! This is not the sweetened fizzy stuff although a bit of that is made too, but scrumpy-style, natural cider that comes to life only when tipped from alarming heights to create a little froth. The professionals don't waste much but a bunch of revellers on the street can create quite a tide. The waft of fermenting apples pervades *sidrerías* (cider bars) and back streets of the local towns year round, reaching a crescendo during the apple-pressing season in late autumn (fall) when merely breathing the cider country air feels intoxicating.

The heavily industrialized valleys and big cities of the region seem a world apart but inevitably they have taken their toll. The rivers of Asturias and Cantabria used to teem with wild salmon and trout, and once such fish were considered very ordinary, everyday fare. Nowadays fly-fishing is an expensive and highly controlled sport and river fish an elusive luxury. Elvers, those tiny eels, stars of the restaurant menu, were once collected by the thousand in river mouths, without a second thought. Today, owing to overfishing, and some pollution, numbers have dwindled and of course prices have soared.

Down on the coast the seafood is superb, unadorned and exquisitely fresh. One of the best places to sample it is the gritty fishing quarter of Santander, the Barrio Pesquero. It's not a place you would stumble upon, being about as far as you can get from the swish *belle époque* villas and sweeping beaches for which the city is famed. The Barrio Pesquero is a strip of unassuming restaurants vying for business, with pans of Paella bubbling on the pavements (sidewalks) and vociferous chefs. Salty locals rub shoulders with suited businessmen savouring the catch of the day. Locals understand and await the various fish seasons with anticipation. In July Gijón's waterfront bars were plastered with hand written signs, "*Hay sardinas*", and that taste of grilled sardine and a first swig of cool cider has still not left me. The fish of the region is legendary, be it the Asturian line-caught hake from the port of Cudilleros or the Cantabrian cured anchovy from Colindres, a mere mention is guaranteed to leave the Spanish gastronome drooling.

The Basque Country

A corpulent taxi driver in San Sebastián once announced rather proudly that while the rest of Spain eats to survive the Basques survive to eat, a fact that I would not dispute after a few months of trouser tightening research. From the scores of Michelin-starred restaurants to the unassuming country bars I have never witnessed such a passion for cooking, such a respect for quality ingredients or such gargantuan appetites in my entire life. Thank heavens for all the macho rowing regattas, the tug-of-wars and Flintstone-style boulder lugging championships or we would be looking at a land of super tubs.

The tempestuous Bay of Biscay has provided the local cuisine with many of its key ingredients. The Basques have always been great sailors; in the old days they combed the high seas in search of whale and cod and were some of

The Asturians consider themselves the world's greatest cider makers and there's no doubting that they are accomplished drinkers!

the greatest navigators on earth. It was, after all, a Basque, Sebastián Elcano, who became the first man to sail around the world. Today the ground floor of the Ribera market in Bilbao is a testament to the local love affair with seafood, an entire floor packed with stunningly fresh fish. A Basque is not content that his fish be just fresh, he wants to know where and how it was caught. The local line-caught hake will fetch exorbitant prices compared with its netted, imported counterpart and most will never make it to the market as the restaurant chefs will have snapped it up. A keen chef will often be looking for a particular cut, the *kokotxas* or hake throats are particularly celebrated for their gelatinous texture. When it comes to tuna, those in the know will be looking for the *mendreska*, the succulently oily flesh from the belly. Tiny meticulously filleted anchovy are lined up ready for the frying pan and the popular, mossy looking snow crabs rustle around in their boxes. Then of course there's the salt cod, an institution and a subject for discussion in its own right (see pages 32–34).

The gastronomic heartbeat of Spain, the *Pais Vasco*, or *Euskadi* as it is known to its inhabitants, is for the most part a damp and mountainous place with plenty of rich pastureland. The heavy industry, and there is plenty of it, is crammed tightly into deep river valleys, and cities turn into rural outback in a matter of moments. Just look at Bilbao, where factories, defunct shipyards, proud avenues and the legendary Guggenheim Museum crowd the banks of the Nervión River. Take a glance above the buildings and on the horizon you will see ancient Basque farmhouses perched serenely like Alpine chalets, and sheep quietly grazing, oblivious to the buzz down below. Follow a small lane through the valleys and you are surrounded by emerald slopes, like folds of card table baize, dotted with sheep, goats and cattle. Here traditional long-haired *latxa* sheep produce a glorious cheese, Idiazábal, and sheep's milk junket is a popular dessert. Lamb, kid and pork are all consumed with gusto, the Basques love their meat, but it is beef that tops the bill. Steak-lovers flock to Tolosa, a busy industrial town surrounded by abundant pastures, to savour the *chuletón*, a well-hung hunk of delicious meat, cooked over coals, often weighing in at over a kilo!

The *Vascos* like their vegetables too. Many star players were brought back from the Americas where intrepid Basques were some of the key figures among the Spanish *conquistadores*. Peppers, tomatoes, potatoes, beans and cocoa were quickly adopted and the local storecupboard (pantry) would be bereft today without them. In summer, markets are filled with delicious misshapen tomatoes, in autumn (fall) balconies hang with curtains of red peppers drying on strings, while winter is time to tuck into glossy black beans from Tolosa or the famous Alava potatoes. The old favourites still have a role to play too: slow cooked onions, delicately fried garlic, sweated leeks and steamed cabbage and of course there are mushrooms. Wild mushrooms are worshipped here. Woodland roads scattered with empty cars bear witness to scores of keen-eyed gatherers scouring the undergrowth for the *perretxiku*, the spring time St George's mushroom or some other jewel. The woodlands are home to wild game too: deer and boar are favourite meats for country gatherings; wood pigeon, woodcock and even thrush finish up on the table too. There's also the odd domestic pig left to snuffle through the leaves, resulting in *chorizos* and black pudding (blood sausage) of outstanding flavour.

What to drink with all this fabulous local produce? Well there are plenty of good local wines too. On the coast, fresh seafood is washed down with young, acidic white wine with a hint of fizz, the cheek-sucking *txacolí*, while inland the Basque territory stretches south into Rioja wine country and produces some of the best reds around, ideal with the heftier carnivorous menu. There is also cider served straight from the barrel, which is fizzier than the Asturian variety and equally delicious.

There is no doubt that the Basques are blessed with some of Europe's finest raw materials but it's the resolve and resourcefulness of the people that has created the show-stopping cuisine. They are fiercely proud of their identity, and just as they have preserved their ancient language and customs so they have clung to their own culinary traditions. Certain recipes are considered almost untouchable among traditionalists, many of whom can be found in the *txokos* or gastronomic brotherhoods. These predominantly male societies have industrial-scale kitchens and unpretentious dining halls where men from all walks of life gather to cook together, chat, eat and drink but above all to savour local food. Age-old dishes are reproduced time and time again, with subtle seasoning adjustments or perhaps a twist in the technique but, God forbid, were some Philistine to introduce a mango or an ostrich steak; that would be pure sacrilege.

At the other end of the spectrum are the distinguished chefs of the *Nueva Cocina* who enjoy cult status both in their homeland and on the international restaurant circuit. Names such as Arzak, Subijana and Berasategui roll off the critic's tongue for they have revolutionized Spanish cooking. "Nouvelle Cuisine", that decidedly French phenomenon of the 1970s was re-interpreted by the Basques, many of who had trained in the kitchens of the legendary French chefs. Basque cooking, with its traditional sauces, had always been influenced by its northern neighbour, hardly surprisingly, since three of the seven Basque speaking provinces lie over the border. The *Nueva Cocina* dissected the ancient cuisine, re-inventing classics with lighter, fresher results with presentation becoming a key feature. Creativity and innovation hit the big time and suddenly going to a restaurant could be a theatrical event entertaining all the senses.

Today a trip to the star-studded food Mecca of San Sebastián is a perfect introduction to the Basque food scene. You could visit the old town and lean up at a bar loaded with so many traditional *pinchos*, the local nibble on a stick, that there is no room even to rest a glass. You might rub shoulders with slick Basque bankers in chic bars serving the *cocina en miniatura*, minuscule re-creations of elaborate dishes that disappear in a bite. You could dine at old family restaurants serving unpretentious classics or internationally acclaimed designer haunts where your dessert may just explode under your nose. Wherever you go you will encounter an indisputable infatuation with food. Just take loose clothing, you may well expand

Navarre and Aragón

Ancient Arab oases and modern mountain ski resorts; scorching summers and bitter winters shrouded in a seemingly endless freezing fog. Wildly extreme describes the character of Navarre and Aragón, the two landlocked provinces that stretch from the Pyrenean mountains to the flat Ebro river valley. Despite their distinctly different cultural roots the two regions share a conservative cooking tradition with similar local ingredients The Basques would claim Navarre as their own, and many of the lush northern valleys are home to their beret-wearing, Euskera-speaking, flag-flying patriots. Yet, a glance at the plains to the south of the capital, Pamplona, and the Moorish ancestry of the people is undeniable. Meanwhile the Aragonese are historically linked to their eastern neighbour Catalonia with whom they once shared a vast Mediterranean empire that stretched as far as Athens. Today the province feels like a harsh outpost with none of the contemporary edge of the coast.

We will begin in the mountains where game has always been top of the menu. *Jabalí* or wild boar is particularly popular and fairly common too, as I discovered when I nearly caught one on my bumper on a misty mountain track. There is venison; traditionally stewed for hours with rich sauces but now often served as a melt-in-the-mouth fillet; divine. Luckless doves are caught in nets; there are plenty of partridge and a few pheasant and woodcock as well. The mountains are also home to *setas*, wild mushrooms (see pages 37–38) and I was amazed to discover some truffle magic too, in the dusty Aragonese town of Graus. The bar of the Hotel de Lleida, seems a most unlikely spot, but on a Monday evening the 1970s formica interior takes on an air of intrigue. Not a truffle in sight but all manner of dealing and the odd whiff of trickery as collectors and buyers try to outsmart each other at one of Spain's largest truffle markets. This may not be the exalted Italian gem but the local black winter truffle can still fetch up to 500 a kilo, when the market is right.

Upland streams are legendary trout waters, although you are more likely to encounter farmed fish in the markets nowadays, nevertheless old local recipes using ham or almonds are superb. Salmon, carp and eels feature strongly in nostalgic fishermen's tales too but appear on the table with rather less regularity. Wild wooded valleys are rich picking grounds for nuts and berries. In Navarre locals collect the sloes, a recipe for painfully scratched wrists but worth the trouble when added to aniseed- (anise-) flavoured liquor along with a few coffee beans and cinnamon to make the delicious digestive, *pacharán*.

Further south you reach rough, scrubby pastureland and misshapen fields of alfalfa and corn. Huge flocks of hardy looking sheep, reared for wool, milk and meat are a familiar sight herded by lonesome shepherds and their hairy hounds. Sheep have been a mainstay of the economy and the diet for centuries. The familiar piggy expression, "everything but the squeak", could be changed to "everything but the bleat": there aren't many omissions in Zaragoza's market. You'll find lamb's heads, brains, tongues, bundles of intestines, livers, kidneys and even the tails that star in a local dish named "mountain asparagus". Nothing is left to the imagination, with pearly white feet lined up as if ready to dance a can-can. For the more squeamish among you there is plenty of delicious roasting lamb, the tiny milk-fed lamb with its pale and tender flesh is a great favourite cooked in the huge igloo-like wood ovens.

Lowland hills are covered with almond blossom like pale confetti in the spring and the nuts play an irreplaceable role in the kitchen in sweets (candies) and savouries alike. There are great swathes of olives too, primarily grown for the all-important oil. Flatter land is increasingly used for vines and with new investment and modern techniques Navarra and Aragón are really hitting their wine pedigreed neighbours of Ribera del Duero and Rioja, to the west.

Once you reach the Ebro River you are among the Mudéjar towns where the converted Moors stamped their style on the Christian conqueror's buildings. Even the churches often resemble mosques with their intricate brickwork, mosaics and horseshoe arches. Perhaps the greatest legacy of those industrious people is the vast network of irrigation channels that transformed an otherwise desert-like plain into one of Spain's most productive vegetable gardens. Today the region is known for white asparagus, beans, artichokes, tomatoes, lettuces and of course the legendary *piquillo* peppers. These roasted peppers are sold in cans and jars and used all over Spain stuffed with seafood, salt cod, cheese or whatever else the local storecupboard (pantry) has to offer. More unusual vegetables such as cardoons, a type of thistle, are grown too. They look most bizarre, swaddled in brown paper sacks with their spiky leaves protruding. Borage, a pre-Roman vegetable, is currently enjoying a comeback. Peeling the furry stalks is a housewife's nightmare, turning fingers black in an instant, but the succulent stems have a wonderful texture when cooked and a flavour reminiscent of cucumber. Espalier fruit trees line the river valleys, looking like sad tortured skeletons in the winter fog but in summer they are laden with peaches, apricots, cherries, plums and figs. Aragón is famous for its candied fruits and poached peaches, a way of conserving the bounty through the long winter months. The Arabs even managed to grow rice in the irrigated valleys, the rice that turns up nowadays in the distinctly non-Muslim *morcilla*, black pudding (blood sausage), along with a few spices.

Pork is popular, as it is everywhere in Spain. The thin *chistorra* sausage, spiced with paprika is a favourite while the cured hams from Teruel in southern Aragón are legendary. Snails creep on to the scene after any rainfall keeping country folk busy scouring the verges. They can be snapped up in the market too, where they hang in yellow nylon nets. They are popular in rice dishes and often combined with rabbit. Salt cod, the great fast-day favourite, features on the local menu too in a dish attributed to the old muleteers, shredded up with lashings of garlic and local peppers. A relative newcomer to the table is duck in every delicious form possible: Navarre currently produces delicious *foie gras*, *magret*, *confit* and all manner of specialities poached from her Gallic neighbours and it seems the Spanish just can't get enough.

The local diet is first and foremost no-nonsense food, created out of the need for nourishing calories to ward off the long winter chill. Now with more sedentary lifestyles some lighter dishes can be savoured in the more contemporary restaurants, though once out of the bigger towns those may be as evasive as the truffles.

Old Castille and Rioja

The vast, landlocked plains of Old Castille and Rioja are fringed by the Cantabrian Mountains. This is the northerly extent of the *Meseta*, or the high plain, where contrary to Eliza Dolittle's proclamations the rain does not mainly fall. This land is a world apart from its damp Atlantic neighbours to the north, and the transformation is startlingly abrupt. Whether you crawl over a steep mountain pass or emerge from a seemingly endless road tunnel the scorched, rugged terrain and cloudless skies will come as a shock. Yet, more arresting, perhaps, is the architecture. Gone are the picturesque Basque chalets and the Asturian farmsteads with their wooden balconies, replaced by

The entire region is peppered with imposing castles and it is easy to imagine the likes of the warrior El Cid galloping across this sparsely populated land.

bleak houses built bang on the roadside. A moment too long dusting the doorknob and you'll be swept away by a juggernaut as it thunders through town. The same no-frills approach applies to the traditional kitchen, where elaborate sauces and new wave sophistication tend to be treated with suspicion.

Today's province of Castilla and León does in fact stretch beyond the Duero riverbanks to the south, but where do I stop? I have chosen the line of the Duero and Ebro Rivers as my culinary boundary, a historical frontier that marked the edge of Christian territory for centuries during the lengthy process of driving out the Moors. The entire region is peppered with imposing castles and it is easy to imagine the likes of the warrior El Cid galloping across this sparsely populated land. More difficult to picture are the great forests and bears that once covered the scorched plain; slashed down by invaders, felled for Armadas and cleared to plant great fields of grain, there is little greenery left today. This is the Spanish breadbasket, where wheat has been grown extensively since Roman times. The endless fields of grain and distant horizons resemble the American Midwest.

Areas of rough grassland that resemble a savannah are home to huge flocks of sheep whose dusty coats seem to meld into the countryside. A meagre diet of herbs and dry grasses results in small quantities of intensely flavoured milk and some fabulous cheeses. When it comes to meat, lamb is top of the menu and the chief claim to fame is the baby milk-fed lamb. Traditional restaurants or *asadores* have wood-fired ovens where their tiny limbs are slow roasted until the meat does, quite literally, melt in your mouth. The word squeamish does not feature in the local vocabulary and offal (variety meats) reigns supreme. Not one to turn down a taste of anything, I must say the lamb's intestines, the *embuchado*, wound up like a ball of wool, did just about push me over the edge. Beef is eaten too, though on a smaller scale – one speciality is the *cecina* or cured beef; sliced paper thin with some good olive oil it is quite delicious.

Pork features, of course, in this very traditional Spanish larder. There is the celebrated suckling pig or *cochinillo*. *Chorizo* sausage and marinated loin are popular too, but in León it is the *morcilla* or black pudding (blood sausage) that tops the bill. Not for the faint hearted, it is served in the bars of the *Barrio Húmedo*, like a pile of deep purple porridge to be scooped up with bread. What a place that "humid quarter" is: teeming with students and lively drinkers, it is one of the few spots in Spain where your *corto*, or short drink, will come accompanied with a complimentary bite. The narrow streets and arcaded squares are packed with *tapas* bars, each with a speciality, guaranteed to draw in the crowds. Those in the know will slug back their drink, demolish their *tapas*, throw their napkin to the floor and move on in a matter of minutes. It is like one gigantic pub-crawl, without the brawl. All that nourishing nibbling sees that the alcohol does not go to your head.

Glancing at a map you will soon see a trail of cities, towns and small villages running across the regions of Castille and Rioja from east to west, like a chain. This is the Camino de Santiago, the Way of St James, trodden for centuries by the penitent in search of salvation. The path is still packed with pilgrims, some in search of spiritual enlightenment, others in pursuit of very firm thighs. One day, after a particularly extravagant meal in a restaurant alongside the pilgrim's path, two ancient ladies, witnessing my postprandial stagger, hailed me with much praise and encouragement: *"Venga valiente"*

"Keep it up, brave one". I just hope they did not spot me as I slunk shamefully back to my car. Along with soaring cathedrals and churches crowned with storks' nests, countless monasteries and convents sprang up along the way. Nuns have always been the nation's great confectioners and there are dozens of different biscuits (cookies), cakes, Moorish-style pastries and sweeties (candies) on offer. One very traditional sweet (candy) is the *yema*, an egg yolk and sugar combination that many attribute to the surplus yolks of the wine trade, where only the egg whites were used to filter the wine.

Now we are, without a doubt, dealing with Spain's most illustrious wine region. The Duero and Ebro river valleys, with their more moderate microclimates, are home to many world-famous vineyards. In Rioja, the Ebro valley is also an immensely fertile vegetable patch where tomatoes, peppers, artichokes and cardoons all grow with the aid of large-scale irrigation. Also renowned for its produce is the Bierzo valley in the west of Castilla y León where huge sweet (bell) peppers, figs and chestnuts abound. But maybe the key ingredients of the *Meseta* are the legumes. Chickpeas, lentils and beans, spiced up with a little pork have seen many a poor household through the bitter winters and the *cocido*, or stew, in its various guises is a staple. Once in a while a little Arab spicing will surprise the taste buds, a reminder of the centuries of Moorish rule.

Some areas of more mountainous terrain are still covered in trees, home to game such as the populous partridge, to wood pigeons and the occasional deer. Such woodland has become an increasingly popular hunting ground for the dozens of different species of mushroom you may now find on the menu in more up-beat restaurants. Creative chefs, often disciples of the Basque and Catalan kitchen deities, are returning to their home turf and spreading the great mycological passion. They are also bringing fresher, lighter flavours to the cities and larger towns but they have a way to go before they persuade the average punter away from his hefty fare: as one local put it, "*no me llena*" it just doesn't fill me up!

Catalonia

This north-eastern corner of Spain has the most incredible diversity of landscape and climate. In the north the Pyrenees rise to about 3,000 metres/ 10,000 feet and spend much of the year capped with snow. Inland are parched, almost desert-like plains, bitterly cold in winter and like a barbecue in the summer months. Meanwhile the mild, humid south coast reaches down to the seemingly infinite flat expanses of the Ebro delta. You are as likely to find roast goose and turnips on the local menu as black rice with squid. The vast variety of local ingredients has led to some fabulous combinations: wild duck and oranges live side by side in the south creating that classic marriage, which the Catalans claim as their own. Meanwhile, up on the north coast, bizarre combinations of lobster and chicken or rabbit and squid, called "*mar i muntanya*", are cooked with quite astonishingly delicious results.

The Catalan people have their own language and customs. Forget the throbbing Spanish guitars and the clatter of gypsy heels, here you find rope-soled *espardenyes*, or espadrilles, jumping and stepping to the measured

rhythms of pipes and drums. The food of the region is equally distinctive, ever evolving and certainly the most progressive in Spain. One chef termed the modern cuisine of Catalonia as "glocal", a fusion of global and local ingredients and techniques. In fact this assimilation of new flavours has been a trait of the Catalans for centuries.

Catalonia is certainly one of the most visited and best-known regions of Spain. Tourists flock in their millions to bake on her sun-kissed Mediterranean beaches and Barcelona is celebrated as one of the most stylish and dynamic cities in Europe. This is no new thing either: the Catalans have received wave after wave of visitors, each adding to the cultural and culinary melting pot. Greeks, Romans, Arabs, French, Andalucians and even the modern day tourists have all left their mark. Add to this the fact that Catalonia and her neighbour Aragón were once the great rulers of the Mediterranean with an empire that, at its height, took in Sardinia, Genoa, Naples and Athens, and you end up with one of the most eclectic kitchens in Europe.

Olive oil, bread and wine, that holy trinity of the ancient Mediterranean kitchen, still reign supreme in Catalonia. Some of Spain's greatest wines come from the region and the local snack, *pa amb tomàquet*, (see page 48) is nothing more than a slice of crusty bread doused in fabulous olive oil with a little salt and tomato flesh. The Greeks introduced the salting of anchovies, an industry that lives on to this day, with the Costa Brava town of L'Escala famous throughout Spain for its preserved fish. You can visit old warehouses, one street back from the ice cream parlours and the tourist scrum to find rows of ladies at trestle tables carefully layering the fresh anchovies in salt just as they would have done centuries ago.

The Arabs have left an unquestionable mark on local dishes where fruit and nuts are combined with meat and poultry, reminiscent of North Africa's tagines. Dishes such as duck with pears or figs, Christmas turkey stuffed with apricots and pine kernels (pine nuts), and apples filled with pork and sultanas (golden raisins) are commonplace. This love of mixing sweet and savoury finds its way into distinctly non-Muslim preparations too such as the unusual *coca de llardons*, a flat bread topped with sugar and pork crackling. Aubergines (eggplants), artichokes and of course rice, that turns the muddy Ebro delta a tropical shade of green, are Arab legacies too.

Many dishes share roots with their neighbours over the French border, *samfaina*, a key Catalan sauce, is very similar to the Provençal *ratatouille*, *allioli* is French *aïoli* minus the egg, the *coca* flat bread is pretty similar to *pissaladière* and so it goes on. Naturally every Catalan will remind you that this is because much of the French south was part of their extensive empire many moons ago. Likewise, Italian dishes such as *cannelloni* and *macaroni*, have become *canalons* and *macarrons* and have been fully fledged members of the local repertoire for well over a century. New World ingredients such as peppers, tomatoes, potatoes and chocolate were snapped up and absorbed by the Catalans into their own distinctive cooking style such as the way that chocolate is still commonly added to many savoury dishes in the typical *picada* seasoning. Today Asian exotica such as soy sauce, ginger, mangoes and seaweed are making their way on to the hip restaurant menus. Give it a few years and they will probably make their way into the home kitchen too, adding to rather than replacing the local fare.

It would certainly be a mistake to imagine the entire region caught up in a culinary revolution as many Catalans love the unadulterated food of their forefathers. The annual *caragolada*, snail "fest", in Lleida is the biggest gastronomic gathering in Spain, attracting thousands of enthusiasts, who consume more than twelve tons of the molluscs (mollusks) in just three days. There are no fancy touches here, just barbecued snails with garlic and paprika or the odd snail stew. Of course it's really an excuse for a very large party, there's plenty of revelry too, along with a bit of snail racing to keep the children happy. Ancient pursuits such as mushroom gathering and hunting are incredibly popular and locals are ever eager to share their passion with a curious and excitable foreigner. One winter's day having spotted a group of proud hunters with a hairy wild boar, I obviously demonstrated just a bit too much interest for I was duly rewarded with its curly tail, hot off the carcass and quite the thing for the hire car. Well it would beat fluffy dice any day.

Meanwhile, fishermen continue to cook time-honoured dishes and many housewives' shopping lists have remain unchanged over the decades.

The restaurant scene is quite another story. In recent years Catalonia has caused a huge stir on the international gourmet scene and the area is glowing with Michelin stars. Just as the Catalan character is a said to be a mix of *seny* and *rauxa*, roughly translated as level-headed sense and capriciousness, so the professional kitchen is packed with contrasts. The two gurus of the kitchen, Santi Santamaria and Ferran Adrià, are like chalk and cheese. While Santamaria is producing glorious contemporary dishes that are rooted in classical cuisine, Adrià is out to turn tradition on its head. His surreal menu includes dishes that would astound Harry Potter, black truffle lollipops (popsicles) and Paella rice-krispies, inventions that have earned him the title of the Dalí of the kitchen.

How the Spanish Eat and Shop

The typical Spanish day is punctuated by breaks for meals and nibbles. Unlike many of us in the frantic western world a Spaniard always stops to eat. It's a matter of great importance and, after all, it's a time for socializing too. The idea of sneaking a chocolate bar, or eating a packet of crisps (potato chips) on the run, just doesn't fit into the Spanish psyche.

The day begins with *el desayuno*, a light breakfast, usually a strong coffee and a sweet pastry at around 8 or 9 a.m. Many have their breakfast in the local bar, catching up with the papers and local gossip. Of course there are exceptions, particularly in rural areas and above all on market day, when it's not uncommon to see old guys downing brandy or wine and demolishing plates of hefty stew and offal at 9 a.m.

By mid-morning the bars and cafés begin to buzz again, it's time for a quick *tentenpié*, quite literally a "keep you on your feet". In Galicia you might nibble a small slice of *empanada*, flat pie, while in Catalonia it might be a slice of *pa amb tomàquet*, tomato bread, with a slice of ham.

By one o'clock the tantalizing smells of freshly cooked food waft on to the streets from the *tapas* bars, luring workers in for a quick snack and a snifter before they rush off for lunch. Croquettes, meatballs or even perhaps a touch of *foie gras*, it all depends on the locale.

La comida, or lunch, is the big meal of the day and begins around 2 p.m. although often much later at weekends. Those who live close enough to their workplace hurry back to the roost for some good home cooking. Local restaurants all offer a three-course *menú del día*, or set menu, at remarkably reasonable prices. The dishes will naturally vary from region to region but everyone seems to manage a pretty substantial lunch. Starters (appetizers) are often fillers such as beans or rice, then comes a plate of fish, meat or poultry, followed by a simple dessert. In recent years, I am relieved to say, I've noticed a few lighter options creeping into these set meals. Maybe a result of an increasing female clientele as more women go out to work or, perhaps, a preoccupation with expanding waistlines?

Lunchtimes do vary according to your profession and the *siesta* is certainly not as common as it is down in the south. However every Spaniard still considers a decent lunch break as his birthright and the suggestion of a sandwich in the office would be absolutely unthinkable. This could be the moment for a slice of plum cake, that rather bizarre Spanish misnomer, a sponge with no hint of a plum – you might find a sultana (golden raisin) if you're lucky.

There's always the possibility of a *merienda*, or teatime snack, between 5 and 7 p.m. The *pastelerías* of the Basque country and Catalonia are certainly quite an inviting prospect if you're really determined to burst your seams, or you've somehow missed out on one of the other half dozen eating sessions of the day.

By eight o'clock people have, rather miraculously, worked up an appetite again. It's time for *tapas*. It could be one or two, snatched with a tipple and a bit of banter with work colleagues before going home, or an appetizer to wake up the taste buds before a dinner out on the town. In Catalonia *tapas* are a fairly new addition to the eating scene. Meanwhile, in the Basque country, bar counters bow under myriads of exotic nibbles, or *pinchos*.

Supper or dinner is late by foreign standards and most restaurants don't even think of opening their doors before nine. Tourist traps tend to be more flexible but then they're probably only reheating the lunchtime paella anyway. Back at home families tend to eat a light meal: perhaps a salad or an omelette (omelet) followed by fish and then fruit. Eating out, however, is quite another matter: I've yet to sit down with friends before 10 p.m. and then, after yet another gargantuan feast, I rarely manage to order my stretcher home to bed before midnight.

When it comes to shopping the average Spaniard spends a far greater proportion of his income, and his time, on food than most of us. But, it would be wrong to paint a picture of an entire nation pottering around local market stalls, however romantic the notion. Supermarkets bustle with busy shoppers, just as they do everywhere else in the world. Yet, thankfully, the aisles of microwave meals and T.V. dinners are happily absent replaced by selections of more basic, raw ingredients. The Spanish do still cook.

Town centres are packed with independent stores for the more discerning shopper. There are the customary butchers, fishmongers, bakers and greengrocers. Then you may find specialist purveyors of salt cod, cured meat, cheese, shellfish or legumes. Many of these stores sell local goods that you're unlikely to find in the next region, let alone abroad. Spanish food is still delightfully provincial. Cake stores, or *pastelerías*, are crammed with regional specialities or sweets of the season, many reserved for particular Saint's days and *fiestas*. There is no real tradition of home baking and people bearing beautiful parcels of pastries and cakes are a common sight at weekends. These packages are miraculous works of origami-style wrapping with ribbons and bows. They might contain a sweet doughy *coca*, a cream filled "gypsy's arm", *brazo de gitana,* or a selection of truly exquisite biscuits (cookies).

Daily markets still thrive in most of the bigger towns and cities. Some have majestic iron and glass structures: food cathedrals packed with seasonal bounty. Whenever I visit Barcelona one of my first stops is the Boquería market. You needn't open your eyes you can virtually smell the season. The citrus scents of winter, the fresh damp leaves of spring, the perfume of soft fruits in the summer heat and the wood-must wafts of autumn (fall) mushrooms. Locals celebrate the arrival of asparagus, of sardines, of fresh beans and figs. Keen cooks will seek out this season's pulses, tomatoes from a particular valley or the freshest curd cheese.

You can't beat the weekly markets that transform sleepy, rural towns into buzzing hives of activity. Bars and cafés are packed; it's the social highlight of the week. There are the full-time traders that tip up with their huge white vans. They do the circuit, a market a day, travelling from town to town. They sell anything from cheeses and hams to wellington boots, tablecloths and lingerie. But, most exciting are the huddles of locals, perched on folding chairs surrounded by their baskets and boxes. They bring home-laid eggs, a few cut flowers, wild mushrooms, herbs from the hedgerows, plaited (braided)strings of sweet onions, misshapen tomatoes. All seasonal, all natural, all mouth-wateringly fresh – it's an epicure's paradise.

Opening hours can be baffling for foreigners but suit the local lifestyle. When it comes to stores and markets, there's no point in being the early bird, the Spanish are night owls and nothing really gets going before 10 a.m. Then it's all go, before everyone shuts down again for lunch at 1.30 or 2 p.m. It's quite logical, who'd want to be out shopping when you should be tucking into a full-scale lunch. A sortie on to the midday streets of Spain in summer will leave you feeling cremated in any case. By 5 p.m. the town centres come to life again, leaving plenty of time to run all the errands before the shutters close at 8 p.m.

Even those who are hard pressed for time can pick up something to throw in the pan: freshly made croquettes, stuffed chicken breasts, ready cooked chickpeas, there's plenty of pre-prepared food available from small stores or market stalls. It's convenience food with a difference; it still has the personal touch and isn't plastered with preservatives.

Food goes far beyond something merely to fill a gap in the stomach or keep you going until the next meal. In Spain eating is a passion, a pastime and a great excuse to meet up with family and friends.

A Few Useful Utensils

The average home kitchen is not stacked with all sorts of specialist gadgetry but there are a few pieces of equipment that will certainly help you to cook like a Spaniard.

The **cazuela** is the most useful dish in the Northern Spanish kitchen. This flat, terracotta dish, with its low, straight sides is the original, all-purpose cooking vessel. You can use it over a gas flame (but not an electric ring, I'm afraid), it's ovenproof and, what's more, wonderful for serving food at the table. The tiny individual *cazuelas* are ideal for Crema Catalana (see page 145) or *tapas*. I always return from Spain laden with the things, in every size, although you can sometimes find them back home too. I could not be without my clay *cazuelas*. Be sure to cure your *cazuela* before you use it the first time around. Soak it in water for a few hours, then fill it with water and place it over a low heat, or in the oven for 10 minutes. A *cazuela* will not last a lifetime, but it is less likely to crack if you always warm it under hot water before placing it over a heat or in a hot oven. Large cast-iron dishes can be used instead: look for something flameproof, ovenproof and attractive enough to put on the table.

Most of you probably don't own a **paella pan**, but nor do many of my Spanish friends and unless you plan to make *paella* your regular weekend treat you probably don't need one either. A very large frying pan (skillet) or sauté pan will do.

The **mortar and pestle** is a must in the traditional kitchen. The bigger, the better – a bowl of about 15 cm/6 inch in diameter is ideal. Those thimble-size affairs sold in most kitchen stores just won't do. You will find it invaluable for crushing seasonings and spices and in Catalan cuisine it's indispensable for sauces too.

The **pasapurés** is best known by its French name, the *mouli-legumes*. This fabulously useful piece of equipment has practically passed the British kitchen by. I have no idea why; it's by far the best way to mash a potato. The *pasapurés* is a rotary sieve (strainer), it does the work of a food processor but miraculously leaves skins and pips behind. It's ideal for all kinds of soups, purées and jams (jellies).

Small metal moulds are really useful for individual puddings. Mine have a 200 ml/7 fl oz/scant 1 cup capacity and are ideal for cooked desserts. The conductivity of metal makes them ideal for gelatine-set mousses, where a quick dip in hot water will be enough to melt and loosen the pudding. China ramekins or cups could be used instead.

A **metal ring** or **cookie cutter** of approximately 12 cm/15 inches in diameter is handy for presenting salads and dishes such as Tuna Tartare (see page 70). Just place the ring on your serving plate, pile in the ingredients (you may need to press gently to retain the form), then remove the ring. Your dish will now have structure and height.

The Storecupboard
and Cellar

Peppers

Peppers play a key role in the Northern Spanish kitchen and their huge variety can be bewildering to the uninitiated. There are dozens of different peppers, ranging from the minuscule chilli (chili) pepper with attitude to the sweet and mellow bell pepper. They appear in so many guises: fresh, roasted, pickled, dried and ground. Spanish peppers are an indispensable ingredient in my larder and soon you may find them irresistible too.

Nowadays it seems almost inconceivable that the pepper appeared on the scene only after the discovery of the Americas. The gold the explorers set out to find has paled into insignificance today; yet the crops they brought back changed the taste of Spain forever. There were potatoes, corn, haricot (navy) beans, tomatoes, chocolate and vanilla. But, none of these have had the impact of the all-pervasive pepper.

A favourite in the *tapas* bar is the simply fried Pimientos de Padrón (see page 46). This small green pepper has aficionados all over Spain and sometimes comes with quite a kick. The entire villages of Padrón and neighbouring Herbón, in western Galicia, are busy cultivating peppers. They have the local monastery to thank for their livelihood. Franciscan missionaries brought the seeds back from the American colonies in the 16th century. The Sunday market in Padrón is packed with ladies selling their peppers from huge baskets. They are sold by the hundred, and not by weight, so the ladies are like croupiers, constantly on the count. In the Basque country the local Gernika pepper is the bar snack celebrity, but it is quite difficult to find elsewhere.

Fresh bell peppers, *pimientos morrones*, are the most commonly used pepper of all. Local summer markets are heaped with the luscious vegetables, ranging in colour from unripe green to mottled orange through to ripe, crimson red. They look reassuringly misshapen compared with their bland, greenhouse relatives from northern Europe. Acidic, green peppers are sometimes used in cooking and salads but the more mature, red peppers are much sweeter and the more common choice. Peppers are used in many dishes but where they play the starring role is in the *chilindrón* dishes of Navarre and Aragon. One of the most celebrated peppers is the *Pimiento del Bierzo*, a plump red pepper from the fertile Bierzo valley in the province of León. The mountains of these voluptuous fresh peppers dominate León's Saturday market. However, many are grilled (broiled) and peeled and preserved in cans or jars, to be snapped up elsewhere in Spain as a delicacy. They are, thankfully, increasingly available abroad.

Spaniards do not regard jars and cans in the same way as serious gastronomes do elsewhere. All manner of fruits, vegetables and seafood are sold as preserves and are in no way considered inferior to their fresh counterparts. A classic example is the *piquillo* pepper. This pointed, or beak-shaped pepper is rarely available fresh, unless you happen to live in Lodosa or one of the neighbouring villages of Navarre or Rioja. Even then you certainly wouldn't eat the peppers raw – a bitter and unpleasant taste – but once roasted they are delicious. In September the entire town of Lodosa seems to be roasting peppers in custom-made iron drums, turned over the flames with handles that make them look like barrel organs. Families and friends gather around wire racks of cooling peppers, putting the world to right while carefully peeling away the skin and painstakingly keeping the flesh intact.

Roasting and soaking peppers
To roast fresh peppers, place them under a preheated hot grill (broiler) until the skin has bubbled and blistered all over. Cover the peppers as they cool. I usually place an upturned bowl over the tray. This will create steam, which helps the skins slip off more easily when it comes to peeling them. When they are cool remove the skin. Don't even think of doing this under cold running water, as you will wash away all the delicious flavour. I like to peel peppers over a sieve (strainer), reserving all the smoky juices, which are then fabulous used in a salad dressing.

To soak dried peppers, just rip out the stalks and pour very hot water over them. Leave to stand for at least 30 minutes if possible. You may need to leave them a little longer if you are scraping the soft flesh from the skins as in the Vizcayan Salt Cod Recipe (see page 109). Then fry or cook the peppers as directed in the recipe.

The pepper's conical shape makes it ideal for stuffing (see page 75) and a ripped pepper is worth a fraction of the price. Well worth keeping in mind, as these *tiras*, or strips, are a great economical alternative to the whole peppers used for salads. Another fabulous preserved pepper to look out for is the *Pimiento de Cristal*. This pepper fetches premium prices as it's difficult to peel, but it's just divine with a slice of toast, oil and garlic.

Pickled peppers are popular too, particular the feisty Basque *guindilla*. This pale green chilli (chili) pepper can pack quite a punch, although there are some sweeter varieties to which I am totally addicted. Such is their popularity that one variety from Ibarra is know by the exalted nickname of *Langostino de Ibarra* or Ibarran king prawn (jumbo shrimp).

Now we get on to the subject of dried peppers, perhaps the most baffling subject to outsiders. In autumn (the fall), balconies are strung with peppers drying before the winter damp sets in. The most common dried peppers are the *choricero* peppers, basically dried red bell peppers. They add an earthy, rich intensity to plenty of Basque and Riojan dishes. Another popular dried pepper is the round *ñora*, that looks more like a tomato than a pepper and plays a star role in the Catalan *Romesco* sauce (see page 135). Then of course we have the dried red chilli (chili), or *guindilla*, with which most of us are well acquainted. This is used sparingly in Northern Spanish cooking while its fresh counterpart is barely used at all. Local dishes will often have a hint of chilli (chili) but are rarely served hot and spicy.

The most common spice in the Spanish kitchen is, without a doubt, *pimentón* or Spanish paprika. *Pimentón* gives its characteristic brick-red colouring and sweetness to all manner of *embutitidos*, or cured sausages. It is worth remembering that there are various types of paprika in Spain ranging from *dulce* (sweet) through *agridulce* (sweet and sour) to *picante* (the hottest). To complicate matters further your *pimentón* may be plain or *ahumado* (smoked) and rather confusingly this is not always noted on the label. In general a *pimentón* from Extremadura, in particular the high-quality spice from De la Vera will be smoked over oak, while to the east in Murcia the paprika resembles its non-smoked Hungarian cousin. I love paprika in every form but do be aware which type a recipe calls for; you don't want to ladle on the hot *picante* in large quantities.

Preserved peppers make fabulous storecupboard stand-bys; great for salads, added to rice and bean dishes or for an instant sauce (see page 139). Dried peppers keep well, and look just stunning as a kitchen decoration, so it's worth buying a string if you visit a specialist Spanish store. Many peppers are sold individually too. If you don't manage to track them down, a spoonful of sweet paprika in their place, will usually do the trick.

Cheese

Gone are the days when Manchego was the only Spanish cheese on the international scene, although it is still without doubt the most famous. I have nothing against Manchego; this sheep's cheese can be sublime, but it's frustrating that people sometimes look no further. Much of north Spain is prime grazing land, producing the majority of the country's fabulous cheese. And, I'm thrilled to say that good delicatessens and cheese stores are on the case at last.

The quality of many of the celebrated Spanish cheeses is controlled by sets of strict regulations. These *denominaciones de origen* maintain local cheese making methods. Thus, a cheese with a DO will have a guaranteed consistency of style and flavour. These are by no means the only cheeses worth eating. There are dozens of incredible artisan cheeses, produced in small quantities supplying just the local market. We will concentrate on the kings of the Northern Spanish cheese board.

Pasteurized cheeses are marked with "P" while "UP" signifies unpasteurized.

Cow's milk cheese

The damp, green pastureland of Galicia, Asturias and Cantabria is cattle country. This is the dairy centre of Spain where milk, butter and, of course, cheese are made.

Galicia has three DO cheeses to be proud of:

DO Arzúa Ulloa (P) is mild and very creamy. The Spaniards don't often cook with cheese but this one does melt very well.

DO San Simón (P) is an ancient pear-shaped cheese formed in conical wooden moulds. It is lightly smoked with birch wood and has a golden rind. A cheese to enjoy as an *aperitivo* or in a salad.

DO Tetilla (P) is supposed to resemble a small breast, hence its name. It's soft and tangy and often teamed with sweet quince paste.

Neighbouring Asturias and Cantabria have plenty of cow's milk cheeses but many do not make it to the international stage. You might come across these:

Afuega'l Pitu (P) or "choke the rooster", is a soft, cream cheese that is sometimes given a rusty coat of deliciously spicy paprika. This is heaven with a little bread and a glass of cider.

D.O De La Peral (UP) is a mild blue cheese from the Picos de Europa Mountains. Fabulous on its own and great for melting in sauces too.

Catalonia produces good cow's milk cheeses too such as the mild DO *Drap* or the more piquant DO *Serrat* but they are rarely found outside the province.

Mixed milk cheese

The idea of blending different milk within a cheese makes sense when you have a variety of livestock. Both these blue cheeses come from the stunning Picos de Europa Mountains where they are aged in limestone caves, rich in penicillin.

DO Cabrales (UP) is the most famous blue cheese in Spain. It is predominantly cow's milk but sheep's and goat's milk are added at certain times of year. The smell of the sticky rind is particularly pungent; I almost passed out, asphyxiated by fumes when I visited a cave in the village of Asiegu. The cheese is a creamy-yellow mottled with blue, and becomes increasingly strong and crumbly as it matures, when it can really "blow your socks off". I love this cheese served with sweet honey (see page 52).

D.O Valdeón, or **Picos de Europa** (UP), as it is sometimes known, is a gloriously creamy and smooth blue cheese. It is made with cow's milk, with the addition of goat's milk during the spring and summer months. This one can "grow hairs on your chest". It also melts well.

Sheep's milk cheese

The quintessential Spanish cheese that evokes memories of the harsh and dusty plains of ancient Iberia

Burgos (UP) is a fresh and soft, white cheese sometimes known as *requesón*, a bit like a *ricotta*. It is very mild, ideal for baking or eaten with fruit and honey as a dessert.

Cuajada (P) is typical of the Basque country and Navarre where it is served as a dessert or breakfast treat. Cuajada has the texture but not the acidity of yogurt. The milk is thickened with animal rennet and heated gently, just like junket.

DO Idiazábal (UP) is from the Basque country and Navarre. It's is an ancient shepherd's cheese that used to mature gently in the smoky mountain huts. Today there are fiercely contested prizes for the best cheese. The winner of the *txapela*, (an over-sized champion's beret) at the fair in Ordizia, is guaranteed to sell his cheese for a fortune. It's a fabulous lightly smoked *tapas* cheese eaten with sweet peppers or dried fruit.

DO Manchego (P/UP) is not from the north at all, but universally popular and available. It is a hard cheese from La Mancha of Central Spain. The *semi-curado*, younger cheese, is mellow and aromatic while the more mature *curado* is usually sweet and piquant. Try it with dried fruit and nuts.

DO Roncal (UP)is Navarre's cheese "extraordinaire". It's quite a pungent "sheepy" cheese that tastes just fabulous with the region's *piquillo* peppers.

DO Zamorano (UP) from Zamora in Old Castille, is quite similar to Manchego, it is traditionally matured in wine cellars, giving a musty grey rind.

DO Castellano (P) and *DO Pata de Mulo* UP) are two other delicious table cheeses to look out for.

Goat's milk cheese

Catalonia is the main producer of goat's cheese in the region. The area is enjoying a cheese-making renaissance, and many ancient traditions are being revived.

Can Pujol-Nevat (P) is a delicate, creamy ripened cheese with a bloomy soft white rind. The cheese is almost sweet with a bitter tang and is ideal in salads.

Garrotxa (UP) is an example of an old cheese being given new life by the new breed of cheese-maker. Entrepreneurial gourmets revived this delicious firm cheese using modern methods. It is a surprise to many who always expect soft or "farmyardy" smelling goat's cheese.

Mató (P/UP) is a fresh curd cheese, with no salt added. It tastes quite tangy and is usually served with honey or fruit as a dessert. It is also fabulous with salted anchovies.

Serving Cheese

Cheese is most often served with something sweet. There is a saying "*miel y queso, saben a beso*" ("honey and cheese taste like a kiss").

The pressed cakes of figs and almonds, *tortas de higos y almendras*, are truly delicious with blue cheese.

The combination of raisins, sultanas (golden raisins), hazelnuts, pine kernels (pine nuts) or almonds is referred to as a *postre de músico*, or musician's dessert, from the days that travelling minstrels were rewarded for their efforts with a handful of fruit and nuts. It's quite an anti-climax if you order the *postre*, with expectations of some luscious dessert as I once did, but it does make a wonderful accompaniment to a mature (sharp) cheese.

Dark pastes of quince, *dulce de membrillo* (see page 138), or less commonly apple, *dulce de manzana* (see page 138) are heavenly accompaniments for hard sheep's milk cheeses.

Restaurants often serve a scale of cheeses, with carefully selected tiny tasters laid out in order of potency of flavour. The platter is sure to have some of the sweet accompaniments listed above and it's a great introduction to Spanish cheeses.

Olives and Olive Oil

The Spanish taste for olives begins virtually in the cradle. Toddlers will snap up an olive with the same glee that most small children reserve for a chocolate button. As an au-pair in Barcelona many years ago, I remember the sight of my first olive stall: an incredible display of bowl upon bowl of green olives, black olives, stuffed olives, stoned (pitted) olives, tiny *arbequinas*, huge *gordales*, and so it went on; it was all most bewildering. Not for my four-year-old charge who dived in with the same energy that I might have displayed at the pick-and-mix sweet (candy) counter at the same age. Olives are part of the Spanish way of life.

Nothing could be more spoiling than a glass of wine and a well-chosen olive, and I say well-chosen as there are some pretty dreadful ones out there too. An olive requires picking at the right moment; some taste wonderful when green and firm, others are better left to ripen, blacken and ooze with oil. It all depends on the variety. An olive eaten straight from the tree is a very bitter experience and not pleasant at all, so olives are cured for at least a month to make them more palatable. It is only then that the business of marinating, stoning (pitting) or stuffing can begin.

Some varieties taste wonderful without any frills. The Catalan *arbequina* is a perfect example, heaven indeed, with no call for fancy marinades. Some olives come into their own when they are combined with another flavour. I have a soft spot for an almond-stuffed *gordal* or an anchovy-filled *manzanilla*. Tasty marinades can transform an olive, and some of the cheap, supermarket jars could do with a little help. You may like to try the one on page 137. My only word of warning would be that the perfectly uniform, stoned (pitted) black olive should be left to lurk in its pot on the shelf. Cardboard would probably taste better. Need black stoned (pitted) olives? Then buy a fabulously soft, delicious variety and stone (pit) them yourself: hard work, messy but worth the effort.

Table olives are one thing but their oil is quite another and in fact most of the olives grown in Spain go straight to the press. Spain is not only the greatest producer of olive oil in the world but the greatest consumer too. Spanish cooking would be inconceivable without the stuff. But, this has not always been the case in the North. Once you reach the misty Atlantic Coast, there's not an olive tree in sight, it's a land of chestnuts and pines. The Galicians and Asturians cooked with butter and pork fat just like their Celtic cousins in France and Britain until relatively recently. The Basques, with their highly developed cuisine used pork fat in many dishes and saved the olive oil for specialities such as the *pil pil* sauce or salads. Even in Catalonia, one of Spain's most ancient olive regions, lard was once at the top of the culinary pecking order. At one time it was considered more distinguished to cook with pork fat, demonstrating that you were wealthy enough to keep enough pigs for an annual supply, than with olive oil, available to the masses. How times have changed.

Today olive oil reigns supreme and its nutritional benefits are widely accepted. An oil that lowers cholesterol and tastes divine too, who could refuse it? With modern transportation olive oil has woven its delicious web throughout the land. It comes as a surprise to many that there are more types of olive than there are grape in the world and factors such as soil and microclimate will affect the flavour of an olive, and thus the oil in just the same way as they will a wine. Just try tasting a Greek oil against a Spanish, or even a Catalan oil against an Andalucian, you will be astounded by the differences between them.

Certain oils come with a pedigree. Look for the letters DO on the label. These oils come from a *denominación de origen*, an area where a governing body controls the quality of the oils by stipulating olive varieties, picking and pressing conditions. Two of the most famous DO oils are from Catalonia: one Siurana, near the Mediterranean coast in the region of the ancient Roman port of Tarragona and the other, Les Garrigues in the dry inland plains of Llérida. Both these oils are made primarily from the tiny *arbequina* olive and produce deliciously light, apple-type oils. Another DO Baja Aragón, in lowland Aragon makes oils from the *empeltre* olive, producing straw yellow, sweeter oils. Small quantities of DO oil are also produced in Rioja but I have yet to come across them outside the region, let alone abroad.

Buying olive oil is just like buying wine – a very subjective business. Some people love their oils peppery and green; others like nutty, riper oils. There is no right or wrong, just personal taste. There are, of course, some better quality oils where extreme care has been taken in their production, where olives have been collected at precise stages of ripening, hand picked to avoid bruising, pressed without heating and carefully blended with no use of chemicals. The resulting oils can be truly exceptional, good enough to drink or certainly to savour with a chunk of decent bread. The best oils of the first cold pressing are the extra virgin olive oils; they must be kept at constantly low temperatures and have an acidity below 1 per cent. I would not dream of using such a delicate commodity in my frying pan (skillet), for that the second pressing, the plain old *aceite de oliva* is sufficient. Extra virgin oil is best enjoyed on salads, on bread or drizzled on food just as it is served.

As a starting point here are a few of my favourite Spanish oils, all available in the UK. In general oils from Andalucia tend to be very fruity and rich while those from the north are nutty and light.

Nuñez de Prado, DO Baena (Andalucia) from *picual, picudo* and *hojiblanca* olives

Lérida, DO Les Garrigues (Catalonia) from *arbequina* olives

Unió, DO Siurana (Catalonia) from *arbequina* olives

I use good quality, branded oils such as Carbonell and Borges for my cooking.

Gourmets will rush to taste the oil within a month of pressing, when it is cloudy and fresh. You may not have this opportunity but you should certainly make sure that oil is used within the year. Olive oil eventually deteriorates losing its glorious flavour and nutritional benefits. Keep your olive oil somewhere cool and dark, as if it were a wine; it is after all, an expensive commodity and certainly worth looking after.

Pork

Pork is the keystone of Spanish cooking. You might be tucking into a plate of fish or vegetables or even nibbling at a breakfast pastry but the chances are that the pig will have snorted it's way into the dish somewhere along the line. On one occasion while I was working as a tour guide in the 1980s it transpired that half my group were vegetarians – a nightmare in rural Spain, they might just as well have had the plague. I dutifully called restaurants to give them plenty of warning and was usually greeted with a less than enthusiastic chef offering *tortilla* or more *tortilla*. One kindly prepared a glorious vegetable *paella*, filled with artichokes and red peppers, the only disturbing part was the rich "porky" aroma. I rushed into the kitchen for an explanation. Did it contain pork? "Good Lord, yes. It wouldn't be worth eating without!" was the stunned reply.

The pig played a symbolic role in the Spain of the Christian re-conquest. Dishes of the recently vanquished Moors were recreated using its forbidden flesh. In the days of the infamous Inquisition, when religious intolerance reached its zenith, clandestine Jews and Muslims were in constant fear of being "outed". One had to show a "healthy" interest in all things porcine or tongues would begin to wag. But, first and foremost, the reason for the nation's love affair with the pig is a basic one: Spain is a country with little grazing land and a pig could be raised in the backyard, eating all the domestic scraps.

To an outsider the celebration of the *matanza*, or pig kill, may seem macabre. But, for many, it was one of the few days of the year when you ate your fill, and with meat, no less. The larder was packed once again with sausages and cured meats to last the rest of the year – a good excuse for a party. All those delicious sausages and hams, collectively known to the Spanish as *embutidos*, allowed a family to flavour cheaper dishes such as beans and provided them with precious protein through out the year. Nowadays times have moved on and there aren't many households with their own pig; most are raised and butchered commercially. Yet the *matanza* lives on and many families still congregate once a year, taking pride in making their *embutidos* in keeping with time-honoured tradition.

The practice is not restricted to country people either. I joined in a massive pig "fest" in Catalonia with a very cosmopolitan crowd. The Roquet family's annual bash lasts an entire weekend. Cousins leave professional jobs in the city behind, children lay down their computer games, elegant ladies remove sparkly wedding rings and it's time to make sausages and the occasional pâté. There's time for plenty of eating and chatting too. By Sunday night every ounce of meat – offal (variety meat) or flesh, cured or fresh, has been efficiently dealt with.

Before we begin to consider the myriad of different sausages and cured meats available across Northern Spain, it is important to realize that there are two distinctly different types of pig involved. Firstly we have the pink European pig, introduced by the Celts – the traditional family waste disposal and provider of Northern Spain's *embutidos*, or cured *Serrano* products. Secondly, there is the legendary indigenous breed, the Iberian pig, the *cerdo Ibérico*. This hairy black pig resembles a small wild boar and thrives in the cork oak forests of the south and west. It eats a diet of acorns and lives a life of relative freedom. The deep red meat has a fabulous flavour and a price tag to go with it – it's quite rightly given caviar-status all over Spain. Thus you will notice a huge gulf in price at the *charcutería* counter between the black footed *Ibérico* meat, be it hams or sausages, and the paler *Serrano* meat.

The Spanish consume virtually every part of the pig in some dish or another, from ears to trotters (feet), nothing edible is thrown aside. Here we will just discuss the most common cured or preserved cuts with which you may not be familiar. Many delicatessens and specialist stores will stock the following:

Manteca as pork fat or lard. It is often combined with olive oil to add depth and flavour to a dish. Some pastries and desserts are even made with *manteca*.

Jamón Serrano is the salted and air-cured leg of pork. It is delicious eaten with figs or melon. It's more chewy and robust than Italian *prosciutto*. The most celebrated hams come from Trevélez in Andalucia and Teruel in Aragon. *Jamón Serrano* is sometimes used in cooked dishes too such as trout (see page 105) or rabbit (see page 122).

Jamón Ibérico or **jamón de Pata Negra** is the ultimate cured ham, from the Iberian pig. It is usually hand-carved and is best savoured on its own. It's prohibitive price means that it is rarely used in cooking. Exquisite hams come from Jabugo and Guijuelo.

Jamón York is the less popular cooked ham – still very good in a cheese sandwich.

Paletilla is the cured shoulder of pork and once again this may be *Ibérico* or *Serrano*.

There is also a cured shoulder from Galicia called **lacón** that's soaked for 24 hours before cooking.

Lomo embuchado is marinated pork loin. It is sometimes only cured, in its typical blend of smoked paprika, garlic and oregano, for a few days and then cooked as fresh meat. The fully cured lomo is sliced paper thin and eaten as an aperitif or with a plate of charcuterie. The Ibérico loin is glorious.

Pancetta or **baicon** is cured belly pork, sometimes with the addition of paprika too. It's a common ingredient in stews and braises.

Chorizo is a pork sausage seasoned with salt and paprika. It may be sold soft and fresh, ready for the pan, or firm and cured to eat straight away or used in cooking. There are two main varieties of chorizo, the dulce (sweet) and the picante (hot) – so do make sure you know which you are buying. Some chorizos will taste smokier than others, depending on the type of paprika used. In damper regions such as Asturias the sausages are not just air-dried but smoked too, to preserve them better.

Salchichón is a sausage cured with just salt and pepper, without the paprika. Some sausages contain garlic too while many are plain and simple, allowing the natural flavour of the meat to come through. The Catalan *longanissa* from Vic is very popular, but there are dozens of varieties on offer. The sausage is often allowed to become really hard and tough, it's then sliced into thin chewy slices and enjoyed with a glass of good wine.

Morcilla is a blood sausage much like the British black pudding (blood sausage). It is often sold soft and fresh, as is the case of the Catalan botifarra negra. There are many varieties some containing rice or spices. The Asturian morcilla is flavoured with paprika and is smoke-cured giving it the distinctive taste so famous in the local Fabada bean dish (see page 95).

Botifarra blanca is a fresh, white sausage from Catalonia. The meat and fat is quite coarsely cut and the only seasonings are salt and pepper.

Pulses

A few decades ago labelling Spain as a nation of bean eaters might have caused huge offence. Back in the old days pulses or legumes, those seeds that mature inside their own protective pod, were considered to be the "*carne de los pobres*", the meat of the poor. Not today. Spain's new federalism has bred an almost fanatical pride in regional dishes and many of the most satisfying classics are made with beans and pulses.

Pulses have been a staple in Northern Spain for thousands of years. Lentils, chickpeas and beans are a great source of protein once combined with grain, fish, poultry or meat. A thrifty housewife could feed an entire family with a tiny quantity of well-flavoured meat and a large pot of beans or chickpeas. Legumes came into their own on the frequent days of Catholic fasting too. In really hard times, and there are still many older people who remember the hunger of the post Civil War years, they sustained whole communities.

The other great plus point of all these seeds is how well they keep. Dried carefully they can be stored for months, even years. Nevertheless the discerning Spanish shopper will seek out fresh stock in the autumn (fall), when the crop has just been harvested and dried, market stalls will be labelled with reassuring signs "*son todas nuevas*", they are all new season.

Chickpeas are the key ingredient in many of the one-pot dishes we associate with Spain. The *cocido*, a stew of meat and chickpeas, exists all over the country in various guises. It can be a humble dish with just a few bones added for flavour or a true celebration such as Castilla y Leon's *Cocido Maragato*, packed with pork, beef and chicken, or the Catalan variation with noodles, the *escudella*, often devoured at Christmas time. There are even cherished regional varieties of chickpea such as the truly delicious Pico de Pardal. This tiny pea with a beak-like point, absorbs its cooking stock and takes on the most glorious flavour and buttery texture. Meanwhile, lentils often end up in simple everyday dishes, served for supper with some *chorizo* thrown in, or as a delicious accompaniment to game. The most famous lentils come from León y Castilla: the tiny dark Pardinas and the bigger green Lentejas de Armuña.

Broadly speaking all dried pulses will double in weight and size once cooked. 75 g/3 oz/½ cup dried pulses will be ample per person for the main dish and 50 g/2 oz/⅓ cup for a side dish or starter (appetizer).

Lentils (lentejas) require no soaking at all, just rinse to remove any dust or grime. Cover them in double their volume of water and boil for anything between 20 and 40 minutes until tender.

Beans (alubias y judías) require at least 8 hours soaking in four times their volume of cold water. Rinse, place in a large saucepan of cold water with plenty of flavourings such as herbs, vegetables, bones and meats. Don't add any salt at this stage, as it toughens the skin. Bring to the boil removing the froth from the top of the pan. Add cold water from time to time to time, cutting the boil, ensuring that the skins do not split. Do not add too much water; you want this to be a thick luscious stock to serve with the beans; it certainly doesn't go down the drain.

Chickpeas (garbanzos) Carlos Cidón, at the Vivaldi restaurant in León, recommends soaking the chickpeas in hot water, this initial heat will help the them soften, and leaving them for at least 12 hours. Spanish chefs may add pig's trotters (feet), ears, snouts for flavour. I find the ears the easiest to deal with, without too much unpleasant cleaning necessary. Go on – be brave!

It's the bean that reigns supreme in the maritime provinces of Galicia, Asturias, Cantabria and the Basque Country. In Santander's covered market there are three entire stalls dealing specifically with dried beans and pulses. I counted over 30 varieties: Tolosa's shiny black bean, Gernika's red, speckled beans from Burgos, the tiny green *verdinas* from Llanes and so it goes on. Each town a different bean, each bean a different dish, each dish a different season. And it's not just the vast choice that can be overwhelming either, it's the price tag too. Certain beans have celebrity status, the *faba de la granja,* star of the Asturian *fabada* (see page 95) can fetch the same price per kilo as steak.

I met a lady in Lodosa, the *piquillo* pepper capital of Navarre who was prepared to risk life and limb for her beans. It was during one of those mad Spanish fiestas when locals throw caution to the wind. Large road signs on the edge of town warned unsuspecting drivers that between noon and two there would be a bull on the loose. So, I found myself cowering in the bandstand while half the town careered around the narrow streets in front of a furious bull. At the cry of "*viene el toro*", "the bull's coming", octogenarians, ladies with pushchairs (strollers) and anyone with a will to live, ran for the bandstand to join me. No sooner had the sweating bull hurtled past, than a genteel lady in her *fiesta* heels announced that she was off home to get her beans on the go. I reminded her that the bull was still loose. "I'll make a run for it, I doubt it will be back this way for a few minutes," she said as she scuttled away, glancing nervously over her shoulder.

Some beans are eaten fresh such as the baby broad bean (fava bean) and the celebrated *pocha*, a haricot, similar to the Italian *borlotti* (cranberry bean), that arrives in late summer and features on every local menu in Rioja and the southern Basque lands. Legumes have found their way into the *Nueva Cocina* too, often in the form of delicious purées, in salads and even in the occasional dessert.

The only drawback with most pulses is the soaking. You certainly have to be organized. It's the kind of thing that springs to mind in bed at 2 a.m. In Spain butchers, delicatessens and market stalls often sell the pulses ready-soaked, or even cooked; an easy way out. However, the best way with pulses is to cook them with stock or flavourings that permeate their creamy flesh during the long, slow cooking.

Salt Cod

Salt Cod, or *bacalao* is a Spanish passion. Most towns will have an entire shop, the *Casa de Bacalao,* dedicated to selling just that. Festoons of the grey, kite-shaped fish are a common sight in Spanish markets. The pervasively pungent smell of salted fish is not likely to leave you salivating, in fact most visitors look on in disbelief or dive hastily towards the more familiar vegetable stalls. Even the texture is off-putting, the fish is so hard that it often takes a guillotine and plenty of elbow grease just to cut it. Yet, one taste of the tender flesh and you will probably be a convert for life. It is a miracle that something quite so unappealing can deliver such magical results. Just give it a try; you will be surprised by the subtle flavour and luscious texture. Most Spaniards would never dream of tucking into fresh cod, as it is widely considered an entirely inferior option.

Soaking or rehydrating salt cod:
This is often a cause for great debate. Some chefs will even require you to use mineral water so as not to taint the flesh with any chlorine flavours from running water. I think this may be a little excessive. What is immediately apparent is that you must be one step ahead when you're cooking bacalao, as it will take anything between 24 and 48 hours to soak out the salt, depending on the size of the pieces.

For the average main course serving 36 hours will suffice and it helps if all your portions are about the same size. Just fill a large pan or bowl with cold, fresh water and leave your fish to soak in the refrigerator. You will need to change the water at eight hourly intervals, four times in total. Many chefs suggest that the last few hours be spent at room temperature. Just nibble a little piece from time to time, the idea is to leave a little saltiness but not have your guests gasping for water.

Once you are ready to cook, carefully remove any scales or bones and dry the fish with a little kitchen paper (paper towel) and hey, at last you're ready to go! Of course if you live in Spain you can pop along to the local market or store and pick up your bacalao ready soaked, but, frankly, that's just cheating.

Bacalao is enjoyed throughout Northern Spain, particularly inland where, in times gone by, with little or no means of refrigeration, it was the only fish available. During times of Catholic fasting when meat was forbidden, including Lent, Wednesdays and Fridays, and whenever else the church decreed, salted fish was a welcome change from beans and legumes. However, paradoxically, it is in the Basque Country, right on the Atlantic coast with an abundance of fresh fish, that *bacalao* is virtually given cult status. Salt cod features on every traditional Basque menu and with rising prices, owing to the depletion of cod fishing stocks, it has shaken off its humble origins and stars in the kitchens of the world class chefs.

It is no coincidence that salt cod should be highly considered in one of the most gastronomically obsessed regions on the planet, for it is truly delicious it also has over three times the nutritional value of the same weight of fresh cod. But most importantly it was the Basques who introduced salt cod to Spain. The Basques were the great whalers of the world back in the sixteenth century, and as their rather too successful techniques depleted the local whale stocks they were forced to travel further and further afield in search of the poor creatures. Then came the problem of how to feed the fishermen aboard. In the seas of the North Atlantic, the summer whaling grounds, there were plenty of cod and the Basques used to gut the fish and then store it in the ship's hold, piled with salt to preserve it. Selling *bacalao* became big business and eventually superseded the whale trade. The fish used to be dried in the sun and wind upon arrival back home in Spain, but now the vast proportion is dried in specially designed chambers. Today most of the salt cod comes from Newfoundland, Iceland and Norway but the Basques remain the most important importers and, without doubt, the most enthusiastic consumers.

Despite the fact that San Sebastián is undoubtedly the gourmet capital of the Basque country it is commonly acknowledged that the *Bilbaínos* are the kings when it comes to salt cod. Gourmets flock to the Guria restaurant in the Gran Vía of Bilbao, a shrine to salt cod where the Chef, Jenaro Pildain, prepares a plate like an artist's palette of "*cuatro sabores de bacalao*", four flavours of *bacalao*. The classic salt cod dishes of *bacalao al pil-pil, a la Vizcaína and club ranero* have been elevated from the food of the working classes to some of the most prestigious dishes of Bilbao, and no chef will be taken seriously until he has mastered their preparation. In fact there are countless weekend gatherings where amateur chefs compete for swanky trophies and titles in the art of cooking salt cod. I even met a chap, proudly proclaimed by his wife to be the "Schumacher of *bacalao*", he had swept away so many trophies. He very kindly gave me a priceless poster, a reproduction of Picasso's Gernika, which on close inspection revealed thousands of pieces of salt cod and skin carefully arranged to recreate a rather unusual copy of the masterpiece!

Here are a few pointers when it comes to purchasing salt cod:
You should be able to track it down in reputable fishmongers (suppliers), any specialist Portuguese and Spanish stores or suppliers from the Caribbean, another area of the world that succumbed to its salty charms. You could even bring some back from Spain. Just wrap it well or you may find your fellow passengers giving you a wide berth.

Bacalao should not be confused with stockfish, which is dried rather than salted cod. Stockfish has a different flavour and is not so popular in Spain.

You will require about 150–175 g/5½–6 oz of dry salt cod per person for a main course. Seek out fish with a grey rather than yellowish hue.

There are many different cuts but the best ones to look out for are *morro* or *lomo,* the thick loin pieces, ideal for serving in main course size portions. If you are shredding your fish for a salad then the *viente* or *loncha,* flatter boneless strips from the belly, are perfect

Seafood

The Spanish consume truly remarkable quantities of seafood. Their fishing fleet is second in size only to the Japanese and every day at dawn coastal motorways (freeways) are packed with white refrigerated vans (trucks) speeding inland with their bounty to the Spanish cities. Most of us are fairly well acquainted with the fish on offer but when it comes to the question of shellfish things get more complicated. Spaniards adore their shellfish and are prepared to spend a small fortune on the extravagance. There are even specialist shellfish stores and stalls, *marisquerías*. They are packed in the lead up to every high day and holiday.

The north coast, and in particular Galicia, is famed for its glorious seafood and it's a real treat to order a *mariscada*, a great platter of mixed shellfish (see pages 102–3). I watched a portly chap sit himself down at a table on the bustling Calle Franja, in the port of La Coruña. Not a word was said; he was obviously a regular. It was like clockwork: first the napkin tucked into the shirt collar, then the half bottle of Albariño wine that miraculously appeared and finally the family-size mound of shellfish. He looked like a surgeon performing a critical operation; the concentration was so intense. Navigating his way around crabs, prawns (shrimp), mussels, razor clams and gooseneck barnacles, he never even stopped for a breath. Then he finally sat back, like a contented cat; pure, unashamed indulgence.

Crustaceans

Shrimp and prawns

There are many varieties of shrimp and prawns in the Spanish Atlantic and Mediterranean waters but these are the most common:

The *quisquilla* or brown shrimp is a tiny creature and it's very awkward to shell, which is why you are likely to find these only in upmarket restaurants or in the markets ready to take home to prepare. Just boil them in salted water until firm.

Gambas, or common prawns (shrimp), are very popular particularly in Catalonia where they are fished in huge quantities in the shallow waters around the Ebro Delta. When eaten really fresh they are fabulously sweet and just to die for.

The *carabinero* and *langostino* are the huge, juicy king prawns (jumbo shrimp). These are often just griddled.

The *cigala*, or Dublin bay prawn (langoustine), more commonly known to us by the Italian name *scampi,* is the one with the pair of pincers, making it look like a miniature lobster.

Tip
Buying prawns
In Spain prawns (shrimp) are most often cooked and served in their shells. Try to buy raw prawns (shrimp) for the recipes in this book. If you can't, then frozen raw prawns (shrimp) will do. Avoid the frozen cooked prawns (shrimp): they taste of little and have a dubious spongy texture.

Lobster

This fine creature is definitely the king of the castle – the most expensive crustacean with reputably the finest flesh.

The *bogavante*, or lobster, has huge claws containing most of the edible meat. When raw it is a dark blue-brown that turns a glorious red once cooked. Such lobsters are few and far between in the Mediterranean but they are still caught in the Bay of Biscay.

The *langosta*, or spiny lobster, is more common. Some fans would say that its meat is the sweetest of all. It has no claws and is naturally deep orange in colour. Lobster must be purchased live or ready cooked. Whether grilling (broiling) or boiling your lobster, place it in the freezer for 2 hours, rendering it unconscious before cooking.

Crab

Crab is highly prized and certainly cheaper than lobster, although only about one-third of its body weight will be edible meat. It's often available ready-cooked from the fishmonger (supplier).

The *buey de mar*, (literally the ox of the sea) is the common crab, with its huge juicy claws, delicious eaten in a *salpicón*, or seafood salad. The Basques are fonder of the spider crab.

The *centolla*, or spider crab, has no claws, just eight spindly legs but the body is packed with fabulous meat. It's used in the legendary dish of Basque Stuffed Crab (see page 69).

The *nécora*, or small swimmer crab, is for the real enthusiasts. It's quite a challenge to crack its tiny shell and then it's a question of sucking and picking to extract the fabulous flesh. There is nothing elegant or precious about tackling this one. It's good for soups too. Crab must always be purchased live or ready cooked.

Molluscs (Mollusks)

There are literally dozens of these tasty sea creatures served up in Spanish *tapas* bars and restaurants. I've enjoyed fried sea cucumber fillets and even eaten tiny whelks with a pin. But here we will deal with the more common varieties that you're more likely to prepare.

Bivalves (two shelled molluscs)

The *mejillón*, or mussel, is the most economical shellfish. It has a thin, light shell and so by weight it's a good deal when compared to a clam. Rope-grown mussels are farmed by the million on rafts in Galicia's estuaries and Spain is the world's leading producer. Their succulent flesh is wonderful steamed or prepared in a spicy sauce (see pages 52–3).

The *almeja* and *almeja fina*, or warty venus (!) and carpet shell, are just two of the numerous varieties of clam on offer. They are glorious just steamed or eaten with beans (see page 94) or rice.

The *berberecho*, or cockle, is commonly used as a filling for Galician *empanadas* (see pages 56–57).

Tip
Make sure that all mussels, clams, cockles and oysters are firmly closed before cooking.

The *ostra*, or oyster, is mostly eaten live from its shell with just a squeeze of lemon juice. The Calle de Pescadería, in the port of Vigo, is crammed with oyster stalls, where you buy them by the half dozen, shucked and ready to go. You just take your plate to a nearby bar and order yourself a drink to accompany them.

The *navaja*, or razor shell, looks like an old-fashioned cut-throat razor. The razor clams are sold in bundles, and unlike most of the bivalves they will not be alive when you buy them. So purchase them from a reputable source. They are usually griddled or steamed.

The *vieira,* or Pilgrim scallop, is the symbol of the great pilgrimage to Santiago. These luscious scallops are farmed in Galicia. I never buy frozen scallops, the texture is just so disappointing. A simple, well-cooked scallop would be my "desert-island" dish (see page 70).

Cephalopods

(All the translucent, tentacled creatures, armed with ink, which the Spanish adore to eat.)

The *pulpo*, or octopus, is a Galician speciality. Huge copper cauldrons of bubbling purple tentacles are an integral part of every fair, market or festival there. Octopus is virtually given away in Britain, try to track some down and have a go at the recipe on (see page 53).

The *calamar*, or squid, is enjoyed in many different dishes. Unfortunately tough, chewy rings in batter have tarnished its name but well cooked squid is exquisite. Squid needs to be cooked very quickly or long and slowly, there's really no in-between. Minuscule squid called *chipirones* are fried whole and then scoffed in *tapas* bars throughout the region. Buy your squid from a reputable fishmonger (supplier) as some is actually bleached to make it seem snowy white and alluring! The ink is often used to colour and flavour dishes such as the *arroz negro* on page 99 or for the famous Basque black sauce. Black ink can be purchased from fishmongers (suppliers) and delis in tiny sachets (envelopes), if your squid is ready cleaned.

The *jibia* or *sepia*, is the cuttlefish. Many of us are only acquainted with the bone in the budgie cage, but the flesh is good eating too. There's enough ink in a cuttlefish to blacken an entire pot of rice or re-decorate your kitchen wall if you're not careful. It can be a little tougher than squid but is prepared in much the same way.

Wild cards

*Erizos de ma*r, or sea urchins, are a delicacy in some areas. Just the orange coral is eaten and it's available in cans (*caviar de erizo*).

Percebes, or goose-necked barnacles, are the most perplexing, and expensive, shellfish of them all. Galician and Asturian fisherman quite literally risk life and limb to pluck these bizarre little creatures from the rocks amidst the pounding Atlantic breakers. *Percebes* are the size of a little finger, a kind of rubbery tube topped by a horny hoof. They are just boiled and served as they are. They actually taste surprisingly good for something resembling an unkempt dinosaur's toe.

Do try to track down some fresh wild mushrooms in stores or markets, they are such a seasonal treat. You could even go out gathering with an expert, but leave nothing to chance, there are some pretty deadly fungi lurking out there. Do not wash them, as they will become slimy. Just a wipe with a damp sponge should do the trick. Some fresh wild mushrooms such as the cep freeze well.

Many varieties of mushrooms are available dried, and seem to be increasingly easy to get hold of. I buy great bags of them in the Boquería market whenever I'm in Barcelona. I put my dried mushrooms in the freezer, avoiding the possibility of little flies hatching. Never a pleasant thing to discover in the kitchen cupboard.

Soak the mushrooms in warm water until they have softened, about 20 minutes. Don't forget to reserve the soaking liquid: it makes the most incredible stock, although you may well need to strain it.

Wild Mushrooms

The mountainous regions of Northern Spain are perfect mushroom territory and when damper weather arrives in the spring and autumn (fall) the woodlands are crawling with professionals and enthusiasts foraging for fungi. Wild mushroom fever is on the up too: where locals used to collect perhaps a couple of varieties now new societies, and even monthly mushroom magazines, are spreading the word about dozens of different edible species. Regions such as Castille, where wild mushrooms have never been fully appreciated, are "catching the bug" too. There is a sense of excitement and mystery that these collectors all share. They are almost evangelical about their passion.

Elbow your way through the bustling crowds of the Boquería Market in Barcelona and eventually, right at the back, you will find Llorenç Petràs presiding over his mushroom stand. Huge ceps spill out of wooden crates, there are trays of bronze-coloured bleeding milk caps, dusky horns of plenty and yellow-legged chanterelles. Baskets of dried mushrooms, jars of preserved, it's a "mycophile's" wonderland. This no local affair either: Petràs supplies the region's top restaurants and he's wheeling and dealing on the international stage too. Mushrooms hold a special magic, since as he says, you never know from one day to the next what will turn up. The Catalans along with the Basques are, without a doubt, the great mushroom fanciers of Spain. In Catalonia the menu stretches to hundreds of varieties, many known only to the likes of Llorenç, and confusingly each will have numerous local names. Then of course there are Basque, Castilian and Gallego translations to contend with too, hence your true mushroom connoisseur will burst into reams of Latin names, the only common language, with the ease of a classical scholar.

Mention wild mushrooms to a Catalan and his eyes will light up, there are so many varieties and everyone seems to have a favourite. They are most commonly served sautéed with a little garlic or added to an egg. Then there are those that are linked to a traditional dish such as the tiny *cama-sec*, fairy ring mushroom, which is cooked with veal in the traditional *fricandó* (see page 125). New wave chefs have included dozens of lesser-known mushrooms in their repertoires. And yet, the *rovelló* (bleeding milk cap) remains the Catalan mushroom "extraordinaire". Delicious just cooked on the grill (broiler) with a little oil and salt, it is perhaps the best known of the lot.

The annual mushroom festival in Berga, in the Catalan Pyrenees, draws thousands of enthusiasts every October. Local shop windows are crammed with wild mushrooms, be they knitted, papier mâché, marzipan or fresh, the entire town goes mushroom mad. There are painting and photographic competitions and an evening cook-off but the festival climax is the Sunday morning *rovelló* hunt. Crowds gather at dawn in a glorious mountain valley for a breakfast of sausage, bacon, hunks of country bread and the odd spoonful of garlicky *allioli*, for a good kick-start. Then the heat is on, just a few hours to collect as many of those bleeding milk cap mushrooms as possible.

The ensuing competition reinforced my love of that Spanish "devil may care" attitude. The first entries seemed fairly credible. Small children proudly bearing baskets of perhaps 20 mushrooms, then rather less plausible were a couple of athletic adolescents who arrived bearing washing baskets crammed with precious *rovellóns* on their shoulders. The final entry was hauled in by a Mr Universe look-alike, straining under a basket of bathtub proportions and weighing in at a ridiculous 75 kg/165 lb. There were a few murmurs of trickery.

How could a man have single-handedly gathered such a quantity of mushrooms in a matter of hours? Had any one in fact gathered their mushrooms this morning? And more over, in that truly Spanish fashion, did anyone really care? The crowd had been entertained, there were plenty of mushrooms to be admired and who could be so petty as to worry about a bit of rule bending?

In the Basque country it's the *perretxico*, the St George's mushroom that has a cult following. The mushrooms pop up as the mountain snows melt in spring, around the time of St George's day on the 23 April. Restaurants and bars rush to serve them first in a typical scrambled egg dish (see page 77). Those *Bascos* also love their *ondo*, the cep, probably best known by its Italian name, *porcini*. There's a glorious bar in San Sebastián's old town, The Gambara, where in autumn (fall), as well as white doily- covered platters of fabulous *pintxos* there are huge piles of fresh *porcini*. You can order a plate of them griddled, no fancy twists and they're to die for.

Once you reach the inland areas of Old Castille there is no real tradition of collecting mushrooms. You will find cultivated button (white) mushrooms, of course, and a few setas de cardo, or oyster mushrooms. When I visited León's beautiful market, set in the old medieval square, there were heaps of oyster mushrooms but not another wild mushroom in sight. Yet, even here, up-beat restaurants are serving huge varieties of locally picked wild mushrooms and locals are developing a taste for them.

Probably the best known and certainly the most expensive of all the wild mushrooms is the truffle. We tend to associate truffles with France and Italy but they grow in Northern Spain too. Admittedly these are not the ludicrously expensive white truffle, so highly prized by gourmets, but the black winter truffles. They still fetch exorbitant prices and are commonly slipped over to Périgord in France when there's a shortage. This tuber grows beneath the ground and is hunted out in Catalonia and Aragón with the help of well-trained dogs. The pigs are too busy being made into sausages.

Which Wine, Which Dish?

Food and wine are inextricably linked in Spain. Even if you just pop out for a quick drink in the local bar you will undoubtedly have a nibble too. It may be just a few almonds or olives, perhaps some traditional *tapas* or even an intricate piece of culinary wizardry, but there will be something to savour with your drink. Meals are invariably accompanied by a glass of wine and it's often a surprise to foreigners that while a glass of the local wine is included in a set-price lunch menu, a soft drink will usually be charged for.

Historically there were plenty of pretty rough Spanish wines to be avoided. As recently as the 1970s Rioja was about the only consistently dependable style sold abroad. Today it's another picture altogether, new technology and big investment have totally transformed the market. Old-fashioned oaky flavours have been increasingly replaced with fruit and freshness that suits the contemporary palate. Spain has more land devoted to vines than any other country in the world, admittedly much of it on the barren Mancha plains where yields are low and sometimes of dubious quality. However, the North is home to some of Europe's greatest wines that will marry beautifully with the recipes in this book.

Ultimately the wine you chose to drink with a particular dish is a purely subjective business; just drink what you love. But, it does seem a shame to get into a rut with a few reliable favourites when there are so many wonderful wines to try. Without delving into too many technicalities, here are a few of my personal suggestions. This book is about food and I shall approach my favourite styles of Spanish wine from that perspective, which is what most Spaniards do in any case.

The easiest way to think about what to drink with a certain dish is to consider its origins. Local wines have evolved to suit local foods. A cool, fishy location will make light crisp wines to match, while big boar country will have some hefty numbers in the cellar. It's worth remembering that the stereotypical pairings of white wine with fish, and red wine with meat are not always the only option, or even the best one. Think about the dish as a whole. A rich tomato sauce with oily fish might call out for a rosé or light red, rather than a white wine. In general, lighter dishes are best balanced with less alcoholic wines, while bigger, richer flavours can take a thumping from a more alcoholic number. The "white followed by red" convention, will also go straight out of the window if you are starting with rich *tapas* such as meatballs (see page 54) or lamb kebabs (see page 55).

Before we look at a few suggestions of some fabulous wine choices to accompany your food it's good to know the following terms that will turn up on some labels. D.O and D.O.C.a are the top wine designations, where quality is strictly controlled. These are not by any means the only wines worth drinking but they are reliable place to begin

The way that a wine has been aged will also usually be indicated. The terms do vary between the regions but these are the guidelines. In general the younger wines will be more acidic and up front, (and tannic in the case of reds), and the *Reservas* and *Gran Reservas* softer, more rounded and complex.

Joven, literally young, a bit like a Beaujolais Nouveau.

Crianza, aged for 2 years with at least 6 months in oak barrels, 1 year and 6 months in the barrel for whites and rosés.

Reserva, aged for 3 years with at least 1 in the barrel, 2 years and 6 months in the barrel for whites and rosés.

Gran Reserva, top end wines aged for 5 years with at least 18 months in the barrel, 4 years with 6 months in the barrel for whites and rosés.

Light Nibbles

If you are having a few pre-lunch drinks you will probably be looking for a light refreshing option, but this should certainly be accompanied by a few *tapas* or at least a bowl of olives or toasted almonds.

Cava, Spain's answer to Champagne is a popular option. It's a light and crisp blend of *Parrelada*, *Xar.relo* and *Macabeo* grapes and sometimes, (a more recent addition) with a little *Chardonnay* thrown in too, which certainly enhances the flavour.

Cava is the number one player in the world of sparkling wines and 95 per cent of it is produced in the Catalan Penedés region. A trip around the cellars at Freixenet, the greatest exporter of Cava reveals the shear scale of it all. You board a small train and whizz off, *Charlie and the Chocolate Factory*-style, into the warren of dark tunnels: mile upon mile of them lined with quite literally millions of bottles. You eventually return, feeling like a mole, to the real world. This is big business.

Sherry, is not a northern wine at all, it's made in the South, in Andalucia among Ibérico pigs and Flamenco dancers. But, this fortified wine, made from *Palomino* grapes, is one of Spain's most popular aperitifs. Although, I must say, that you may get a blank expression if you demand a *Manzanilla* in the depths of Aragon or an Asturian cider bar. Rural Spain remains very provincial.

The light and pale *Fino* and *Manzanilla* sherries, are glorious with virtually every truly Spanish flavour. From olives to cured ham, from spiced *chorizo* to prawns (shrimp): they are absolute winners.

The nuttier *Amontillado* sherry is divine with almonds, and perhaps a more comforting winter drink.

Do buy sherry in half bottles, as contrary to popular belief, it does not like to be left for months on end once opened. I am amazed by the number of my friends who still think of sherry as a drink for octogenarians in tweed. It's anything but, just visit a swinging *tapas* bar and dive into a glass. It's heaven you can't deny it. Serve some chilled, back at home and no schooners please!

Simple Shellfish, Steamed and Grilled (Broiled) Fish

Txacolí (chacolí) is a lip-puckering, acidic, slightly fizzy Basque wine. The locals love to drink it in the bars with the huge selection of seafood *pinchos* (nibbles) on offer and it's used in plenty of cooking too. The *Txacolí* vineyards, with their *Hondaribbi Zuri* grapes, cling to the drizzly slopes of the

Labels to look out for
Cava – Cavas Hill, Cordoníu, Freixenet, Juvé y Camps, Marqués de Monistrol, Raimat, Seguras Viudas
Sherry – Lustau (who export a fabulous range of styles), Barbadillo, Hidalgo, Gonzalez Byass, Valdespino

Labels to look out for
Rias Baixas – Martín Codax, Lagar de Cervera
Rueda – Alvarez y Diez, Marques de Griñon, Hermanos Lurton, Marques de Riscal

San Sebastián coastline on the Bay of Biscay. This wine is rarely available outside the Basque lands, but can be tracked down by mail order. See suppliers on page 157.

The DO of *Rias Baixas*, literally the "shallow estuaries", is the most westerly of Spain's wine regions. The estuaries are packed with mussel-farming platforms and busy clam beds. So, it comes as no surprise that the local wine is a crisp, dry white that tastes just wonderful with the local seafood. The *Albariño* grape produces the most aromatic and exotically scented white wines of Spain; they command high prices on the local market so don't expect a bargain. As one local lady put it, an Albariño always deserves a tablecloth, it's just not the thing to take to the beach. The peachy scent is unforgettable and a delicious pairing with the classic, simply prepared fish and shellfish of the region.

Rueda is an ancient wine region that's been recently injected with a huge, new lease of life. Experienced winemakers have come in from areas such as Bourdeaux and Rioja bringing modern winemaking methods with them. The old style, traditional wines made predominantly from the *Verdejo* grape are rich, highly alcoholic and taste a bit like rough sherry. Today the region is producing zippier, herby tasting wines made from *Verdejo* and smaller quantities of *Viura* grapes by cold fermentation, these are light and ideal to drink with fish or grilled (broiled) vegetable dishes. Also from *Rueda* are increasing numbers of delicious wines made from more recently planted French *Sauvignon Blanc* grapes.

Rich, Oily Fish, Creamy Sauces, Poultry and Light Meat

Labels to look out for

Conca de Barberá – Torres, Costers de Segre Castell de Remei

Navarra – Chivite, Principe de Viana

Penedés – Bach, Jean León, Torres

Somontano – Enate

Rioja – Marqués de Murrieta, Muga, Sonsierra

A richer, fuller wine would be ideal with salmon, tuna, trout, sardines or any of the oily fish. Salt cod has a great depth of flavour and is often served with rich sauces too. Creamy dishes such as the Catalan Cannelloni (see page 74) or light poultry and veal dishes fit into this category.

Many areas such as *Costers del Segre, Navarra, Penedés* and *Somontano* are all producing wines made with the French **Chardonnay** grape. Some of these fit into the subtle, steely bone-dry style; wonderful with clean, fresh fish flavours and therefore slip into the crisp white category above. Others are fat and buttery, after barrel fermentation, fabulous alongside rich fish and poultry. Unfortunately the label is unlikely to tell you which you a dealing with. A deep, yellow wine will give a pretty good indication of oak fermentation and ageing, but your wine merchant or supplier will certainly be able to advise you.

The legendary *Rioja D.O*, is producing progressively less of its characteristic oaked, oxidized white wine. The most traditional wines, made primarily with the **Viura** grape, are intense and could almost taste corked to the uninitiated. You'd need a pretty rich chicken or veal dish to cope with one of these. Young whites, **blancos jóvenes** are taking over and these may be lightly oaked, with hints of vanilla and lemon or rather nondescript cool-fermented wines. It's time for another chat with the wine merchant.

Barbecues, Rice Dishes, Lentils, Pastas and Tortillas

Labels to look out for
Navarra – Chivite, Gran Feudo, Ochoa, Castillo de Monjardín.
L'Ampordà – Costa Brava Castillo Perelada
Catalunya – Torres

Many wine buffs are a bit sniffy about *rosados* (rosé wines) but I can think of nothing more fitting for lunch on the beach, the shady terrace or the aft-deck. Great with relaxed outdoor meals such as barbecues, traditional rice dishes, lentils, pastas and *tortillas*. Rosé tastes of holidays (vacations).

D.O Navarra is, without a doubt, Spain's most prolific producer of pink wines, mainly made from the *garnacha* grape. Meanwhile a few of the Riojan producers make rosés from *garnacha* grapes in the lower, hotter *Rioja Baja* region. Many of the Catalan *denominaciones* produce easy drinking *rosados* too, the ideal seaside quaffing wine.

Light Meat Dishes, Chicken, Rabbit and Big Flavoured Fish

Labels to look out for
Valdepeñas – Casa de la Viña, Pata Negra
El Bierzo – Descendientes de J Palacios, Prada a Tope, Vinos del Bierzo

Now you might chose to drink a creamy, white or a rosé wine with this type of food but don't forget that a light red wine could be a winner too. Take the trout and crisp *jamón* on page 105; well that would be fabulous with a light red wine.

Reds from *Valdepeñas*, from the seemingly endless plains of Don Quijote's La Mancha, would be an option. They are made from the *Cencibel* grape (which is just the favourite Spanish *Tempranillo* in disguise) and are generally softer and rounder than their Riojan or Ribero del Duero counterparts.

Delicious light reds from the up and coming *El Bierzo* region, in the mountainous west of Castille and León made with the local *Mencía* grape could be interesting. The area has its own almost mild microclimate resulting in wines a world away from the muscley numbers of nearby *Toro*.

Rustic Fodder: Chorizo, Cured Meats, One-pot Bean Dishes

Labels to look out for
Toro – Bodegas Fariña
Somontano – Enate
Cariñena – Torrelongares
Campo de Borja – Borsao

Here are flavours that you'll often encounter in the *Tapas* bar, or in a one-pot bean dish such as the Asturian *Fabada* laden with rich smoked sausages. These are robust, uncomplicated flavours that require plenty of acidity and tannin to cut through the fat. It's time to hit the sturdy reds, loaded with tannin. This is not the moment to splash out on a complex *reserva*, the wine will be quite simply over powered by the food. If you're heading for a *Rioja* or *Ribera del Duero* go for a younger Crianza style or you could try one of these:

The beefy wines of *Toro*, have always been renowned for their kick, with massive alcohol levels. Nowadays it would seem that the bull has been tamed and more rounded wines are emerging. They'd still stand up to good *tapas* session though, the question is will you still be standing too?

Traditional wines of *Somontano*, *Cariñena* and *Campo de Borja* from *Garnacha* and *Cariñena* grapes are packed with robust flavours and alcohol to match the rich lamb casseroles (see page 128) and rustic fare However, these areas are re-inventing themselves producing higher quality wines using *Tempranillo* and new grapes such as *Cabernet Sauvignon*.

Lamb, Lamb, Pork and Lamb

Labels to look out for
Rioja – Marqués de Cáceres, Marqués de Griñon, Muga, Marques de Murrieta, Palacio, Marques de Riscal
Ribera del Duero – Alión, Dehesa de los Canónigos, Pesquera, Pingus, Protos.
Cigales – Marques de Pagollano, Museum

Once you reach the arid inland plains of Spain you are in the *asador*, or roasting, country. Dusty fields of sparse grass and aromatic herbs are, miraculously, all a sheep needs to thrive, and the lamb is legendary. Restaurants roast baby, milk-fed lamb in huge wood-fired ovens and the meat just melts in your mouth.

The regions of *Rioja* and *Ribera del Duero*, are both in the heart of lamb country and so of course the wines are absolutely ideal for this style of food. These are Spain's best-known, most recognizable and celebrated wines.

Rioja's top wines mainly emerge from the *Rioja Alta* and the key grape is the *Tempranillo* usually blended with *Garnacha*, and smaller quantities of *Graciano* and *Mazuelo*. But, grapes apart, the one thing synonymous with *Rioja* is oak and that's all down to the French! The winemakers of Bordeaux made *Rioja* their home in the mid nineteenth century when their own vineyards were stricken by the dreaded Phylloxera bug. They brought centuries of refined technique with them including the practice of ageing the wine in oak. *Rioja* wines are herbaceous, smoky and underpinned with the vanilla flavours of oak. Anything from a fruity *Crianza* to a smoother oaky *Reserva* will be wonderful; it just depends on the budget.

A little further west, beside the Duero river we find the *Ribera del Duero*. This area of ancient castles and sugar beet is the golden goose of the Spanish wine makers. Its rise was meteoric in the 1980s and now it's often known for more sophisticated and richer wines than *Rioja*. The key grape is the *Tinto Fino*, which is in fact a variation of that old coconut, the *Tempranillo* again. The legendary *Vega Sicila* wine is actually made from French grape varieties too but celebrities such as *Pingus* and *Pesquera* have proved that *Tinto Fino* can come up with the goods all by itself.

Nearby *Cigales* is an area to keep your eye on, with plummy, fruit-led wines with a bit of oak ageing thrown in. A *Cigales reserva* can be an absolute bargain compared to a more distinguished *Rioja* so do give it a try.

Elegant Red Meats and Game Dishes – the Big Splash Out

Labels to look out for
See **Rioja** and **Ribera** suggestions above
Priorat –Alvaro Palacios
Costers de Siurana – Scala Dei

Refined food with great depth of flavour will be heaven indeed with a complex, rounded wine to match. It may be a piece of fine beef fillet (tenderloin) or a venison casserole packed with flavour. There's nothing to stop you pulling the stops out for a leg of lamb either.

Now it's time to splash out on the *Reservas* and *Gran Reservas* of the great *bodegas* or wineries.

A fabulous *Rioja* or *Ribera del Duero* would be an absolute treat with lamb(see above) or you could go for the rising star of the Spanish wine industry from *Priorat*. Winemakers and big investors are descending upon the region like bees to a honey pot. The wines are not for the faint hearted and certainly require a pretty robust and rich dish of red meat or game to balance them. They vary from 13.5 percent to over 16 percent alcohol so you'd better factor in a *siesta* too. Talented modern winemakers have planted *Cabernet Sauvignon* and *Syrah* alongside the traditional *Garnacha* and *Cariñena* with astounding results. These wines already have a cult following, although the ageing potential is only beginning to be realized as the style is so young, but they are tipped to last a massive thirty years. *Rioja* and *Ribera* step aside!

Cheeses

I have to say that invariably I carry on with what ever I'm drinking! It's a tricky business if you're serving a variety of cheese, as a soft goat's cheese might call for a Sauvignon Blanc while a hard sheep's cheese would be better with a more commanding red. So, I'll be a complete heathen and say a tasty Rioja is pretty good with the lot.

Desserts

Labels to look out for
Catalayud (Moscatel) – Torres
Jeréz – Lustau, Sacrístia

A voluptuous, golden *Moscatel*, clinging like honey to the side of the glass is glorious with fruity or custard-based desserts. I fell in love with its orange-marmalade charms as a child in the seaside town of Benicasim and have never forgotten it.

When tackling desserts of a "death by chocolate" nature or rich sweets packed with dried fruits then there is nothing better than a *Pedro Ximénez* sherry from *Jeréz*. It tastes of ripe raisins, it's absolute nectar.

Other Bottles to Keep in Store

Aguardiente de Orujo is the fire water spirit, distilled from grape skins and pips (seeds) left over from winemaking. The Galician *Orujo* is legendary, particularly when it is burnt as a *quiemada* with lemon zest, sugar and coffee beans.

Pacharán (*patxarán*) is a delicious liqueur from Navarre made with sloes and *anís* (an aniseed liqueur).

Vi Ranci is an oxidized, sweetened white wine from Catalonia. It can be replaced with an Oloroso sherry in the recipes.

3
Light Bites and Tapas

This is one of the classic *pinchos* of the Basque country. Spicy and salty, you will be gasping for a slug of cool wine or refreshing beer. If you find this combination too salty then try using the delicious pickled anchovies, *boquerones*, instead of the cured. I find *boquerones* even more delicious with a little crushed garlic and parsley added.

Gilda

Anchovy, Pepper and Olive Pincho

Serves 4

8 salted anchovies
8 sweet *guindilla* peppers
16 green stoned (pitted) olives

Thread the anchovies, peppers and olives on to 8 wooden cocktail sticks (toothpicks), curling the peppers and anchovies around the olives. Hey presto, you have it.

Tetilla is a deliciously creamy cow's milk cheese from Galicia. The name, "little tit" derives from its conical, breast-like shape although you could drop the "little", it is more like a double D cup! The combination of cheese and sweet quince jelly is just magical, so do try using other cheeses too.

Pincho de Tetilla y Membrillo

Tetilla Cheese and Quince Jelly

Serves 4

100 g/4 oz *tetilla* cheese
50 g/2 oz *membrillo* (quince jelly)

Cut the cheese and *membrillo* into small cubes or slices. Place the *membrillo* on top of the cheese and spear with a wooden cocktail stick (toothpick).

Tip
* In Spain, and increasingly elsewhere, you can buy ready grilled (broiled) and peeled red peppers in a jar. I would go for *El Bierzo* red peppers, rather than the more gutsy *pimientos de piquillo* in this recipe.

Pimientos de Padrón

Fried Padrón Peppers

6 tbsp olive oil
200 g/7 oz *pimientos de Padrón*
1 tsp coarse grain salt

Heat the olive oil in a large frying pan. Add the peppers and cook over a high heat until they begin to blister and colour. Place the peppers on a serving plate using a slotted spoon to drain off the excess oil. Serve at once sprinkled with salt.

And

These peppers are usually eaten with fingers as a bar snack or appetizer but could also make a fantastic accompaniment to grilled (broiled) meat and fish.

Tuna canning is big business on the north coast of Spain, particularly in Cantabria and the Basque country. Canned tuna is completely different from its fresh counterpart and, I think, equally delicious in its own way. The pale fleshed *bonito del norte* is the most highly prized and is really worth seeking out.

Pincho de Atún y Pimiento

Tuna and Pepper Pincho

Serves 4

75 g/3 oz canned best quality tuna in olive oil
3 tbsp mayonnaise, (see page 134 or use a good, preferably organic store-bought one)
Salt and freshly ground black pepper
Fresh lemon juice (optional)
8 slices baguette
1 red (bell) pepper, roasted and peeled (see page 24), to garnish

Drain and flake the tuna into tiny pieces and mix with the mayonnaise until soft and creamy. If you are too generous with the tuna the result will seem dry. Season with salt, pepper or a squeeze of fresh lemon juice if necessary.

Pile the tuna mayonnaise on to the slices of bread, be generous, the Basques are. The bread is there to hold the *pincho* together, not as the main player. Garnish with red (bell) pepper and eat as soon as possible.

Every year in San Sebastián there is a fiercely contested prize for the very best *pincho* on offer. Patxi and Blanca, the husband and wife team at the Bar Bergara are always among the hot favourites with their elegant, new-wave nibbles. The counter is crammed with tiny tarts, croquettes, stuffed croissants and bread, precariously piled with goodies. As if this were not enough, there is also a small blackboard of hot pinchos made to order. This is one of them and the combination is just out of this world.

Foie gras is easily accessible in both the Basque Country and Catalonia and the lightly cooked *mi-cuit foie gras* is used here. I find the *bloc de foie gras*, is much easier to get hold of and the results are equally delicious.

Foie Templado con Mango

Foie Gras and Mango Pincho

Serves 4

8 slices baguette
100 g/4 oz mi-cuit *foie gras* or *bloc de foie gras*, cut into 8 thin slices
8 thin slices mango
Coarsely ground black pepper
Balsamic vinegar

Preheat the oven to 200°C/400°F/Gas Mark 6.

Begin by toasting the baguette. Place the *foie gras,* then the mango on top. Place in the oven for a couple of minutes, just enough to warm through. Sprinkle with black pepper and a splash of balsamic vinegar. Heaven.

Pa amb tomàquet is a Catalan institution. In a land where olive oil has always been plentiful and tomatoes easy to grow, this is the distinctly healthy answer to Northern Europe's bread and butter.

The Catalans are proud of their cuisine and even such a simple combination is prepared with great love and care. I once witnessed an unsuspecting tourist being accosted by a fellow diner, when he began to slice his tomato instead of squeezing. After a meticulous demonstration the local chap returned to his seat with a contented nod, happy in the knowledge that he had educated another, somewhat bemused, foreigner in the ways of Pa amb tomàquet.

Pa Amb Tomàquet e Pernil

Grilled Bread with Tomato and Cured Ham

Serves 4

4 slices country bread
1 garlic clove, sliced in half
2 ripe tomatoes, halved around their equator
Extra virgin olive oil
Salt
4 slices *jamón*, such as Ibérico or serrano

Begin by toasting the bread, it will taste best on a barbecue or ridged griddle pan (stovetop grill pan) but a toaster will do. While the bread is still hot rub with a little garlic. Next squeeze the tomato over each slice to release a juicy pulp. Finish with a good drizzle of your favourite extra virgin olive oil and a little salt.

Place the jamón on top, fold and tuck it a little rather than placing it flat. It looks much more appetizing.

If you are making a large quantity of *Pa amb tomàquet* it is worth grating the tomato flesh into a bowl and spooning it on as required. The skin will miraculously remain intact during the procedure.

A fabulously simple dish made with two favourite ingredients of Asturias: pork and apples. The sweet smell of smoky cured sausage and fermenting apples that pervaded the *chigre*, or cider bar, where I first encountered this dish is just unforgettable.

Try cooking this dish with red wine instead of cider. But beware, the combination of red wine and *chorizo* is guaranteed to stain anything and everything, so not a moment for the favourite white linen tablecloth.

Chorizo con Sidra

Chorizo with Cider

300 g/10 oz hot or sweet *chorizo*, preferably the softer, less cured variety
300 ml/10 fl oz/1 ¼ cups dry (hard) cider
Crusty country bread, to serve

Preheat the oven to 200°C/400°F/Gas Mark 6.

Using a sharp knife, slice the *chorizo* into discs (disks) about 2.5 cm/1 inch thick and place them in a small ovenproof dish, such as a terracotta *cazuela*. Pour over the cider and bake in the oven for about 15 minutes. As soon as the surface of the cider is glistening with paprika and *chorizo* juices it is ready.

Serve with plenty of very crusty, country bread to mop up the smoky cider.

Opposite: Tortos de Maís con Queso Cabrales y Miel, page 52

Croquetas are a favourite all over Spain. They are popular toddler's teatime fodder as well as a welcome offering in the *tapas* bar. They take me back to my days at the high chair, as an au pair, when it was certainly a case of "one for you, one for me".

The options are limitless from the more usual chicken or ham croquettes to salt cod or wild mushroom. They can be truly sublime, a crisp crunchy shell with an oozing, creamy stuffing.

Croquettes are fiddly to prepare but are certainly worth the effort. They are great family party food as their appeal stretches from teenagers to toothless great-grannies.

Variations

* Try using finely chopped *jamón serrano* instead of the chicken, about 100 g/4 oz will be plenty, a great way of using the scraps around the bone if you happen to have a whole ham.
** Wild mushrooms make wonderful *croquetas,* fry them with the onions and evaporate as much liquid as possible. Continue as before using vegetable stock instead of the chicken stock, if you prefer.

Tip

* *Croquetas* are best served straight away but can easily be made ahead of time and reheated in a hot oven, as they do in the *tapas* bars.

Croquetas

Croquettes

Makes 12–16 croquettes

Chicken Croquettes

2 tbsp olive oil or butter
½ small onion, very finely diced
4 tbsp plain (all-purpose) flour
250 ml/8 fl oz milk, chicken stock or a mixture of the two
400 g/14 oz very finely chopped or minced (ground) cooked chicken (poached or leftovers from a roast)
Salt and freshly ground black pepper
Freshly grated nutmeg
200 g/7 oz/1¾ cups fine white dried breadcrumbs
2 medium eggs, beaten with a little water
Olive oil, for frying

Heat the olive oil or butter in a frying pan. Add the onion and cook gently until it becomes soft and transparent. Sprinkle over the flour and cook for a few more minutes. Slowly add the milk, stirring constantly as if you were making a white sauce. Now boil the mixture for 1–2 minutes until it becomes really thick, but take care because it will spit!

Next add the chicken. Season the paste with salt, pepper and nutmeg. Place the mixture in a flat dish or tray and place in the refrigerator for at least 2 hours, or preferably overnight, to cool and firm up.

Once thoroughly chilled, you should be able to divide the mixture into small bricks.

Now for the production line, and mid operation, the inevitable phone call from the double glazing salesman! Have your breadcrumbs and beaten eggs ready in 2 wide shallow bowls and a tray for the finished croquettes.

Roll the mixture into a ball or cylinder, then dip in the breadcrumbs, then the egg and then back in the crumbs. The croquettes can be chilled at this stage until ready to use. You can even make a few extra and store them in the freezer.

Heat the oil in a deep-fat fryer or deep frying pan to 190°C/375°F, or until a cube of bread sizzles immediately when added. Deep-fry the *croquetas* until golden brown, drain on kitchen paper (paper towels) and serve at once. You will need to cook the *croquetas* in batches.

Opposite: Pa amb Oli i Xocolata, page 61

The potato omelette (omelet) graces virtually every bar in Spain. It is eaten for breakfast, as a pre-prandial snack and enjoyed among a myriad of *tapas* along with a drink. When travelling by train, I am always intrigued by the carefully wrapped foil parcels that emerge from bags and baskets at lunchtime, more often than not there will be a wedge of juicy *tortilla* among them: the perfect transportable picnic food. The Cirera family's cook, Isabel Jiménez, makes the best *tortilla* I have ever eaten. I spent a morning with her learning a few of her secrets.

The plain and simple potato omelette (omelet) is perhaps the best of the lot. Isabel uses a bland sunflower oil to cook the potatoes but you may prefer to use a light olive oil. Do not be put off by the amount of oil, it really must cover the potatoes, you will strain it off anyway.

Tortilla Española

Spanish Omelette

Serves 4

300 ml/10 fl oz/1¼ cups sunflower oil or olive oil
700 g/1½ lb waxy potatoes, peeled, cut into chips (french fries),
    then sliced into thin squares
1 medium onion, diced (optional)
Salt
5 medium eggs
2 tbsp olive oil

Heat the sunflower oil in a deep frying pan (skillet). Add the potato and onion and cook gently over a medium heat for about 20 minutes, or until well cooked. Make sure that they do not fry or colour. Stir occasionally so they don't weld together.

Once the potatoes are thoroughly cooked, place them in a colander and strain off and reserve the oil (It can be used for another *tortilla*). Leave the potatoes to cool for a few minutes.

Beat the eggs together thoroughly with a fork, then add the potatoes and stir well. Season with salt to taste.

Heat the olive oil in a small frying pan (skillet), about 20 cm/8 inches in diameter. Once the oil is really hot, add the omelette (omelet) mixture; it should fill the pan to achieve a traditionally thick and juicy *tortilla*.

Reduce the heat to medium and cook for about 5 minutes until the base has just set. Loosen the sides of the omelette (omelet) with a wooden spatula and shake the pan well.

Now for the fun: take a plate a good deal larger than your pan or use a flat upturned saucepan lid that has a handle to grip on to. Invert your omelette (omelet) on to the flat surface. Beware, as the base will still be quite runny.

Add another tablespoon of oil to the pan and slide the *tortilla* back in. Continue to cook for a few minutes until the centre of the tortilla feels almost set. If you can bear it, turn the omelette (omelet) a couple more times, cooking briefly on each side. You will be much more confident by now and your tortilla will have the traditional rounded sides of a professional.

Serve the omelette (omelet) while still warm or at room temperature. When serving straightaway I love to leave the centre a little juicy and soft, but do cook it thoroughly if the *tortilla* will be standing for a while.

This is a really refreshing summer *tortilla*, great when broad (fava) beans are in season. In Barcelona's Boquería market the ladies busy themselves podding tiny, tender broad (fava) beans between customers so you can buy them ready for the pot. If you are the "podder", a more likely scenario, and discover that your beans are a little larger and more leathery than hoped, then it really is worth skinning them too – a true labour of love or a good excuse to sit down with a glass of wine. Blanch the beans in a pan of boiling water for a couple of minutes, cool, then pinch the skin between your fingertips and the glorious bright sweet bean will emerge. Frozen beans are very good too and will just slip out of their skins once thawed.

Tortilla de Habas

Spanish Omelette with Broad Beans

250 ml/8 fl oz/1 cup olive oil
450 g/1 lb waxy potatoes, thinly sliced
1 onion, finely diced
5 medium eggs
200 g/7 oz/1⅜ cups young broad (fava) beans, cooked in boiling water until just tender
Small handful fresh mint, finely chopped

Follow the method for the *Tortilla Española* opposite. Add the broad (fava) beans and mint to the beaten eggs and continue as before. You could even add a few small pieces of *jamón serrano* or cooked bacon too.

When cooking with *chorizo* it is always best to buy the softer sausage that has not been fully cured. The drier harder variety is usually eaten raw and can become really rather tough once cooked. If you can only get hold of the fully cured one, just make sure that you slice it very finely. It's your choice whether you go for the sweet smokiness of the *dulce* or the spicy kick of the *chorizo picante*, just as long as you are aware of the difference.

Variation

* As you can see, once you can make a good tortilla the world is your oyster – ham, asparagus, artichoke, spinach, salt cod; you can add what ever you fancy.

Tortilla de Chorizo y Pimientos

Chorizo, Pepper and Potato Omelette

450 g/1 lb waxy potatoes, thinly sliced
200 g/7 oz sweet or spicy, soft cured *chorizo*
250 ml/8 fl oz/1 cup olive oil
2 onions, finely sliced
2 red (bell) peppers or 100 g/4 oz preserved *El Bierzo* or *piquillo* peppers
5 medium eggs

Follow the recipe for *Tortilla Española* opposite and, while the potatoes are cooking, heat the olive oil in a frying pan (skillet). Add the *chorizo* and fry for a few minutes, then drain off the excess oil. If you are roasting and peeling your own (bell) peppers, rather than using a preserved variety, then this is the time to do it (see page 24). Slice the peppers into thin ribbons.

Add the cooked *chorizo* and peppers to the beaten eggs together with the potato and onion mixture and proceed as before.

Corn once played a vital role in the peasant diet of northwestern Spain. Introduced from America, it flourished here and the countryside of Asturias and Galicia is still studded with *horréos* or granaries. These small buildings on pillars were built to store and protect the cobs. Corn bread and *tortos* were absolute staples, later superseded by wheat bread.

I came across these tiny corn cakes in the village of Asiegu, high in the Asturian Picos de Europa. The views are apparently quite stunning, not that I saw them as we were engulfed in a thick Atlantic fog. I drowned my sorrows with some home-made cider and these tasty corn cakes topped with the local Cabrales blue cheese and heather honey from the mountainside.

Variation

* You could double the size of the *tortos*, making sure that they are still 1 cm/½ inch thick (or they will be very stodgy), and serve them for breakfast with fried eggs and *chorizo*.

How these deliciously spicy mussels earned their name, "rabid tigers", I have yet to discover but they are a popular nibble in many bars. The sauce is fabulous mopped up with bread .

The Rias Baixas, or estuaries of western Galicia, are the world's most productive mussel beds. The mussels grow on ropes suspended from fleets of rafts that occupy the inlets. They are glorious just steamed with a little water and served immediately with a squeeze of lemon but for something spicier and great to prepare ahead, try this recipe.

Tortos de Maís con Queso Cabrales y Miel

Corn Cakes with Cabrales Blue Cheese and Honey

Serves 4 (makes about 12 small tortos)

100 g/4 oz cornmeal, *masa harina* or *polenta* (the polenta processed in a blender until fine and soft)
25 g/1 oz/¼ cup plain (all-purpose) flour
1 tsp salt
120 ml/4 fl oz/½ cup boiling water
Olive oil, for frying
200 g/7 oz Cabrales, Picos de Europa or Roquefort cheese
6 tbsp runny heather honey

Place the cornmeal, flour and salt in a bowl. Pour the boiling water over the flour and stir with a wooden spoon until the mixture is a doughy consistency. You may need a couple of extra tablespoons of water. Leave to cool.

Once cool enough, roll the dough into walnut-sized balls and lay them on a damp cloth. With dampened hands, flatten them to about 1 cm/½ inch thick. You should finish up with about 12 small discs (disks).

Heat the olive oil in a frying pan (skillet). Add the *tortos* and fry until they are completely golden and cooked through. Drain well on kitchen paper (paper towels), then top each cake with a little Cabrales cheese and a drizzle of honey.

Serve at once, otherwise the corn cakes will become tough and rubbery.

Tigres Rabiosos

Spicy Mussels

Serves 4

About 150 ml/5 fl oz/⅔ cup water
24 live mussels
2 tbsp olive oil
1 large onion, chopped
3 garlic cloves, chopped
1 small dried red chilli (chili pepper), crushed

1 tsp sweet or hot paprika, depending on how rabid you like your tigers
4 ripe tomatoes, peeled and diced
4 canned anchovy fillets, diced
150 ml/5 fl oz/⅔ cup dry white wine
Salt and freshly ground black pepper
Crusty bread, to serve

Begin by cleaning the mussels. Scrub the shells and pull away any turfy beards. Now discard any mussels that remain open or have damaged shells. These mussels are

* You could add 100 g/4 oz/²/₃ cup of diced, stoned (pitted) olives to the sauce.
** Alternatively, place the mussels in a flat dish or terracotta *cazuela*, sprinkle with a tangy cheese and some breadcrumbs and place under a preheated hot grill (broiler) to brown.

dead and could cause food poisoning.

Bring the water to the boil in a large saucepan. Add the mussels and cover with a tight lid. Give the saucepan a shake every couple of minutes, then turn off the heat as soon as the mussels have fully opened.

Leave the mussels to cool then remove the lids leaving the juicy flesh in the half shells.

Heat the olive oil in a frying pan (skillet). Add the onion and fry until soft and golden. Add the garlic, chilli (chili pepper) and paprika and stir until the aroma really hits you. Add the tomatoes, anchovies and wine and boil to reduce the sauce a little. Taste and adjust the seasoning if necessary.

Once you are ready to eat, add the mussels to the hot sauce and cook briefly to heat them through but do not boil. Serve with crusty bread.

A traditional Galician market would be unthinkable without the *pulperías*, or octopus stands that pop up among the stalls of umbrellas, vast flesh-coloured corsets, bedroom slippers, cheese and bread. Translucent octopus are dunked on long metal hooks into copper cauldrons of swirling pink water. Later they emerge plumped and violet. They are snipped with scissors on to small wooden platters and promptly eaten with olive oil, salt and paprika.

At Ribadavia's twice-monthly market the local men, sporting curiously small berets, are in the bar by ten, enjoying their breakfast: octopus, hunks of bread and bottles of Ribeiro wine from the surrounding vine-clad banks of the Miño river. I managed to resist. An hour later a serving of warm, salty-sweet *pulpo* proved an unexpected treat as I wandered in the persistent October drizzle.

Variation

* Potatoes are sometimes boiled in the octopus water to accompany the dish; they turn a fantastically lurid violet colour.

Pulpo á Feira

Galician Octopus

Serves 8

1 octopus, weighing about 1–1.8 kg/2–4 lb
½ onion, left in one piece
Extra virgin olive oil
1 tsp sweet paprika
Salt

Begin by cleaning the octopus. Turn back the tentacles and slice through the muscles that hold the innards inside the head. Next turn the head inside out and wash thoroughly. Pop the head back the right way and the job is done. Now freeze the octopus for at least 48 hours. This will save you all the thrashing and pounding that used to be necessary to tenderize the flesh.

Place the onion in a large saucepan, then fill with water and bring to the boil.

As soon as the water is boiling hard, using a pair of tongs, dip the octopus in and out of the water 3–4 times until the tentacles begin to curl. This will keep the skin intact and give a deliciously tender result. Place the octopus in the boiling water and cook for about 30–45 minutes, or until a skewer slides easily through the flesh.

Turn off the heat and leave the octopus to rest in the water for 10 minutes. Slice the tentacles into discs (disks) and pile them on to a wooden board, drizzle with olive oil and sprinkle with salt and paprika to taste.

Tuck in with a cocktail stick (toothpick) while the octopus is still just warm. You may store the cooked octopus for a couple of days in the refrigerator, just make sure you let it come back to room temperature and add the seasoning at the last minute.

Meatballs are standard fare at *tapas* bars, on restaurant set menus and in the home kitchen. Most Spanish cooks wouldn't even require a recipe to prepare them; it's just second nature. Meatballs vary but most are made with a combination of pork, and beef or lamb. I ate an exquisite wild boar meatball stuffed with a chestnut in the Pyrenean foothills. Another rather bizarre, but tasty, combination was a dish of meatballs served with squid that I ate in the chic Catalan resort of Cadaqués. But perhaps my all-time favourites are these meatballs with ceps that I tasted in the Basque city of San Sebastián.

Tips

* You could of course omit the mushrooms altogether and the meatballs would still be delicious.
** Try adding pine kernels (pine nuts) to the meatballs instead of mushrooms and add a stick of cinnamon to the tomato sauce.
*** You could use lamb instead of beef and spice up the meatballs with a little cumin and handful of fresh mint.

Albóndigas de Setas

Wild Mushroom Meatballs

Makes about 24 meatballs

15 g/¹⁄₂ oz dried ceps, or any other tasty
   dried wild mushroom
2 tbsp olive oil
1 onion, finely diced
3 garlic cloves
280 g/10 oz minced (ground) beef
100 g/4 oz minced (ground) pork
2 tbsp fresh breadcrumbs
2 tbsp fresh flat-leaf parsley, chopped
1 medium egg, beaten
Salt and freshly ground black pepper
3 tbsp plain (all-purpose) flour,
   for dusting
2 tbsp olive oil, for frying

For the sauce
2 tbsp olive oil
1 onion, finely diced
1 red (bell) pepper, finely diced
2 garlic cloves, crushed
900 g/2 lb ripe tomatoes, peeled and
   chopped or 800 g/1 ³⁄₄ lb canned
2 tbsp fresh flat-leaf parsley,
   finely chopped
5 tbsp white wine
200 ml/7 fl oz/scant 1 cup mushroom
   soaking water (see method)
Salt and pepper, and sugar, to taste

For the meatballs, place the wild mushrooms in a bowl, pour in enough hot water to cover them and leave to soak for 20 minutes.

Heat the olive oil in a frying pan (skillet). Add the onion and fry until soft, then add the garlic and fry, taking care not to burn it, until it just turns gold.

Next drain the mushrooms, reserving the soaking water, and chop them very finely. Add the mushrooms to the onions and cook for 1–2 minutes.

Place the beef, pork, breadcrumbs, parsley, egg and mushrooms in a large bowl and mix together. Season with salt and pepper to taste.

If I am making a lot of meatballs I fry a little ball of the mixture to check the seasoning at this point.

Roll the mixture into walnut-sized balls and dust with the flour. Heat the olive oil in a large frying pan (skillet). Add the meatballs and fry until they are well browned and just cooked through.

For the sauce, heat the olive oil in a pan. Add the onion and red (bell) pepper and fry until soft. Add the garlic and continue to cook until the garlic begins to turn golden. Add the tomatoes, parsley, wine and the reserved mushroom soaking liquid (it's worth straining, as it can be a little gritty).

Season with a little salt, pepper and sugar and leave to simmer for 20 minutes, then taste again and adjust the seasoning if necessary.

Add the meatballs to the sauce and cook at a gentle simmer for about 20 minutes before serving.

Pinchos Morunos can be found all over Spain, their delicious aromatic spicing harks back to centuries of Moorish rule. One of my favourite haunts is the Café Iruña in Bilbao, a *belle époque* gem of arabesque archways and glorious Spanish tiles. Here the waft of freshly cooked lamb and cumin is irresistible as Ahamed Belkhir, seated in his own corner of the bar, carefully turns kebabs over the hot coals as he has done for the last 35 years.

Tips

* Double the quantities and this will serve 6 as a main course. It is fantastic served with the *Escalivada* on page 90.
** Use lean pork instead of lamb for a delicious alternative.
*** If using wooden skewers soak them in a bowl of cold water for at least 30 minutes to prevent them burning while cooking.

Pinchos Morunos

Moorish Meat Kebabs

Serves 4

450 g/1 lb lean lamb, cut into large dice
Salt
Juice of 1 lemon

For the marinade
2 garlic cloves, crushed
3 tbsp olive oil
2 tbsp sherry vinegar
1 tsp ground cumin
1 tsp smoked sweet paprika
Pinch of hot paprika or cayenne pepper
½ tsp dried thyme

Mix all the marinade ingredients together in a bowl large enough to hold the meat. Add the lamb and leave to marinate for a few hours, or preferably overnight.

Preheat a ridged griddle pan (stovetop grill), grill (broiler) or barbecue. Thread the lamb dice on to wooden or metal skewers and sizzle for about 3 minutes, then turn over and cook for a further 3 minutes. Be sure not to overcook the lamb as it will dry out; I love mine slightly pink. Add a little salt, plenty of fresh lemon juice and serve at once.

Almost a sandwich and not quite a pie: this is perfect picnic food, ideal for wandering pilgrims on their way to Santiago, for farmers in the fields, for lunch on the beach or a snack in the bar. There are countless recipes and a never-ending debate as to whether the puff pastry, corn pastry or bread dough variety is the most authentic or the best. It all depends on the filling; a lamprey or baby clam *empanada* would be unthinkable without it's traditional cornmeal pastry but most varieties are made with a crisp bread dough, and delicious they are too.

I spent the morning cooking with Fernando Asensio in his restaurant in Goian, just a hop over the Miño river from Portugal, and learned this fantastic foolproof recipe.

Empanadas

Galician Flat Pies

For the crust
20 g/³⁄₄ oz fresh yeast or 1 tsp easy-blend dried (active dry) yeast
350 g/12 oz/2³⁄₈ cups strong white flour
125 g/4¹⁄₂ oz/³⁄₄ cup cornmeal, *masa harina* or finely ground *polenta*
¹⁄₂ tbsp salt
100 ml/3¹⁄₂ fl oz/generous 1/3 cup white wine
50 g/2 oz/¹⁄₄ cup lard or vegetable fat, chopped into 1 cm/¹⁄₂ inch dice
8 tbsp olive oil
1 medium egg, lightly beaten
Water, to bind the dough
1 medium egg, lightly beaten, to seal and glaze

Combine the yeast with about 3 tablespoons of hand-hot water and mix to a paste.

Pour the flour and cornmeal into a large bowl, then add the salt, wine, lard, olive oil, egg, yeast paste and enough water to make a soft, but not too sticky, dough.

Stir the mixture, then pull it together with your hands. If there is any dry flour left in the bowl, then add a splash more water. If the dough is too dry it will be difficult to roll it out thinly later.

Knead the dough for a couple of minutes until smooth and well mixed. Place the dough back in the bowl and cover with clingfilm (plastic wrap). Leave to rise for at least 1 hour, or until it has doubled in size.

Make the filling (see opposite).

Preheat the oven to 200°C/400°F/Gas Mark 6.

Roll out half the dough to a 5 mm/¹⁄₄ inch thick rectangle, disc (disk) or square. It does not matter; just make sure it will fit on your baking (cookie) sheet or Swiss roll tin (jelly roll pan). Oil the baking (cookie) sheet and lay the dough on top.

Next add the filling, spreading it evenly, leaving a 2 cm/1 inch margin around the edge. Brush the edge with a little beaten egg.

Roll the rest of your dough to the same size and lay it over the filling. Pinch the edges together, then twist over the dough to form a rope-like edge. Brush the whole *empanada* with beaten egg and, using a fork, pierce the top all over with little holes.

Leave to rest for 10 minutes, then bake in the hot oven for 20–30 minutes, or until the crust is really crisp and golden.

Every morning, in the Vista Alegre bakery in Santiago de Compostela the floury-faced baker is surrounded by a motley selection of pots and pans containing his clients own home-made fillings. He makes up the *empanadas*, carefully decorating each with a number or symbol to ensure that they return to their correct homes.

The universal ingredient is the onion, cooked long and slow until sweet and soft, then you may add whatever flavouring you please. Here are some of the most traditional and tasty.

Variations

* Octopus makes a fabulous filling – just fry the onions in olive oil, then add 2 crushed garlic cloves, 2 tablespoons of fresh flat-leaf parsley, 1 teaspoon of sweet paprika, continue to fry for a couple of minutes and then add about 900 g/2 lb cooked octopus (see page 53), cut into small chunks. Season with salt and pepper to taste and add to the empanada.

** Salt cod is another favourite – just add 400 g/14 oz of de-salted fish (see page 33) to the onions together with 2 crushed garlic cloves and 2 tablespoons of fresh flat-leaf parsley. Add 50 g/2 oz/ 3/8 cup of raisins and 200 g/7 oz/ 1 1/8 cups of well-drained cooked spinach and use as in main recipe.

Relleno de Atún

Tuna Filling

150 ml/5 fl oz/2/3 cup olive oil
4 onions, finely sliced
1 red (bell) pepper, finely sliced
1 green (bell) pepper, finely sliced
1 tsp sweet unsmoked paprika
175 g/6 oz canned tuna in olive oil
Salt
3 hard-boiled (hard-cooked) eggs, sliced (optional)

Heat the olive oil in a frying pan (skillet). Add the onions and fry until sweet and golden, then add the (bell) peppers. The longer and more gently you fry this base the sweeter and more delicious the result.

Sprinkle with the paprika, stir in the tuna and cook for a further 2 minutes. Season with salt to taste.

If you are using them, lay the slices of egg on top of the filling in the empanada before adding the lid.

Relleno de Lomo

Pork Filling

150 ml/5 fl oz/2/3 cup olive oil
450 g/1 lb pork loin, cut into fine strips
4 onions, finely sliced
1 red (bell) pepper, finely sliced
1 green (bell) pepper, finely sliced
2 garlic cloves, crushed
1 tsp sweet smoked paprika
1/2 tsp dried oregano
2 tbsp tomato purée (paste)
Salt and freshly ground black pepper

Begin by heating the olive oil in a large frying pan (skillet). Add the pork strips, a few at a time, and allow them to brown slightly, then remove them from the pan.

Cook the onions in the same oil until really soft, stirring occasionally.

Next add the (bell) peppers and continue cooking until these soften. Add the garlic and paprika, fry for a moment, then add the oregano and tomato purée (paste). Season with salt and pepper to taste.

A *coca* is really a Catalan pizza, although once in a while it may be made with pastry rather than bread dough. *Coques* can be sweet or savoury, square, round or oval but they are always flat.

The *coca* is often fiesta food, eaten on midsummer night and other festive occasions. In the Catalan town of Falset, surrounded by vines, olives, almonds and hazelnuts, they even have a *Ball de Coques* where the men are required to give a *coca* to every lady they dance with. Some young girls stagger home with enough to feed the five thousand, but according to tradition, every maiden, mother or widow should leave the square with at least one *coca*.

Coques

Flat Breads

For the dough - enough for 1 large coca
15 g/½ oz fresh yeast or 7 g/¼ oz easy-blend dried (active dry) yeast
300 ml/10 fl oz/1¼ cups hand-hot water, or enough to make the dough
450 g/1 lb/4 cups strong white flour, plus extra for dusting
1 tsp salt
4 tbsp olive oil
2 tbsp white wine
Oil, for greasing the baking (cookie) sheet

Place the yeast in a small bowl with 4 tablespoons of the hand-hot water and stir to form a loose paste. Tip the flour into a large mixing bowl and add the salt, olive oil, wine and yeast mixture. Add enough water to make a soft, but not too sticky, dough.

Turn the dough out on to a work surface and knead for about 5 minutes until silky and stretchy. Transfer it to a lightly oiled bowl and cover with a baking (cookie) sheet or some clingfilm (plastic wrap). Leave to rise for at least 1 hour at room temperature, or until it has doubled in size.

Preheat the oven to 200°C/400°F/Gas Mark 6.

Roll out the dough on a lightly floured work surface to a thickness of about 2 cm/¾ inch. The shape is not too important, usually round or oval for a sweet coca and rectangular for savoury. Lay the dough on an oiled baking sheet (cookie) and proceed with a topping of your choice , see opposite.

This is often made with a cake mix (batter) too although I prefer this bread dough version. Delicious dipped in black coffee and great for breakfast.

Coca de Pinyons

Pine Kernel Coca

1 x recipe *Coca* dough (see above)
1 tbsp olive oil
50 g/2 oz/¼ cup white sugar
100 g/4 oz/¾ cup pine kernels (pine nuts)
2 tbsp *anis* or any aniseed-flavoured liqueur

Once you have shaped your dough into 1–2 long ovals on an oiled baking (cookie) sheet, brush with a little olive oil.

Next cover the surface with sugar, sprinkle on the pine kernels (pine nuts) and drizzle with a little *anìs*.

Leave the *coca* to rise for 10 minutes before baking for about 20 minutes until golden.

* My great friend Mercè Brunés has a wonderful restaurant and guesthouse near Vic where she makes a delicious *coca* using courgettes (zucchini) in the dough. The result is a moister, softer bread. Just add about 250 g/9 oz/ 1¼ cups of grated courgettes (zucchini) together with the flour. Mix thoroughly before adding water to the dough; you really won't need much at all as the courgettes (zucchini) are packed with moisture. If the dough becomes sticky while you are kneading, just add a bit more flour.

Tip

* You could use anchovy or herring fillets instead of the sardines or even replace the fish with some stoned (pitted) olives.

Coca D'espinacs

Spinach Coca

1 tbsp olive oil
1 onion, finely sliced
2 garlic cloves, crushed
1 x recipe *Espinacs Amb Pases y Piñones* (see page 87)
1 x recipe *Coca* Dough (see opposite)
Plain (all-purpose) flour, for dusting

Heat the olive oil in a frying pan (skillet). Add the onion and fry until just soft and translucent. Add the garlic and cook for just long enough to release its fabulous aroma. Next stir in the spinach, raisins and pine nuts.

Roll out the coca dough on a lightly floured work surface and spread the spinach mixture over the top.

Bake for 20 minutes, or until the crust is crisp and golden.

Coca de Cutxipanda

Roasted Vegetable and Sardine Coca

1 x recipe *Coca* dough (see page opposite)
1 tbsp olive oil, plus extra for drizzling
1 x recipe *escalivada* (see page 90)
6 medium sardines, filleted
Salt

Brush the *coca* with olive oil, then arrange the roast vegetables in attractive strips across the top. Add the sardines, skin-side up. Drizzle the coca with olive oil, season with salt to taste and bake for about 20 minutes, or until the crust is crisp.

Galician bread is some of the best in Spain; it often contains plenty of rye, making it chewy and delicious. A wood-fired oven would add even more flavour but the home baked variety is still fabulous. This bread is sold by weight in many small stores, you can even buy it by the slice; great with a slither of local *tetilla* cheese for a meal on the hoof.

When making almost any bread I like to use a starter dough, it will always add flavour and texture to the dough.

This loaf keeps well for a few days.

Tips

* This bread is equally delicious without the raisins.
** Placing a saucepan or roasting tin (pan) of water in the oven below the bread will give a wonderfully crispy crust.
*** The remaining starter dough should go into the refrigerator with 4 tablespoons of plain [all-purpose] flour and 150 ml/5 fl oz/⅔ cup more water. This will hopefully encourage more bread baking.
**** Try incorporating it into any bread recipe for extra depth and flavour. Always use just half the starter and then add water and flour as above.

Pan Gallego con Pasas

Galician Bread with Raisins

You will need to begin the bread at least 24 hours in advance if you are making the starter dough. Otherwise continue with the recipe below – just add an extra 1 teaspoon of yeast.

For the starter dough
15 g/½ oz fresh yeast
300 ml/10 fl oz/1¼ cups water
250 g/9 oz/1¾ cups strong white bread flour

Cream the yeast with a little of the water in a large bowl then stir it in with the remaining water and flour. Make sure your bowl is large enough to allow plenty of room for expansion. Cover with a damp cloth and leave at room temperature for at least 24 hours and better still for 2 days. If you are not ready to use the starter yet, you may keep it in a jar in the refrigerator. It should smell almost champagne-like. Place the raisins in a heatproof bowl and add enough boiling water to cover. Leave to soak while you make the bread.

For the bread
150 g/5 oz/scant 1 cup raisins
600 ml/1 pint/2½ cups hand-hot water
20 g/¾ oz fresh yeast
450 g/1 lb/3 cups strong white bread flour
300 g/10 oz/2½ cups rye flour
50 g/2 oz/½ cup cornmeal, *masa harina* or finely ground *polenta*
Salt
Oil, for oiling
Sifted plain (all-purpose) flour, for dusting

Add a few tablespoons of water to the yeast and stir to a creamy paste.

Place the bread flour, rye flour and cornmeal in a large mixing bowl. Add a generous tablespoon of salt, the creamed yeast and half of your starter dough. (See left for advice on using up left-over dough.)

Next add enough water to make a soft but not too sticky dough. Tip the dough on to a large flat surface.

Now for the action, this is so much more rewarding than a trip to the gym. You must knead the dough for about 10 minutes. It will be hard work with all that heavy rye flour and cornmeal. Once the dough feels quite elastic, drain the raisins, add them to the dough and knead in.

Transfer the dough to a lightly oiled bowl and cover with a baking (cookie) sheet or some clingfilm (plastic wrap). Leave to rise at room temperature for at least 1 hour, or until it has doubled in size.

Knock back (punch down) the bread and shape it into a large, flat round, about 30 cm/12 inches across. Place the bread on an oiled baking (cookie) sheet, cover with a damp tea (dish) towel and leave to rise again until doubled in size.

Preheat the oven to 220°C/425°F/Gas Mark 7.

Sprinkle the loaf with the sifted plain (all-purpose) flour and bake for 10 minutes. Reduce the oven temperature to 190°C/375°F/Gas Mark 5 and bake for a further 40 minutes. Once the bread just slips off the baking (cookie) sheet and the bottom sounds hollow when tapped underneath, place it back in the oven, directly on the oven shelf for a couple of minutes longer until the base is crisp.

Leave to cool on a wire rack.

Pa amb Oli i Xocolata

Chocolate, Olive Oil and Rock Salt Toastie

This unlikely, but fabulous, combination is all about using the best quality ingredients you can get your hands on. Use a really delicious bitter chocolate and extra virgin olive oil good enough to drink. The young chefs of Barcelona are constantly trying to challenge the taste buds and this simple combination from the Estrella de Plata Bar really works.

Serves 4

50 g/2 oz best quality plain dark (bittersweet) chocolate, at least 70% cocoa solids
4 small slices of good white country bread
Extra virgin olive oil
Rock salt, for sprinkling
Sifted (unsweetened) cocoa powder, for sprinkling

Preheat the oven to 180°C/350°F/Gas Mark 4.

Place a chunk of chocolate on each slice of bread and warm through in the oven for 5 minutes, or until the chocolate just begins to melt.

Drizzle with extra virgin olive oil, sprinkle with rock salt and a little sifted cocoa. Serve at once.

High in the Asturian Mountains, among the eagles and clanking cowbells, Paula Valero runs her beautiful guest house, La Valleja. The food is organic and much of the fruit comes from the slopes below the house where blueberries, kiwis and raspberries grow between the apple trees and plum trees.

Paula is a wonderfully creative cook. She dreamed up this breakfast cake for a guest with a dairy allergy. The result, using olive oil, is fabulously light and moist. It makes a healthy teatime treat too, topped with a little fruit and honey.

Tips

* Do not use a loose-bottomed tin (pan) for this cake because the cake mixture (batter) will be quite runny.
** Delicious served as a dessert accompanied by sherry-plumped sultanas (golden raisins) (see Tip on page 143).

Marmalade Cake

Bizcocho de Naranja

Makes a 23-cm/9-inch cake

100 ml/3½ fl oz/generous ⅓ cup olive oil, plus extra for oiling
4 medium eggs
100 g/4 oz/½ cup caster (superfine) sugar
175 g/6 oz/⅔ cup marmalade
100 ml/3½ fl oz/generous ⅓ cup apple juice
200 g/7 oz/1⅜ cups plain (all-purpose) flour
1 tbsp baking powder
1 tbsp icing (confectioners') sugar, for dusting

Preheat the oven to 180°C/350°F/Gas Mark 4.

Oil a 23-cm/9-inch cake tin (pan) with olive oil and line the base with greaseproof (waxed) paper.

Place the eggs and sugar in a free-standing electric mixer or large bowl and beat together until soft and mousse-like. Add the marmalade, apple juice and olive oil and continue to mix together. Lastly, sift the flour and baking powder together and beat them into the mixture. Pour the thick cake mixture (batter) into the prepared cake tin (pan).

Bake the cake in the middle of the oven for 30–40 minutes until the top is browned and the centre is cooked through. (To test, insert a skewer into the middle of the cake and check that it is clean when pulled out.) Turn the cake out on to a wire rack to cool.

Serve dusted with a little icing (confectioners') sugar.

4

Soups and Starters

This recipe is inspired by a fabulous soup that I ate at the truly innovative restaurant, Casa Marcelo, in Santiago de Compostela. It was a steaming hot day in June and the chilled, intensely flavoured soup was just so refreshing. Once cut, the warm yolk flooded the soup while the crunchy salt and a drop of truffle oil just added the final magic touch.

The combination of asparagus and egg is a classic. Stumpy, white spears are topped with a soft poached egg in the traditional *Espárragos a la Tudelana* – do try it, it's fabulous. Marcelo made his soup with the spindly, wild asparagus that pops up in the hedgerows while I am using the more readily available, green asparagus. The most important consideration is the freshness of the asparagus, whatever its variety. Those tender stalks taste so much better when really fresh, so avoid the bundles that have been shipped from the other side of the planet, however good they look. Buy asparagus in season from a local greengrocer (grocery store) or, better still, the grower.

Variations
*   This soup can be served hot too, but keep it as an early summer treat.
** You could leave out the egg altogether. In which case add the potato and a few tablespoons of double (heavy) cream.

Gazpacho de Espárragos con Huevo Pochado

Chilled Asparagus Soup with a Warm Poached Egg

Serves 4

2 tbsp olive oil
2 small leeks, white parts only, chopped
600 ml/1 pint/2½ cups water
1 potato, peeled and diced (optional)
450 g/1 lb fresh asparagus, trimmed of the tough stalks and chopped
Salt and freshly ground black pepper
4 medium eggs, the freshest and best possible
1 tsp vinegar
Pinch of sea salt flakes
Few drops of truffle oil or extra virgin olive oil

Heat the olive oil in a saucepan. Add the leeks and stew slowly until soft.

Next add the water, a little salt, pepper and the potato, if you are using one. The potato will slightly thicken the soup making the whole dish seem a little more substantial. When I ate this at Casa Marcelo it was the first of a long succession of courses and so the soup was left naturally light and potato free. The soup will need to cook for about 10 minutes until the potato has softened. Next add the asparagus and boil for 5 minutes, no longer, or you will lose the glorious colour.

If you have a *pasapurés* push the soup through it leaving any stringy fibres behind. Otherwise you will need to purée the soup in a blender or food processor, then push it through a sieve (strainer). Do be careful, too much hot soup in the blender can result in dangerous eruptions.

Leave the soup to cool, then chill until ready to serve. When you are almost ready to serve pour the soup into some wide, shallow bowls.

Now for the eggs. Fill a wide saucepan or frying pan (skillet) to a depth of about 5 cm/ 2 inches of water. Add the vinegar and bring the water to a simmer, rather than a boil. Crack the eggs and drop them carefully into the water. Simmer, a couple at a time, for about 3 minutes, or until the white is set.

Remove the eggs with a slotted spoon and leave them to drain. You can even trim the edges of the white with scissors, if you are a true perfectionist. Place an egg in the centre of each bowl of soup. Sprinkle the egg with some flakes of sea salt and add a couple of drops of truffle oil. Be careful, truffle oil can be overpowering and is not to everyone's taste. You could serve it at the table with a glorious extra virgin olive oil as an alternative.

Opposite: Tortilla de Habas, page 51
Following page: Migas con Uvas y Granades, page 76

Tomato *gazpacho* is enjoyed all over Spain, although the dish originated in Andalucia, in the south. Charged with vitamins and fresh flavours, this chilled vegetable soup is fabulous on a sweltering summer's day. I tasted a striking beetroot (beet) version in the Izaga restaurant in Vitoria, the capital of the Basque country. The stunning fuchsia soup had an earthy dimension – just a few beetroot (beet) added to a traditional *gazpacho*, I was told. So, here you have it and believe me this is divine.

Nowadays, in some restaurants, your *gazpacho* will arrive in two halves; the first a plate resembling a modern artwork of carefully placed garnishes such as king prawns (jumbo shrimp) or more traditional accompaniments and the second half, a jug (pitcher) of soup.

Tips

* For a conventional *gazpacho* just replace the beetroot (beet) with tomatoes.
** Great served in chilled shot glasses at a drinks party or as an aperitif at the table.

Gazpacho de Remolacha

Beetroot Gazpacho

Serves 4

1 slice white country bread
450 g/1 lb beetroot (beet), cooked and peeled
250 g/9 oz ripe tomatoes, peeled and de-seeded
½ cucumber, peeled and roughly chopped
1 red (bell) pepper, de-seeded
1–2 garlic cloves, roughly chopped
2 spring onions (scallions) or a little sweet Spanish onion to taste
100 ml/3½ fl oz/generous ⅓ cup extra virgin olive oil
3 tbsp sherry vinegar
Salt

Place the bread in a bowl, add just enough water to cover and leave to soak. Chop the vegetables roughly, place in a blender or food processor and process briefly. (You may need to do this in stages.) Squeeze the bread to remove the excess water, then place in the blender and process with the vegetables until it is a really smooth purée.

Pour the soup into a large bowl and add the olive oil, vinegar and salt to taste. You may also need to add a little water if the soup seems too thick. Chill in the refrigerator until ready to serve.

Serve with your choice of garnishes below

Traditional garnishes

Hard-boiled (hard-cooked) egg finely diced and spring onion (scallion), sliced.
Cucumber, finely diced and red (bell) pepper, finely diced.
Small croûtons, fried in olive oil and tiny cubes of *jamón serrano*.

Delicious alternative garnishes

Diced cooked squid with beautiful tentacles intact if small enough, diced cucumber.
Or Tartar de Atún, (see page 70) moulded with a small biscuit (cookie) cutter.
Or cooked and peeled (shelled) king prawns (jumbo shrimp).

Opposite: Gazpacho de Remolacha
Previous page: Vieiras Gratinadas, page 70

The *hongo* (*Boletus edulis*), or cep in English, is perhaps the king of wild mushrooms. It is often better known by its Italian name the *porcini*, as these are widely available dried.

The *Boletus* is, without a doubt, my favourite mushroom. I vividly recall an early morning jaunt to the market in Vic with my wonderful friend Mercè. We bought a plump cep, shaped like a huge champagne cork, and whisked it home for breakfast. We gorged upon fried mushroom on toast with a splash of olive oil, salt and garlic – nothing could taste better.

This soup is a glorious extravagance made with fresh ceps but you can always use field (portobello) mushrooms instead and add a few dried ceps for flavour. The recipe also uses butter and cream, pure Basque indulgence, but after all you don't get to eat wild mushrooms everyday.

Variations

* I have used canned beef consommé instead of beef stock with great results, just remember not to add any salt to the soup. Two cans (400 g/14 oz) were ample with a little water to make up the quantity.
** This soup is stunning served in tiny shot glasses or demi-tasse coffee cups as an aperitif. You may like to froth the top of the soup with a whisk or cappuccino whisk just before serving.
*** You could fry some extra mushrooms, place them in the serving bowls and pour the soup at the table – very *Nueva Cocina*!

Crema de Hongos

Boletus Mushroom Soup

Serves 4

400 g/14 oz fresh ceps *or* 400 g/14 oz field (portobello) mushrooms
   and 25 g/1 oz/¼ cup dried ceps
100 g/4 oz/1 stick butter
1 onion, finely diced
2 garlic cloves, crushed
Salt and freshly ground black pepper
1 litre/1¾ pints/4 cups beef stock
6 tbsp double (heavy) cream

If you are using dried ceps, begin by covering the dried mushrooms in warm water and leaving them to soak for at least 30 minutes.

Melt half the butter in a large, heavy-based saucepan. Add the onion and cook gently for about 10 minutes until really soft. Add the garlic and stir for a moment.

Next cut fresh mushrooms into rough chunks and add them to the pan together with a little salt. Stir-fry for 5 minutes.

Add the dried mushrooms, if you are using them, together with their soaking liquid (taking care to strain the liquid as it can sometimes be gritty). Pour in the beef stock and leave to simmer for about 20 minutes.

Transfer the soup to a blender and blend until really smooth. Alternatively, use a hand-held blender. Now, if you are being a perfectionist, you should strain the soup through a fine sieve (strainer).

Pour the soup back into a clean saucepan, add the cream and bring to a simmer. When the soup is simmering, whisk in the remaining butter a little at a time. Add salt and pepper to taste and serve.

Marmitako is a classic Basque dish, cooked aboard the fishing boats for generations. It was a staple on long trips when onions, dried peppers and potatoes were the only ingredients that kept well for weeks on end and accompanied the seemingly never ending supply of tuna. The dish is usually eaten as a starter (appetizer), but would make a delicious light lunch or supper dish, mopped up with some crusty bread.

One Sunday morning in the streets of Galdakao I watched over 30 teams battling for the local *Marmitako* trophy. The basic recipe comes from Valentín, the electrician, one of the chefs, who spends his weekends touring the Basque countryside competing on the cooking circuit. He swept up a cup on this occasion too: just one more to add to the collection.

Tips

* If you cannot buy *choricero* peppers you could use any mild dried pepper or 2 tablespoons of sweet paprika (but not the smoked variety).
** If you want to prepare ahead, just follow the method until the potatoes are almost cooked through, then leave to cool. About 30 minutes before you are ready to serve heat the potatoes through, then once really hot add the tuna as before.

Variation

* You could add the flesh of 2 peeled tomatoes together with the potatoes.

Marmitako

Tuna and Potato Hotpot

Serves 4

5 tbsp olive oil
2 red onions, finely sliced
2 green (bell) peppers, finely sliced
2 garlic cloves, crushed
2 *choricero* peppers, soaked for at least 30 minutes
900 g/2 lb firm, waxy potatoes, cut into 4 cm/1½ inch dice

50 ml/2 fl oz/¼ cup *txacolí* or any dry white wine (optional)
50 ml/2 fl oz/¼ cup Cognac (optional)
600 ml/1 pint/2½ cups fish stock
Salt
450 g/1 lb tuna loin, cut into 4 cm/ 1½ inch dice

Heat the olive oil in a pan. Add the onions and fry very gently over a low heat until really soft. This is easier in the traditional terracotta *cazuela* or *marmita* (after which the dish is named) but you could use a sauté pan. If you are using a metal pan take care not to burn the onions, you may want to cover them with a lid. The longer the onions cook the sweeter the dish will be.

As soon as the onions are really soft, add the (bell) peppers and garlic and continue to cook gently for a further 15 minutes.

Next cut open the *choricero* peppers and scrape the flesh from the inside of the skin with a spoon. Add the flesh to the onions together with the potatoes and stir well, making sure that the potatoes are covered in the delicious oil.

Add the alcohol and just enough fish stock to cover the potatoes. The wine and Cognac are optional. Traditionalists like Valentín would probably not approve, but alcohol is often added by restaurant chefs and does give an extra dimension to the dish.

Season with salt to taste, cover the pan and leave to simmer until the potatoes are cooked through. The stock should begin to thicken a little with the potato starch but do not let the potatoes collapse and turn into a purée.

Once you are happy that the potatoes have reached perfection, remove the pan from the heat, taste the stock and add more salt if necessary.

Now, while everything is still piping hot, add the tuna, stir gently and replace the lid. You do not need to continue cooking. Just give the pan a few shakes to help the potato break down slightly and leave to stand for 10 minutes. During this time the tuna will cook through, remaining deliciously tender and slightly pink in the middle.

If you prefer your tuna cooked for slightly longer, then place the pan over a low heat for 5 minutes after adding the fish and leaving it to rest for 5 minutes.

This delicious combination of tiny, tender squid and caramelized onions is a Basque favourite and such a welcome change from the more ubiquitous fried squid in batter found all over Spain. At Victor Montes, a wonderfully civilized bar and restaurant in Bilbao's Plaza Nueva, they piled warm cherry tomatoes on the plate too, giving a wonderfully fresh dimension to the dish.

It is traditional to use small squid for this recipe so that you can serve them whole, although there is nothing to stop you cutting larger squid into sections. Just remember that squid requires minimal cooking, either that or a long slow simmer, anything in between and you will end up with a distinctly rubbery result.

Tip

* It is worth caramelizing double the onion and (bell) pepper quantity and keeping some in the refrigerator. It is a delicious accompaniment for charred tuna, cold meats or pâté.

Chipirones Encebollados (a lo Pelayo)

Squid with Caramelized Onions

Serves 4

2 tbsp olive oil
3 large onions, finely sliced
1 green (bell) pepper, finely sliced
2 garlic cloves, peeled and cut in half
8–12 small squid, about 450 g/1 lb, cleaned
12 cherry tomatoes
2 tbsp dry white wine
1 tbsp chopped fresh flat-leaf parsley, to garnish

Heat 1 tablespoon of olive oil in a saucepan. Add the onions and green (bell) pepper and cook over a very low heat for at least 1 hour. The idea is to caramelize the onions until they become tawny and sweet but do not let them burn.

Meanwhile, prepare the squid by pushing the tentacles and wings into the empty body cavities.

Preheat the oven to 180°C/350°F/Gas Mark 4.

Heat the remaining olive oil with the garlic cloves in a heavy-based frying pan (skillet) until the garlic turns golden and its flavour infuses the oil. Remove the garlic from the pan.

Add the squid, a few at a time to the frying pan (skillet) and fry over a high heat until the flesh turns opaque and browns a little. As soon as the squid is cooked, transfer it to the onion mixture and continue until all the squid is fried.

Place the cherry tomatoes on a baking (cookie) sheet and heat in the oven to warm through for about 10 minutes. They may split but this is not a problem.

Once all the squid has been cooked, pour the wine into the empty frying pan (skillet) and scrape around with a wooden spoon to loosen up all the fabulous flavours. Add this to the onion and squid mixture then return to the frying pan (skillet) and cook over a medium heat for a further 5 minutes. Transfer to individual plates, garnish with a sprinkle of chopped parsley and serve with the warm tomatoes.

Donostia is the Basque name for San Sebastián and this recipe is a local classic, served in some guise or another in all the Basque harbour towns. The spider crab, or *txangurro* as it is known in Basque, certainly doesn't look particularly appetizing with its encrusted shell, like a miniature rock garden, and its spindly little legs; yet the meat is truly delicious. The shell traditionally serves as a case for the stuffing although I prefer to serve this in individual ramekins.

You can cheat and use any good crab instead. You may like to make your life really simple and buy the crab meat ready cooked from your fish supplier.

Tip

* If you prepare these ahead of time, reduce the oven temperature to 180°C/350°F/Gas Mark 4 and cook for 15 minutes.

Txangurro a la Donostiarra

Stuffed Spider Crab

Serves 4

400 g/14 oz cooked crabmeat (about 2 large or 3 medium spider crabs see page 35)
4 tbsp olive oil
1 medium onion, finely diced
1 leek, finely chopped
1 carrot, finely diced
1 garlic clove, crushed
1 small fresh red chilli (chili pepper) *guindilla*, chopped very finely or a dash of cayenne pepper
1 small fresh tarragon sprig, finely chopped
3 tomatoes, peeled, de-seeded and chopped or 200 g/7 oz canned chopped tomatoes will do
3 tbsp brandy
100 ml/3½ fl oz/generous ⅓ cup white wine
Salt
5 tbsp fresh breadcrumbs
1 tbsp chopped fresh flat-leaf parsley
50 g/2 oz/½ stick butter

Preheat the oven to 200°C/400°F/Gas Mark 6. Begin by rubbing the crabmeat through your fingers to check for any bits of shell. Keep the white meat separate from the creamier brown meat, if you have any (the spider crab has none at all).

Heat the olive oil in a pan. Add the onion, leek and carrot and fry over a gentle heat until they are really soft. Now stir in the garlic and the chilli (chili pepper) or cayenne and cook for 1–2 minutes.

Next, add the tarragon, tomatoes, brandy, wine and about a quarter of the crabmeat, or any brown crabmeat you may have. Add a little salt to taste and bring to the boil for 1–2 minutes.

Add about half the breadcrumbs and all the parsley. The breadcrumbs should thicken the sauce slightly.

Place the remaining crab in the base of the ramekins, then pour over the tomato mixture. Sprinkle with the rest of the breadcrumbs and add a tablespoon of butter on the top. Bake in the oven for about 10 minutes, or until lightly browned.

For centuries pilgrims have made their way to Santiago de Compostela in Galicia to visit the shrine of St James the Apostle. In the Middle Ages this route across Northern Spain was the most trodden path in Europe. The pilgrims used to wear a scallop shell, the saint's symbol, around their neck to ward off thieves and earn the odd free meal. They must surely have eaten its contents too, as a sweet fresh scallop is a heavenly experience in itself.

Vieiras Gratinadas

Grilled Pilgrim Scallops

1 medium onion, chopped
2 tablespoons of olive oil
1 garlic clove, crushed
100ml/3½ fl oz/generous ⅓ cup dry white wine or dry sherry
4 tablespoons of breadcrumbs
50g/2 oz/4 tbsp butter, melted

Salt and pepper
1 tablespoon parsley, chopped
12 large fresh scallops, cleaned and with their shells
50g/2 oz/4 tbsp butter
Lemon juice

Preheat the oven to 200°C/400°F/Gas Mark 6.

Begin by frying the onion in the olive oil until it softens and then add the garlic. Cook for a moment or two until the scent of garlic takes over and then it is time to add the splash of wine. Let the alcohol boil and reduce and next stir in the melted butter, seasoning, parsley and breadcrumbs.

Take four small ovenproof dishes, or better still the scallop shells, and grease with a little butter. Now place your scallops three to a shell, or five if that seems stingy, and top with the breadcrumb mixture.

Dot the scallops with a little butter and pop into the hot oven for 12–15 minutes, until crisped on the top. You could even put them under a grill (broiler) to finish but be careful not to burn the breadcrumbs.

For a more contemporary look you may choose to roast the scallops on skewers. (Make sure you soak wooden skewers for at least 30 minutes before using.)

The Spanish, particularly the Catalans, have embraced Japanese cuisine with open arms. Sushi is all the rage and now, as a result raw, fish pops up in many guises. This lightly spiced combination is fabulous.

Buy the fish from a trusty fish supplier, it's got to be as fresh as possible.

Tip

* For a more elegant presentation, place a small ring mould or biscuit (cookie) cutter on the plate and push the tartar inside it. Lift off the cutter giving you a neat little tower of tuna. Garnish with a fresh flat-leaf parsley sprig.

Tartar de Atún

Tuna Tartar

300 g/10 oz really fresh tuna loin, skinned
Pinch of salt
5 drops Worcestershire Sauce
2 drops Tabasco sauce
1 tbsp soy sauce
½ small red onion, finely diced
2 gherkins (dill pickles), finely chopped
1 tbsp capers, finely chopped

1 egg yolk
2 tbsp olive oil
1 tbsp finely chopped fresh flat-leaf parsley

To serve
Crispy toast
Small bunch of radishes

Chop the tuna very finely into tiny dice. This is a sharp knife job and not one for the food processor.

Place the tuna in a shallow dish, add the salt, Worcestershire sauce, Tabasco and soy sauce and leave to marinate while you prepare everything else.

Add the onion, gherkins (dill pickles) and capers.

Whisk the egg yolk in a bowl and slowly add the olive oil as if you were starting to make mayonnaise. Next stir this into the tuna together with the parsley.

Serve the tuna in small bowls or ramekins with crispy toast and a few radishes.

Ensalada Marinada de Lubina
Marinated Sea Bass with Dill

Serves 4

300 g/10 oz sea bass fillet, skin and
   bones removed
Pinch of salt
Freshly ground black pepper
2 tbsp extra virgin olive oil, a lighter
   flavoured one if possible
Juice of 1 lemon
1 tsp chopped fresh dill

1 handful of curly endive or other tasty,
   attractive green leaves

To garnish
8 cherry tomatoes, cut into quarters
4 physalis (Cape gooseberries), cut into
   quarters (optional)

Begin by slicing the fish as thinly and neatly as you can. If you are having problems place the slices between 2 sheets of clingfilm (plastic wrap) and press them out, very gently, with a rolling pin.

Arrange the fish, just one layer thick, on 4 cold serving plates. If you want to prepare ahead of time, cover the plates with clingfilm (plastic wrap) and place them in the refrigerator until you are ready to serve.

A couple of minutes before you are going to eat, sprinkle the fish with a little salt and pepper, drizzle with olive oil and lemon juice, then sprinkle the dill over the top.

Next dress the salad leaves (greens) with a little salt, olive oil and lemon juice and place in a tiny pile in the centre of the plate, on top of the fish.

Garnish with the tomatoes and physalis (Cape gooseberries) if you are using them.

Marinated, paper-thin slices of raw fish or meat have become a popular starter (appetizer) in upbeat restaurants. They often appear on the menu as *carpaccio*, harking back to the Italian dish of raw beef that started the craze. This is such a delicate starter (appetizer) to begin a meal with, the lemon juice will "cook" the fish in seconds and you can have everything sliced ahead of time. Sea bass is expensive but you won't need much, just make sure it is wonderfully fresh.

I ate this salad at Toñi Vicente's restaurant in Santiago de Compostela, it was gloriously light and refreshing. Toñi is one of the new breed of highly respected females who has broken into the male-dominated star chef scene.

Variations
* You could use pomegranate seeds instead of the tomatoes and physalis (Cape gooseberries).
** Very finely sliced scallops would be delicious prepared in the same way with perhaps a little chilli (chili pepper) added.

Escabeche

One of the most ancient means of preserving food, the *escabeche*, was brought to Spain by the Arabs. Fish and poultry will keep for a couple of weeks when pickled with vinegar and so a large catch or a successful day's hunting could feed the family for a while.

Nowadays, with refrigeration the *escabeche* is appreciated more for its delicious flavour than its keeping qualities. It is such a useful storecupboard (pantry) standby that I have included two recipes; an aromatic herbed version for poultry and a spicier one for fish.

Perdiz y Verduritas en Escabeche

Pickled Partridge and Baby Vegetables

Partridge can sometimes be a little dry, but left in this marinade for a few days it will tenderize quite beautifully.

This is excellent served as a starter (appetizer) or could be the star of a salad with a few slices of ripe plum, toasted almonds and some bitter green leaves.

Variation

* The recipe also works well with whole quail or chicken quarters. The quail will require only 30 minutes' simmering while chicken will need at least 1 hour. Make sure to check that the chicken is completely cooked through before leaving to cool.

Serves 4. Prepare at least 24 hours in advance.

2 partridge (4 if you have large appetites), split in half, seasoned with salt and freshly ground black pepper
2 tbsp olive oil
12 button (white) onions or shallots, peeled but left whole
3 garlic cloves, peeled but left whole
300 ml/10 fl oz/1¼ cups white wine
300 ml/10 fl oz/1¼ cups wine vinegar
300 ml/10 fl oz/1¼ cups water or chicken stock

12 black peppercorns
2 cloves
Salt
3 bay leaves
1 fresh thyme sprig
1 celery stick (stalk)
12 baby carrots, peeled but left whole

To garnish
Small bunch watercress
Dash of extra virgin olive oil

Heat the olive oil in a large pan. Add the partridges and fry until they begin to brown. Remove the partridges, add the onions and fry for 10 minutes until soft and browned. Add the garlic and fry, taking care not to burn it, until it just turns pale gold.

Pour in the wine, vinegar and water together with the peppercorns, bay, thyme and celery. Bring to the boil, then return the partridges to the pan. Reduce the heat and leave to simmer, covered, for 30 minutes. Add the carrots and cook for a further 10 minutes.

Place the partridges and vegetables in a small dish and pour over the liquid. Now the important bit; the marinade must completely cover the partridges if it is to act as a preservative. Once cool, place in the refrigerator. Ideally, if you can resist, leave the *escabeche* for a few days to marinate before eating, it will keep in the refrigerator for at least a week.

Serve the partridge and vegetables with a little juice ladled over them. Don't forget the peppercorns, they add a piquant crunch. Garnish with the watercress and a little really good extra virgin olive oil.

Oily fish tastes glorious after a couple of days in this sweet and sour marinade. Whole fish are often used but for a more elegant starter (appetizer) I prefer to use fillets; they are just so much easier to eat. Try to get your fish supplier to do the filleting for you; it will save a lot of time.

Tips

* *Escabeche* works wonders with sardines, tuna, red mullet (red snapper) and trout. Just fry your fish, filleted or whole, until it is cooked and proceed as above.

** You may like to substitute roasted cumin and coriander seeds for the cloves; about a teaspoon of each is delicious.

Caballa en Escabeche

Sweet and Sour Mackerel

Serves 4. Begin this recipe at least a day in advance.

8 mackerel fillets
2 tbsp plain (all-purpose) flour
½ tsp salt
8 tbsp olive oil
1 red onion, finely sliced
6 garlic cloves, peeled but left whole
1 tsp sweet paprika
3 bay leaves
3 cloves
12 black peppercorns
2 tbsp sultanas (golden raisins)
300 ml/10 fl oz/1¼ cups red wine vinegar
150 ml/5 fl oz/⅔ cup water

To garnish
2 tbsp pine kernels (pine nuts) or chopped almonds, toasted
1 tbsp fresh flat-leaf parsley, roughly chopped

Dust the fish with flour and salt. Heat 2 tablespoons of olive oil in a large frying pan (skillet). Add the fillets, a few at a time, and cook until golden and just cooked through. Arrange the fish in a single layer in a large, flat dish.

Heat the remaining olive oil in a clean pan. Add the onion and fry until it becomes quite soft. Add the garlic and continue cooking until you see the cloves just beginning to colour.

Stir in the paprika and fry for a moment, taking great care not to burn it. Next add the peppercorns, sultanas (golden raisins), vinegar and water and bring to the boil, then pour the marinade over the fish, making sure that it is completely covered. Leave to cool before placing in the refrigerator.

Leave the fish to marinate for at least a day but preferably two, before serving topped with toasted pine kernels (pine nuts) or almonds and chopped parsley.

Cannelloni have featured on Catalan menus for centuries. Catalans will claim that they gave the Italians their *risotto* rice and took back the *cannelloni* in exchange. *Canalons* are comm on fare while other Italian dishes such as lasagne are unheard of, a strange state of affairs. This is a popular Boxing Day dish and although it's quite a fiddle it's great to prepare ahead for easy entertaining.

Many traditional recipes call for lamb's brains to be added with the rest of the meat, I have opted to leave them out as they are difficult to come by and not everyone's cup of tea. I find that plenty of chicken livers give the required richness instead. If I'm getting around to making this, I would always make at least enough for six people. You could always pop half in the freezer.

Canalons

Catalan Cannelloni

Serves 6 (makes about 12 large cannelloni)

Béchamel sauce
1 litre/1 ¾ pints/4 cups creamy milk
1 onion, peeled and cut in half
50 g/2 oz/4 tbsp butter
50 g/2 oz/generous ⅜ cup plain (all-purpose) flour
Salt and freshly ground black pepper
Freshly grated nutmeg

For the filling
3 tbsp olive oil or pork lard
2 onions, diced
6 garlic cloves, crushed
2 tomatoes, peeled, de-seeded and chopped

300 g/10 oz pork, minced (ground)
300 g/10 oz chicken breast, minced (ground)
4 chicken livers, finely chopped
100 ml/3½ fl oz/generous ⅓ cup *vi ranci* or Oloroso sherry
Salt and freshly ground black pepper
Ground cinnamon, to taste
1 medium egg, beaten
2 tbsp breadcrumbs
12-18 cannelloni sheets (depending on size), or fresh pasta cut into 13 cm/5 inch squares
Olive oil, for cooking
6 tbsp freshly grated Parmesan cheese

Begin by bringing the milk and the onion to boiling point in a small saucepan, then setting the pan aside to allow the milk to infuse.

For the filling, heat the olive oil or lard in a pan. Add the onion and fry until really soft, then add the garlic and tomatoes and cooking until the tomatoes have reduced.

Add the pork, chicken and chicken livers and heat, stirring for a few minutes until cooked through.

Next add the *vi ranci* or sherry and stir for a moment or two before seasoning with salt, pepper and cinnamon to taste.

Take the pan off the heat and stir in the beaten egg and breadcrumbs.

Meanwhile, cook your pasta in a large saucepan of boiling salted water for about 3 minutes. A little oil added to the water will help to prevent sticking, but don't attempt more than 5 sheets at a time. Lay the pasta on a clean tea (dish) towel to drain.

For the béchamel. Melt the butter in a saucepan and add the flour. Cook for 1–2 minutes then take the pan off the heat. Remove the onion from the milk, then slowly add the milk to the butter and flour mixture, stirring constantly. Bring the sauce to boiling point, still stirring all the time, and simmer for 2–3 minutes. Add a little salt, pepper and nutmeg to taste.

Preheat the oven to 200°C/400°F/Gas Mark 6. Next place a little sauce in the base of an ovenproof dish.

Fill the pasta by placing a couple of spoonfuls of meat mixture down one side of each square, roll up, then place seam-side down in the dish, side by side.

Pour the sauce over and top with grated Parmesan cheese. Bake for about 10–15 minutes until bubbling and golden.

Piquillo peppers are fabulously tasty and make wonderful containers for all kinds of stuffing. The peppers are the pride of southern Navarre where they are grown by the thousand, then roasted, peeled and preserved in jars and cans. The process is a lengthy one, since the skins are meticulously removed by hand without ripping the triangular pocket of the pepper. *Piquillo* peppers are available at specialist Spanish stores and some deli's – a really useful treat to keep in the cupboard for impromptu entertaining.

The peppers are often filled with a stuffing of shellfish, salt cod or tuna bound together with a béchamel sauce. Their scarlet flesh is sometimes camouflaged with fried batter in *tapas* bars. I just adore this recipe where the fresh, piquant flavour of the pepper comes through.

Tip

* You could prepare the entire dish in advance. Arrange the stuffed peppers in the sauce and cool. Allow an extra 5–10 minutes in the oven to heat through.

Variation

* *Piquillo* peppers are delicious stuffed with goat's cheese and herbs and then served with a salad. If you buy a larger can, fry any leftover peppers gently in a little olive oil with a touch of garlic for a glorious toast topping.

Pimientos de Piquillo Rellenos de Morcilla

Piquillo Peppers Stuffed with Black Pudding

Serves 4

200 g/7 oz *morcilla* (see page 31) or
    black pudding (blood sausage)
1 medium egg, beaten
1 x 225 g/8 oz jar of *piquillo* peppers
    (about 16 peppers)
2 tbsp olive oil
2 onions, finely diced
1 green (bell) pepper, finely diced

3 garlic cloves, crushed
1 tsp fresh thyme leaves
150 ml/5 fl oz/⅔ cup cream

To garnish
2 tbsp roasted pine kernels (pine nuts)
1 tbsp chopped fresh flat-leaf parsley

Preheat the oven to 180°C/350°F/Gas Mark 4.

Remove the skin from the *morcilla* and fry it in a frying pan (skillet) for 5 minutes, breaking it up as you go. Leave to cool slightly, then stir in the beaten egg.

Using a small spoon, stuff 12 *piquillo* peppers extremely carefully with the *morcilla* filling. Don't throw away any juices from the jar, you'll need those later.

Heat the olive oil in a pan. Add the onion and green (bell) pepper until really soft and beginning to brown. Add the garlic and thyme and cook until the garlic is golden.

Transfer the onion mixture to a blender or food processor, add the cream, the juices from the peppers and any leftover peppers you may have and process briefly. Season with salt and pepper to taste.

Pour the sauce into a *cazuela*, or ovenproof dish large enough to hold all the peppers in a single layer. Place the peppers on top of the sauce and bake in the oven for 10 minutes until really hot.

Serve the peppers with the sauce, sprinkled with the pine kernels (pine nuts) and a little chopped parsley.

An age-old dish, born out of necessity among the shepherds: *migas* are made with fried stale bread and a little salt pork or bacon. Traditionally served for breakfast along with a fried egg, they sometimes have a little chorizo and even fruit thrown in too.

This recipe is inspired by a version I ate as a wonderful starter (appetizer), in a country restaurant beside the ancient Cistercian monastery of Veruela, in Aragón. It was a freezing December day, the olive groves were thick with mist and once in a while you could make out an ethereal monkish figure wafting through the fog.

The *migas* will only be as good as your bread, so use a good rustic loaf, preferably a sourdough. You will need to begin this recipe a few hours ahead of time.

Migas con Uvas y Granadas
Shepherd's Crumbs with Grapes and Pomegranate

Serves 4

200 g/7 oz stale bread
3 tbsp olive oil
75 g/3 oz *panceta* or bacon, diced
75 g/3 oz spicy *chorizo*, diced
3 garlic cloves, peeled but left whole
1 tsp ground cumin
Salt (optional)

To serve
1 tart apple, cut into chunks and tossed in the juice of 1 lemon
1 pomegranate, just the seeds (you can drink any leftover juice)
200 g/7 oz green, seedless grapes

Begin by ripping or cutting the bread into small croûton-sized pieces, then place in a bowl and sprinkle with a few drops of water. Toss the bread around, then sprinkle again with more water. The idea is to dampen rather than soak the bread. Cover with a tea (dish) towel and leave to stand for 2 hours.

Heat the olive oil in a large frying pan (skillet). Add the *panceta* and *chorizo* and fry until most of the fat has rendered. Add the garlic, stirring, until it just begins to colour.

Add the bread pieces and cumin and stir until the bread turns crisp and golden.

Check the seasoning, you may not need any salt at all if your bacon and *chorizo* are quite salty.

Serve the bread with the apple, pomegranate seeds and grapes. If you are tossing them together, be sure to serve at once before the *migas* become soggy.

In spring the Basques await the arrival of the first wild mushroom of the season, the *perretxico,* or St George's mushroom, with great anticipation. The *perretxico* heralds the return of warmer weather as the last snow finally melts away. The mushrooms grow in magical fairy rings and pop up in the same spot year after year. These locations have become precious family secrets passed from one generation to the next. Country bars and restaurants rush to serve *Revuelto de Perretxicos* and locals dive in with gusto.

The marriage of very creamy, softly scrambled eggs and delicate wild mushrooms is just sublime. It is a wonderful way to stretch a few elusive mushrooms among a crowd.

Variations

* *Revuelto* is fabulous with prawns (shrimp) fried in a little butter and some wilted spinach stirred in.
** Try cooking asparagus, then cutting the tender heads and stalks into bite-sized pieces. Fry them with a little *jamón* or bacon, then add your beaten eggs.

Revuelto de Setas

Scrambled Eggs with Wild Mushrooms

Serves 4

250 g/9 oz fresh St George's mushroom, chanterelle or any other tasty
   wild mushroom
2 tbsp olive oil
1 garlic clove, crushed
6–8 eggs
Salt and freshly ground black pepper
2 tbsp cream (optional)
4 pieces of white bread, toasted

Clean the mushrooms carefully with a damp cloth, removing any soil. If they are larger mushrooms, then cut or tear them into smaller pieces.

Heat the olive oil in a frying pan (skillet). Add the mushrooms and garlic and fry over a low heat for about 5 minutes.

Beat the eggs with a good pinch of salt, and add the cream if you are feeling indulgent.

Add the eggs to the pan and stir until the eggs just begin to set. A *revuelto,* should have the texture of a very thick custard rather than dry granular scrambled eggs, so beware.

If you're a real perfectionist, you may like to place the cooked mushrooms and the beaten eggs in a double boiler and stir the *revuelto* over a low heat to thicken.

Serve at once with a good sprinkle of black pepper, if you like, (the locals probably wouldn't but I can't resist), and white toast.

Ferran Adrià, that magician of the Catalan kitchen, suggested that a fried egg could reach true perfection only if cooked in two halves, allowing a deliciously firm fried white and a hot runny yolk. I have to agree after this amazing starter (appetizer) at the Restaurante Antigua Bodega de Don Cosme Palacio, in Laguardia (now there's a mouthful in itself!). The chef Javier Ramos Alvarez let me into the secret, which, with a little twiddling, is perfectly possible for the home cook.

Baby broad (fava) beans are held in high esteem in Spain, and so they should be, they eat them when they are sweet, tender and no bigger than a pea. While Javier carefully "confits" his own beans, I suggest that you seek out a jar of Spanish *habitas* in oil since I have yet to find the tiny fresh ones at home. Alternatively, the frozen variety work really well too.

Variations
You could:
* Make your life easier by just poaching or frying a whole egg.
** Sprinkle croûtons around the plate instead of serving toast.
*** Fry an onion and 2 garlic cloves with the beans, splash with a little dry sherry and serve on their own with a pinch of chopped fresh mint.

Huevo Desmontado con Habitas Salteadas

"Dismantled" Egg with Sautéed Baby Beans

Serves 4

500 g/1 lb 2 oz *habitas* in oil, drained or 600 g/1¼ lb fresh or frozen baby broad (fava) beans
2 tbsp olive oil, plus extra for oiling
160 g/5¼ oz *jamón Ibérico*, sliced and cut into tiny squares
4 medium eggs
4 slices of white bread
Salt and freshly ground black pepper

Preheat the oven to 180°C/350°F/Gas Mark 4.

If you are using fresh or frozen beans, then I really recommend you remove the skins off the individual beans, or at least half of them to reveal their tender lime-green flesh. (You will need to blanch them first if using fresh beans.)

Heat 1 tablespoon of olive oil in a saucepan. Add the *jamón* and beans and fry for about 3 minutes if you are using *habitas* in oil, or for 6 minutes if you are using fresh beans.

Next heat the remaining oil in a large frying pan (skillet).

Separate the eggs, taking great care not to break the yolks. Place the yolks in 4 oiled ovenproof dishes, such as ramekins, while pouring the whites into the frying pan (skillet) in 4 small circles, a biscuit (cookie) cutter will help. Alternatively, fry all the whites together and cut out the circles later.

While the whites are cooking begin toasting the bread.

As you place the egg yolks in the oven, warm your serving plates. The yolks need only 45 seconds to heat through. Meanwhile, reheat the beans and ham if you need to.

As soon as the egg yolks are hot, place the egg whites on the warmed plates, pile the beans and ham on top and carefully tip the egg yolks over. Season with a little salt and pepper and serve with squares or fingers of toast on the side.

5

Salads and Vegetable Dishes

The quintessential Spanish Salad; it may be simple but the ingredients will invariably be of the highest quality. Tomatoes and lettuce snapped up from the local market will always taste better than anything out of the refrigerator. Use a delicious extra virgin olive oil. I am totally enamoured with the Catalan oils from Siurana and Les Garrigues, made with tiny, herby *arbequina* olives but any really good extra virgin olive oil will do.

You may like to add boiled eggs, cucumber, roasted (bell) peppers or grated carrot to the salad too.

Ensalada Mixta

Mixed Salad with Tuna

Serves 4

½ head of cos (romaine), or any other crisp flavoursome lettuce, iceberg is off limits!
2 ripe tomatoes, sliced
½ sweet Spanish onion, or perhaps a red onion
200 g/7 oz canned best quality tuna in olive oil
8 fingers of thick white asparagus or 12 stalks of green asparagus, cooked
12 plump green olives

For the dressing – usually DIY at the table
Fabulous extra virgin olive oil
Red wine vinegar or sherry vinegar
Salt

Arrange the salad on individual plates or a platter.

All the dressing ingredients are usually placed on the table for everyone to help themselves.

And for something more elegant
I had a delicious variation on this salad, minus the asparagus in a small restaurant overlooking the fishing harbour of Laredo in Cantabria. It was a perfect example of the simplest dish lifted to new heights by the most wonderful quality ingredients.

The canned tuna was the highly prized *ventresca,* the most succulent cut of the fish from the belly, juicy and flavoursome. It's worth looking out for in specialist delicatessens and Spanish stores. The tomatoes had been finely diced, with the addition of a little fresh oregano. Each ingredient was carefully layered, dressed with oil and vinegar and pressed into a ring mould of about 12 cm/5 inch diameter. A little extra oil had been drizzled around the plate and hey presto a delicious result!

Opposite: Ensalada de Espinacas Tiernas, Jamón y Queso de Cabra, page 82
Following page: Caballa en Escabeche, page 73

An absolute favourite: crunchy leeks and velvety soft peppers topped with sweet prawns (shrimp) and barely set boiled quail's eggs. What a fabulous combination, inspired by my delicious starter (appetizer) at the Restaurante La Escalinata. I felt rather undeserving as I tucked into this salad in the little town of Vilafranca: the place is swarming with pilgrims, resting up before the last gruelling leg of the Camino de Santiago.

The local *El Bierzo* red peppers are famous throughout Spain; they are roasted over wood fires, giving a distinctive smokiness then packed into jars. If you can't buy *El Bierzo* peppers, then just roast and peel some red (bell) peppers of your own.

Tips

* This makes a great starter (appetizer) but I have also served the salad as a light lunch dish with the addition of some cold new potatoes, a bit of a British touch but great all the same.
** If you make this ahead of time, do not dress the salad until the last minute or your leeks will flop.

Ensalada de Pimientos, Puerros y Langostinos con Huevos de Cordoníz

Roasted Pepper and Leek Salad with King Prawns and Quail's eggs

Serves 4

For the salad
Sunflower oil, for frying
2 medium leeks, trimmed and cut into the finest julienne possible
Salt and freshly ground black pepper
6 quail's eggs
1 x 280 g/10 oz jar of *El Bierzo* peppers or 6 red (bell) peppers, roasted and peeled
12 cooked king prawns (jumbo shrimp), peeled (shelled) and deveined
1 tbsp roughly chopped fresh flat-leaf parsley

For the dressing
5 tbsp extra virgin olive oil
2 tbsp sherry vinegar
1 garlic clove, crushed
Salt and plenty of freshly ground black pepper

Pour sunflower oil to a depth of about 7.5 cm/3 inches into a small deep saucepan. Heat the oil; it should bubble and fizz when you add a few leek shreds. Cook the leeks a handful at a time, frying them for 2–3 minutes, or until crispy. Remove them from the oil and blot them well with kitchen paper (paper towels), sprinkle with salt and pepper and reserve.

Next cook the quail's eggs in a saucepan of boiling water for 2 minutes and 15 seconds, or 2 minutes and enough time to fill a bowl with really cold water, if like me you don't have a stopwatch! Pop the eggs into the bowl of cold water to stop them cooking. The yolks will remain a wonderful canary yellow, overcooked and they turn a less inspiring powdery grey. Once cold remove the shells and cut the eggs in half.

Now make the dressing according to your taste in a screw-top jar and give it a vigorous shake.

Place the pieces of red pepper on individual plates and drizzle with plenty of dressing. Add the crispy leeks, arrange the prawns (shrimp) and quail's eggs on top, drizzle with the remaining dressing and sprinkle with a little fresh parsley.

Opposite: Ensalada de Pimientos, Puerros y Langostinos con Huevos de Cordoníz
Previous page: Menestra de Tudela, page 87

There was a time when a salad in Spain was a rather predictable affair but now creative chefs are having a field day combining fresh flavours from the plentiful local larder.

I ate this fabulous salad at the La Galana cider house in the seaside city of Gijón. It was a steamy day and I staggered in from the long sweeping beach, backed by row upon row of old fashioned, striped changing tents. A light dish was the order of the day and this salad was perfect.

Most Spaniards would never consider eating a salad as a main course, so this is enough for four starters (appetizers), just up everything by half again for a main course.

Ensalada de Espinacas Tiernas, Jamón y Queso de Cabra

Spinach, Cured Ham and Goat's Cheese Salad with a Hazelnut and Honey Dressing

Serves 4 as a starter (appetizer) 2–3 as a main course

4 thin slices of *jamón Serrano*
Oil, for oiling
200 g/7 oz/4 ⅜ cups baby spinach leaves
12 ripe cherry tomatoes, quartered
6 sun-dried tomatoes, finely chopped
150 g/5 oz fresh soft goat's cheese, cut into small chunks

For the dressing
1 tbsp honey
5 tbsp extra virgin olive oil
Juice of ½ lemon
Salt and freshly ground black pepper
25 g/1 oz/¼ cup toasted hazelnuts, roughly chopped

Preheat the oven to 160°C/325°F/Gas Mark 3.

Place the *jamón* on a lightly oiled baking tray (cookie sheet) and cook in the oven for 10 minutes, then leave to cool and crispen. The ham should be really brittle as it cools, if not just return it the oven for a few more minutes.

Meanwhile, place all the dressing ingredients in a screw-top jar or container with a tight fitting lid. Give the jar a good shake, then taste. You may need to adjust the quantities. It can be quite sweet since the *jamón*, sun-dried tomatoes and cheese are quite salty (If you are making the dressing ahead of time just add the hazelnuts at the last minute so they keep their crunch).

Next, combine the spinach leaves with the tomatoes, add most of the dressing and toss together.

Break the crispy *jamón* into bite-sized pieces and sprinkle these over the salad with the goat's cheese. Drizzle over the remaining vinaigrette and serve.

A celebration of Asturian flavours and a delicious salad to eat in the autumn (fall) when rosy red apples and walnuts have just come to the market. The slightly bitter curly endive gives a wonderful bite and harks back to the more traditional presentation of the dish with Cabrales blue cheese being piled on to chicory (Belgian endive) leaves and topped with walnuts.

The Cabrales cheese is decadently creamy and pungent at the same time. If you can't get hold of Cabrales, do try the recipe with Picos de Europa or even French Roquefort instead.

Ensalada de Cabrales, Manzana y Nueces

Blue Cheese, Apple and Walnut Salad

Serves 4

I head of curly endive or any other tasty salad leaves (salad greens)
200 g/7 oz Cabrales blue cheese
2 sweet apples, cut into eighths
75 g/3 oz/¾ cup walnut halves, as fresh as possible
75 g/3 oz/½ cup blueberries

For the dressing
Extra virgin olive oil
Cider vinegar
Salt and freshly ground black pepper

Wash the salad leaves (greens), ripping them into bite-sized pieces, then give them a whirl in a salad spinner.

Next, cut the cheese into large chunks, allow a little extra in the recipe as half of it will never hit the salad if you are anything like me, just a little quality management!

Reserve a few walnuts and blueberries for the garnish and place everything else in a large bowl. Add the dressing ingredients, toss well, garnish and serve.

This salad is a Catalan classic – a really light and refreshing starter (appetizer). Once the cod has been soaked adequately it really won't be too salty at all but the texture will be divine. The idea of raw salt cod can be a little scary for the uninitiated, but just think of *bacalao* as the ham of the sea, and suddenly it seems much more appealing.

A few traditionalists will insist that a true *esquiexada* is nothing but cod and a marinade of exquisite extra virgin olive oil; the more popular approach includes some really fresh salad vegetables. Use the best quality tomatoes possible, the large rippled Montserrat variety are to die for. Don't keep tomatoes in the refrigerator because the flavour dies instantly, let them sit in the fruit bowl. Should they ripen too fast you could always use them for *gazpacho* (see pages 64–65) or *pa amb tomàquet* (see page 48).

Tip

* I ate a delicious version of the salad where the tomatoes had been replaced with orange segments; you could try the sweet pink grapefruit too.

Esquiexada

Salt Cod Salad

Serves 4. You will need to begin this recipe 48 hours in advance.

400 g/14 oz salt cod loin or *morro* (dried weight), soaked (see page 33)
2 large or 4 small ripe tomatoes, peeled, de-seeded and diced
1 green (bell) pepper, diced
½ large sweet Spanish onion, very finely sliced (or red onion will do)
2 tbsp extra virgin olive oil, plus extra to serve, Arbequina if possible
Freshly ground black pepper
100 g/4 oz/⅔ cup tasty black olives, to garnish

Remove the cod from the soaking water and dry off with kitchen paper (paper towel). Using your hands, rip the cod into thin strips, removing any bones or skin as you go.

Next mix the cod, tomato, (bell) pepper, onion and olive oil together in a large dish and season with pepper to taste. Leave to marinate for at least 1 hour before serving.

When ready to serve, pile the salad on to individual plates, a ring mould will help to give it structure, and garnish with olives and a tiny splash of olive oil.

Variation

To create a traditional *empedrat* salad add cooked white beans such as Santa Pau, haricot (navy) or cannellini beans. Halve the quantity of salt cod and add about 400 g/ 14 oz/2¼ cups of cooked beans, plus a little fresh parsley and a dash of wine vinegar to taste.

Sahagún has a dusty, one-horse town kind of appeal; set on the arid Meseta between León and Burgos, it's a resting place for pilgrims on the Camino de Santiago. In the Middle Ages this was a bustling town of Jews, Moors and Christians nowadays it's a country backwater, but it does have one claim to fame, its deliciously sweet leeks.

This is a simple recipe that gets even better after a few hours, or even a night, in the refrigerator. But do make sure it is at room temperature when you serve it.

Puerros a la Vinagreta

Sweet Leek Vinaigrette

Serves 4

8 leeks, trimmed and washed, leaving just about 2.5 cm/1 inch of green
Salt and freshly ground black pepper
1 egg
3 gherkins (dill pickles), finely diced
1 tbsp very finely diced onion

1 red (bell) pepper, finely diced
1 green (bell) pepper, finely diced
1 tbsp fresh parsley, finely chopped
1 tbsp mustard
2 tbsp red wine vinegar
8 tbsp extra virgin olive oil

Boil the leeks in a saucepan of salted water until they are soft, about 15 minutes. Drain, then leave them to cool. Cut them in half lengthways and reserve until required.

Next boil the egg for 8 minutes, then cool under cold running water. Reserve. Place the remaining ingredients and seasoning in a screw-top jar and shake well to mix.

Pour the dressing over the leeks and set them aside until ready to eat. When you are ready to serve grate or chop the egg very finely and sprinkle over the top.

This makes a wonderful accompaniment to fish, lamb or vegetables cooked in a griddle pan (stovetop grill pan). The typical Spanish mash is really quite liquid, there's no hiding any lumps so a potato ricer or *pasapurés* is the best option.

Do not be tempted to use canned, stoned (pitted) black olives for this; they have absolutely no flavour at all. Buy some delicious loose olives and stone (pit) them yourself, just don't eat them all in the process.

Puré de Patata con Aceitunas

Mashed Potato with Black Olives

Serves 4 as a side dish

900 g/2 lb floury (mealy) potatoes, peeled and cut into even chunks
Salt and freshly ground black pepper
5 tbsp extra virgin olive oil
50 g/2 oz/⅓ cup stoned (pitted) black olives, finely diced

Place the potatoes in a large saucepan of cold salted water, bring to the boil and cook until tender.

Drain the potatoes, reserving half of their cooking water for later. Next, mash the potatoes, if you don't own a potato ricer or *pasapurés,* then push the potato through a sieve (strainer) using a rubber spatula.

Stir the olive oil through the mashed potatoes, then add enough of the reserved cooking water until you reach the desired consistency. Add the black olives and salt and pepper to taste. Serve at once.

This is an ancient recipe that pops up all around the Mediterranean; it is equally good made with Swiss chard. You could add a little ham or bacon too if you like.

I remember spending hours as a teenage au pair combing the ground below the umbrella pines for nuts. It was the daily post-*siesta* challenge with my toddler charges; we rarely managed more than a fistful of pine kernels (pine nuts) and they certainly never made it as far as the kitchen.

Espinacas con Pasas y Piñones

Spinach with Pine Kernels and Sultanas

Serves 4

1 kg/2 lb 4 oz fresh young spinach, washed
3 tbsp olive oil
25 g/1 oz/⅛ cup pine kernels (pine nuts)
25 g/1 oz/⅛ cup sultanas (golden raisins), soaked in warm water for 30 minutes
Salt and freshly ground black pepper

Place the spinach in a large saucepan with a tightly fitting lid; you will not need to add any more water if the spinach is still damp from washing, otherwise a splash will do. Cook the spinach over a medium heat until it has wilted, you may want to give it a stir after a couple of minutes. Drain the spinach, oh and do save the juice, it makes a delicious drink. Chop the spinach roughly.

Heat the olive oil in a frying pan. Add the pine kernels (pine nuts) and fry until they begin to brown, then add the spinach and sultanas (golden raisins). Toss everything in the oil and heat through. Taste for salt and pepper and serve.

The Spanish, like the French, love their asparagus white and as fat as your thumb. You can even buy cans of preserved white asparagus from Navarra, so highly prized that they are given the title of "*espárragos cojonudos*", quite literally "asparagus with balls". Now there's a rather disturbing thought. Green asparagus is available in the markets too. I had never considered barbecuing or chargrilling asparagus until I came upon this recipe. You can place the stalks over the hotter flame allowing the delicate heads to cook more gently.

Tip
* No griddle pan (stovetop grill pan) or barbecue? Just pop the asparagus under the grill (broiler) for a few minutes.

Espárragos y Salsa Romesco

Asparagus with Romesco Sauce

Serves 4 as a side dish or starter (appetizer), double up for a delicious light lunch

24 green asparagus spears
2 tbsp olive oil
Salt
1 x recipe *Romesco* Sauce (see page 135)

Preheat a ridged griddle pan (stovetop grill pan) or barbecue.

Brush the asparagus with olive oil and sprinkle with a little salt.

Next place the spears on a very hot, ridged griddle pan (stovetop grill pan) or over a barbecue. You will need some tongs to turn the asparagus, it should turn a vivid green and char in a few places. The entire process will only take a few minutes and the spears should bend rather than flop as you remove them from the heat.

This dish is best eaten with fingers, dipping the asparagus in the sauce as you go.

Now, I have to admit my first encounter with a *menestra de verduras* was not a good one. I was in Rioja, and opted for a light supper, or so I thought. It arrived, the delicious virgin vegetables had been given a thick coat of batter and worse still they were submerged in a murky stock – a soggy flaccid batter. What could be worse?

Thankfully I ate this lighter, fresher version on a trip to Tudela, a city steeped in Moorish history, in the fertile Ebro valley of Navarra. The area is famous for its tiny Little Gem (Boston) lettuces, *cogollos* and the delicious artichokes, a legacy of the Arabs. In the old days vegetables were cooked to death, I suggest that you leave them crunchy and packed with vitamins.

Tips

*   You can prepare ahead to the point of adding the vegetables to the ham, just make sure that you cool the vegetables with ice cold water after boiling so that they do not continue to cook and become soggy.
** Vegetables can be alternated: pumpkin, courgette (zucchini), potatoes or whatever is in season may be added to the pan.

Menestra de Tudela

Tudelan Vegetable Medley

Serves 4

4 medium artichokes
1 lemon
8 thick white, or 12 thin green asparagus spears
8 baby carrots or 4 medium carrots, sliced
200 g/7 oz/1¾ cups shelled green peas (frozen are fine)
200 g/7 oz podded broad (fava) beans (frozen are fine)
2 tbsp olive oil
1 onion, finely diced
2 garlic cloves, crushed
100 g/4 oz *jamón Serrano*, diced with the fat left on
1 tbsp plain (all-purpose) flour
Salt and freshly ground black pepper
Extra virgin olive oil, for drizzling
1 tsp chopped fresh mint (optional, unorthodox, but delicious all the same)

Begin by preparing the artichokes. Cut the lemon in half. Half fill a large saucepan with water and add the juice of half of the lemon. You will need to submerge the cleaned artichokes as you prepare them to stop them oxidizing and turning black.

Next trim the stalks and peel off the rough skin, then remove the tough outer leaves. Chop across the remaining leaves, about a third of the way down, you should now be able to delve into the centre with a teaspoon and scrape out the hairy choke. Cut the artichokes in half. Now you are ready.

Place the artichokes in a saucepan of water. Add the juice of the remaining half of lemon and a pinch of salt. Bring to the boil and cook until the artichokes are tender, about 20 minutes.

Next boil or steam your remaining vegetables, separately, until they are a little undercooked and crunchy. Reserve the cooking water. I find that thawed, frozen peas and beans can just be added to the pan at the next stage.

Heat the olive oil in a large, terracotta *cazuela* or saucepan. Add the onion and fry gently until it begins to soften. Add the garlic and *jamón* and allow any fat to render down.

Carefully add all the vegetables and sprinkle with the flour. Add about 150 ml/ 5 fl oz/⅔ cup of the reserved vegetable water, then give the pan a few shakes to mix the flour with the liquid. Bring to the boil for a minute or two before serving.

Season with salt and pepper to taste, drizzle with olive oil, add the mint, if using, and serve at once on a platter or arranged in individual portions.

Rioja's wines enjoy worldwide fame but within Spain the region's vegetables receive cult status too. It would be difficult to imagine the local cuisine without peppers, introduced in the sixteenth century from the Americas. This dish is a pepper "fest" with fresh green (bell) peppers, dried red *choricero* peppers, a chilli (chili pepper) and the even *chorizo* flavoured with paprika.

This is real comfort food: fantastic left sitting in the pan to be devoured after a bracing winter's walk.

Variation
* You can use the recipe as a wonderful base for steamed fish. Lay fillets of seasoned, firm white fish on top of the potatoes once they are almost cooked. Cover with a lid and allow the fish to steam through. Sprinkle with a little parsley and lemon juice.

Patatas a la Riojana

Rioja-style Potatoes with Peppers and Chorizo

Serves 4

4 tbsp olive oil
2 onions, sliced
2 green (bell) peppers, sliced
250 g/9 oz *chorizo* sausage
5 garlic cloves, crushed
900 g/2 lb potatoes, peeled and "broken" (see page 24) or cut into small pieces
4 dried red *choricero* peppers, de-stalked, de-seeded and roughly chopped, or 1 tbsp sweet paprika
1 dried red chilli (chili pepper) or *guindilla,* finely chopped
1 bay leaf
100 ml/3½ fl oz/generous ⅓ cup dry white wine
200 ml/7 fl oz/scant 1 cup vegetable stock, chicken stock or water
Salt
Crusty bread, to serve

Heat the olive oil in a large pan. Add the onions and green (bell) peppers and fry until they begin to caramelize.

Next, add the *chorizo*, garlic and potatoes, stirring around until everything is covered in wonderful oil. Once you can smell the glorious waft of cooked garlic, add the dried red *choricero* peppers, the chilli (chili pepper) and bay leaf.

Pour over the wine and just enough stock or water to cover the vegetables. Bring to the boil, then reduce the heat and continue to simmer for about 15–20 minutes until the potatoes are tender and their starch has thickened the juice a little.

Season with salt to taste and serve with some really crusty bread.

This stew of summer vegetables is a key feature in the Catalan kitchen, it is a close relative of the Basque *pisto* and the Provençal *ratatouille*. The vegetables are often cooked until they become soft and almost jammy, they can then left whole or puréed and used as a sauce.

In fact Samfaina has been cited by many chefs as one of the keys of Catalan cooking, along with the Sofregit, Allioli (see page 132), Picada (see page 136–7) and Romesco (see page 135). Master these five and you will have the Catalan kitchen at your fingertips!

Variations

* This is fabulous served on toasted country bread, with lamb, rabbit, chicken or fish.
** Add a couple of courgettes (zucchini) to the pan together with the aubergines (eggplants) if you are being traditional, with the tomatoes if you'd like them a little crunchy.
*** If you want to add a little more punch, you could add a little chopped chilli (chili pepper) and a few diced sun-dried tomatoes.
**** A sprig of fresh thyme added with the garlic would be delicious to serve with lamb.

Samfaina

Catalan Cooked Vegetables

Serves 4–6 as a vegetable side dish or 6–8 as a sauce

5 tbsp olive oil
2 onions, finely diced
2 green (bell) peppers, finely diced
2 red (bell) peppers, finely diced
2 aubergines (eggplants), diced in 2.5 cm/1 inch cubes
3 garlic cloves, crushed
6 ripe tomatoes, peeled, de-seeded and diced
Salt

Heat the olive oil in a large saucepan. Add the onions and fry until they are really soft, then add the (bell) peppers and aubergines (eggplants). The aubergines (eggplants) will absorb the oil at once but after a few minutes, as they begin to cook and turn translucent, the oil will seep out again.

When the vegetables are soft and cooked through, after about 15–20 minutes, add the garlic and stir until its fragrance hits you. Next, add the tomatoes, then reduce the heat and simmer until any juices have evaporated. Season with salt to taste.

If you are going to use the *samfaina* as a sauce, continue to cook, covered, for a further 20 minutes, stirring occasionally.

I never tire of these wonderful Catalan charred vegetables. *Escalivada* translates as "cooked in the embers" and the vegetables do taste great prepared in the barbecue coals or even placed in the embers of your log fire, if you are lucky enough to have one. However, I usually end up cooking this in the kitchen with astonishingly good results, you just can't tell the difference if you take the time to really blacken the skins.

This is a fabulous starter (appetizer) served with good crusty bread and great as a side dish too, with grilled (broiled) meats such as lamb.

Variations
* *Escalivada* is sublime served on crisp toast and topped with good quality salted anchovies.
** You could add the Moorish touch with a tablespoon of roasted cumin seeds along with the garlic, this is especially good with lamb.

Escalivada

Charred Summer Vegetables

Serves 4 as a starter (appetizer) or side dish

4 aubergines (eggplants)
4 red (bell) peppers
4 small onions or 12 tiny pickling (pearl) onions, skin on
2 garlic cloves, crushed
4 tbsp extra virgin olive oil
Salt and freshly ground black pepper

Preheat the oven to 180°C/350°F/Gas Mark 4.

Char all the vegetables until their skins are black. I always place my aubergines (eggplants) and (bell) peppers on top of the gas hob (stove) and turn them carefully with some tongs, a kind of indoor barbecue but a spurt under a very hot grill (broiler) will do.

Once the skins are completely charred, then place the vegetables in the oven until they have cooked through. The (bell) peppers are ready once soft and blistered, they won't take long at all. The aubergines (eggplants) should feel like feather pillows when squeezed. The onions, which need a little longer, will have squashy flesh under the crisp skins.

Once the vegetables are cooked it's an idea to cover them as they cool, I just use an upturned bowl, to create plenty of steam so the skins slip off more easily.

Peel all the vegetables, remove the seeds and cut the (bell) pepper and aubergine (eggplant) into strips.

The onions can be sliced or left whole if they are tiny.

Next add the garlic and olive oil and season with salt and pepper to taste.

6 Rice and Pulses

In late summer the regions of Rioja and southern Navarre celebrate the arrival of the *pocha,* a fresh white bean that's sold in its withering pod. "*Hay pochas*", "we've got beans", announced the sign outside a tiny restaurant in a Logroño back street. The place was packed, so I finished up sharing a table with hungry Juan, an ageing *pocha* enthusiast.

Today's dish was vegetarian but Juan assured me that, further south in Tudela, eels were a common accompaniment. In Álava, to the north, you might get a lamb's tail thrown in while *pochas* and quail were a traditional dish throughout the region with the onset of the game season. Juan demanded a couple of mild chillies (chili peppers) to nibble on between mouthfuls. I followed suit and they really spiced up the dish.

I have never found fresh *pochas* outside Spain but they are available cooked, in jars. However, you could use fresh Italian *borlotti* or French *flageolets* instead, or even substitute a dried bean (soaked before cooking).

Variations

* These beans are fabulous with any game such as squab, quail, partridge or pheasant. I ate a wonderful version with fried oyster mushrooms stirred in just before serving.

** You could cheat with ready-cooked beans. Just cook all the vegetables, purée them and add to the drained beans together with a little vegetable stock to loosen the sauce.

Pochas a la Riojana

Fresh Rioja Beans

Serves 4

900 g/2 lb shelled pocha, flageolet, borlotti or cannellini beans
  (or 450 g/1 lb dried if you are using)
1 bay leaf
2 tbsp olive oil
1 onion, finely diced
2 red (bell) peppers, finely diced
2 green (bell) peppers, finely diced
2 carrots, diced
3 garlic cloves, crushed
1 tomato, peeled and diced
1 tsp unsmoked sweet paprika
Salt
2 tbsp extra virgin olive oil
8 pickled *guindilla* chillies (see page 24) or 4 mild fresh chillies (chili peppers)

Place the beans in a large saucepan and cover with cold water. Add the bay leaf and bring to the boil (don't add any salt at this stage). Cover the saucepan and simmer for about 20 minutes.

Meanwhile, heat the olive oil in a frying pan (skillet). Add the onion, (bell) peppers and carrot and fry until they are soft and golden. Next add the garlic and tomato to the pan and stir for a moment or two.

Stir in the paprika and cook for a moment longer, it's delicate stuff and you don't want to burn it.

Now it's up to you. You may like to process the vegetables to a paste or just leave them as they are. Add them to the beans and stir well.

Continue to cook the beans for a further 20–30 minutes, or until tender. You may need to add a little water as you are cooking. You should end up with plenty of creamy, orange juices around the beans.

Season the beans with salt and serve hot, with a drizzle of extra virgin olive oil and the *guindilla* chillies or fresh chillies (chili peppers) on the side.

There are numerous recipes for this soup. Many leave out the *chorizo* replacing it with *unto,* a type of aged pork fat. If you are in Spain or close to a specialist Spanish store, do try to get hold of some *unto,* this will give the *caldo* the most authentic flavour, but a good soft *chorizo* is fabulous too.

I ate one delicious variation that contained no beans. The beans were, the chef assured me, an Asturian influence and not authentic at all. So, forgotten to soak the beans? No problem, just add a few more potatoes instead. The greens may vary according to the season but the classic *caldo* is made with *grelos* or turnip tops (turnip greens).

Tips

* This soup is often made in vast quantities and reheated; it often tastes even better second or third time around.
** If you would like your greens to remain crunchy and bright green, not traditional at all but delicious nonetheless, just add them much later, about 5 minutes before serving.

Variation

* A chicken carcass can be added to the stock too, just make sure to remove all the bones before serving the *caldo.*

Caldo Gallego

Hearty Galician Vegetable Soup

Serves 6–8

200 g/7 oz/1⅛ cups dried white beans such as haricot (navy) or even *fabas de la Granja* if you are splashing out, soaked overnight
1 ham bone, traditionally *Serrano* but any unsmoked ham bone will do
1 beef bone
1 small onion, quartered
2 litres/3½ pints/8½ cups water
450 g/1 lb potatoes, peeled and diced or "broken" into small pieces
450 g/1 lb greens, such as turnip tops (turnip greens), spring greens (collards), kale, Swiss chard or Savoy cabbage
100 g/4 oz sweet, soft *chorizo* in one piece
Salt and freshly ground black pepper
½ tsp paprika, or to taste

Drain the white beans and place them together with the meat bones, onion and water in a large, heavy-based saucepan or casserole. Bring to the boil, skimming off any foam, then simmer for about 1½ hours, or until the beans are almost tender. Occasionally add a small glass of cold water to "shock" the beans and help keep the skins intact.

Add the potatoes, greens and *chorizo* and continue to simmer for a further 20–30 minutes, or until the potatoes are cooked.

Remove the bones and season with a little salt, pepper and paprika. Using a slotted spoon, remove the *chorizo* from the pan, cut into slices, then return to the pan.

If you would like to thicken the soup a little, you could ladle a few beans and potatoes into a blender or bowl and purée or mash them with a fork. You could even process the *caldo* itself, just for a second or two with a hand-held blender.

This recipe comes from Llanes, a busy little fishing port on the Asturian coast, which overflows with lots of Spanish tourists in the summer.

The Asturians are bean-mad; their Fabada (Pork and Bean Stew opposite), made with the buttery *fabes de la Granja,* is renowned throughout Spain, but that's not the end of the matter. There's a bewildering selection of beans available and dozens of different dishes to cook with them. The *verdina* is a tiny green bean that many locals insist is peculiar to the area around Llanes. I am convinced that it's a *flageolet* bean or certainly a very close relative. Whatever the case, the *flageolet* works very well and the combination of shellfish and beans is just glorious.

Variation

* You could also add some prawns (shrimp) to the beans. I have even eaten one version where tiny fried elvers were sprinkled over the beans as a delicious (and rather extravagant) garnish.

Verdinas con Almejas

Beans with Clams

Serves 4

250 g/9 oz/1½ cups dried *verdinas*/*flageolet* beans, soaked overnight
1 onion, peeled and quartered
1 bay leaf
1 fresh thyme sprig
5 tbsp olive oil
Salt
4 garlic cloves, crushed
2 tbsp fresh flat-leaf parsley, finely chopped
100 ml/3½ fl oz/generous ⅓ cup dry white wine
900 g/2 lb fresh clams, cleaned and closed
Large pinch of saffron strands

Drain the beans and place them in a large saucepan with the onion, bay leaf, thyme sprig and enough water to cover them. Do not add any salt at this stage otherwise the bean skins will become tough. (If your water is particularly hard, bean lovers would have you use mineral water too!)

Bring the beans to the boil skimming off any foam with a slotted spoon. Reduce the heat and simmer gently, adding a little cold water every 20 minutes to "shock" the beans, helping the skins to stay intact and making sure that they are just covered.

After about 1 hour add 2 tablespoons of olive oil and 1 teaspoon of salt and continue to cook the beans until tender (anything between 10–40 minutes).

Once the beans are ready, and there's nothing to stop you cooking them ahead of time, it's time to cook the clams.

Heat about 3 tablespoons of olive oil in a large saucepan. Add the garlic and fry gently until golden. Add half the parsley and wine and bring to the boil. Once the wine is boiling add the clams and cover the pan. Give it a little shake occasionally and cook until the shells open. Discard any clams that remain closed.

Shuck half of the clams and leave the rest in their shells.

If the clam pan looks gritty, and some clams can be quite sandy, then you will need to strain the liquid before adding it to the beans.

Grind the saffron with a pinch of salt in a mortar and pestle and add to the beans. Add all the clams and simmer for 1 minute. Check the seasoning, sprinkle with the remaining parsley and leave to stand for a few minutes before serving.

This simple and hearty one-pot stew is often considered the pinnacle of Spanish bean cuisine. You will certainly require a good appetite and some time to recover. It is, as the locals would put it, "*un plato fuerte*", a hefty dish. Maybe it's just a question of training, I have seen Asturians demolish a vast plate of *fabada* and then tuck eagerly into a main course and dessert too.

The true *fabada* is made with buttery, melt-in-the-mouth beans, the local *fabes de la Granja*, a hybrid of the haricot (navy) bean brought back from the Americas, that can fetch ten times the price of a humble kidney bean. When not available I find that good quality white haricots (navy beans) work very well. The local *chorizo* and *morcilla* are oak smoked and it's a good idea to rinse them well or their smokiness can overpower the dish. At home I often add some smoked *pimentón* to give the dish its trademark flavour.

Tip

* If the stock seems watery then remove a few beans and mash them with a fork, add them to the pan and give it a good shake.

Fabada Asturiana

Asturian Pork and Bean Stew

Serves 4

225 g/8 oz smoked *chorizo* sausage
225 g/8 oz *lacón* or raw ham, soaked overnight
100 g/4 oz *tocino*, unsmoked streaky bacon, in one piece
1 bunch fresh parsley, tied
1 onion, peeled and left whole
450 g/1 lb dried Asturian *fabes de la Granja* or large white haricot (navy) beans, soaked overnight in cold water
Large pinch of saffron strands
225 g/8 oz Asturian *morcilla* or black pudding (blood sausage)
1 tsp smoked Spanish paprika
Salt

Place the *chorizo*, ham, bacon, parsley, onion and beans in a large wide pan and cover them with cold water. Sit the *morcilla* on top of the beans and bring them slowly to the boil, skimming off any foam with a slotted spoon.

"Shock" the beans with a cup of cold water and reduce the heat to a low simmer. Don't be tempted to stir the beans, just give the pan a good shake occasionally, otherwise the beans will break up.

Toast the saffron in a dry frying pan for a matter of seconds until the filaments become quite brittle, then grind it in a mortar with a pestle.

Sprinkle the ground saffron over the pan, cover and continue to simmer until the beans are soft and tender. The large local beans will take anything up to 4 hours while smaller haricots (navy beans) may take only 2 hours. The beans should be totally submerged in water as they cook, so top them up with a little cold water occasionally. This also helps to keep the skins intact.

Once the beans are cooked leave the stew to stand for at least 1 hour. Many people even prefer their *fabada* made a day in advance.

When ready to serve remove the meat, parsley and onion from the pan. Cut the meat into slices and season the beans with a little salt, just remember the meat will be salty too.

You may like to place all the meat back in the pan and warm everything through or you could serve the meat on a separate dish altogether.

This is a really speedy dish; it can be thrown together in minutes when you run in from work. The ingredients are all great storecupboard (pantry) standbys so there's no last minute shopping to do either.

I always keep the vacuum-packed, soft, cooking *chorizo* in my refrigerator for such occasions but you could use the firmer rings that are more readily available in supermarkets. I love the spicy heat of the *chorizo picante* but the choice is yours, the sweet *dulce* is delicious too.

I am using canned chickpeas in this recipe for convenience. In Spain you can pick up cooked chickpeas at the market or butcher's store or, of course, you could cook them yourself with the odd pig's ear thrown in.

Tip
* Any leftovers are wonderful blended in a soup with some vegetable stock.

Variations
* Fresh spinach is great stirred in with the canned tomatoes and just allowed to wilt.
** *Morcilla*, black pudding (blood sausage), could replace the *chorizo* or you could use a mixture of the two.
*** *El Bierzo* roasted peppers could be added straight from the jar or you could roast your own (bell) peppers and throw them in.

Potaje de Chorizo y Garbanzos
Chorizo and Chickpea One-pot Supper

Serves 4–6

2 tbsp olive oil
2 onions, diced
2 garlic cloves, diced
250 g/9 oz *chorizo*, hot or sweet, sliced
800 g/1 lb 8 oz canned chickpeas
400 g/14 oz canned chopped plum tomatoes
2 tbsp sultanas (golden raisins)
Juice of ½ lemon
Salt and freshly ground black pepper
1 tbsp toasted pine kernels (pine nuts)
1 tbsp roughly chopped fresh flat-leaf parsley
Drizzle of extra virgin olive oil

Heat the olive oil in a large frying pan (skillet). Add the onions and fry until they are soft, then add the garlic and *chorizo*.

Once the pan is swirling with the smoky, red *chorizo* fat add the chickpeas, stirring to cover them in the delicious oil.

Add the tomatoes and sultanas (golden raisins) and cook until everything is completely heated through.

Taste – I usually find that the chickpeas need a little lemon juice to liven them and a bit of salt and pepper.

Sprinkle with pine kernels (pine nuts), parsley and a dash of extra virgin olive oil.

Opposite: Potaje de Chorizo y Garbanzos
Following page: Lomos de Salmonete con Vinagreta de Pimientos y Alcaparras , page 107

This is perhaps the signature dish of Spain, prepared in one form or another all over the country. Chickpeas, bones, meat and vegetables are cooked long and slowly to create a two-course feast. The stock is consumed as a broth, often with the addition of rice or pasta, followed by platters of vegetables and meat.

A multitude may be fed from one pot, as I witnessed at a Shrove Tuesday festival in the Catalan town of Ponts. There the *cocido*, known as *escudella*, bubbled in vast cauldrons over fires in the square and the entire town turned out to fill their pots and pans – One last meat marathon before the Lenten fast.

The *cocido's* origins are the Jewish *adafina*, a huge pot that was left to stew during the Sabbath, when cooking was out of the question. The Catholics threw in the pork and made the dish their own.

Variation

* You could fry a chopped onion, 2 crushed garlic cloves and 2 peeled tomatoes together and stir these into the broth together with the potatoes.

Tip

* Some perfectionists insist on keeping their chickpeas completely separate from the vegetables. Should you decide to follow their example you can cook the chickpeas in the pot in a netting or muslin (cheesecloth) bag.

Cocido

Feast in a Pot

Serves 6–8

About 3 litres/6 pints/12¾ cups water
450 g/1 lb chuck steak, in one piece
1 *serrano* or any unsmoked ham bone
1 salted pig's trotter (foot), soaked overnight (optional)
450 g/1 lb dried chickpeas, soaked overnight
1 chicken, jointed into 8 pieces
200 g/7 oz *chorizo* (see page 30) left in whole links
3 carrots, chopped into large chunks
3 leeks, trimmed, cleaned thoroughly and chopped in half
4 celery sticks (stalks), chopped in half
1 onion, halved and stuck with 2 cloves
2 bay leaves
4 medium potatoes, peeled and cut in half
200 g/7 oz *morcilla* (see page 31) or black pudding (blood sausage)
Swiss chard or cabbage
200 g/7 oz *fideos*, *vermicelli* or other tiny pasta

Pour the water into the largest saucepan you have. Add the beef, the bone and the pig's trotter (foot), if you're using one. Bring to the boil, skimming off any foam with a slotted spoon. Add the drained chickpeas, the carrots, leeks, celery, onion and bay leaves.

Make sure that everything is covered in water, bring to the boil and skim off the foam again. Continue to cook, covered, at a steady simmer. Topping up with hot water as necessary.

After 1 hour add the chicken and *chorizo* together with a good pinch of salt and cook for about 30 minutes, or until the chickpeas are almost tender.

Add the potatoes and *morcilla,* then after a further 10 minutes add the Swiss chard or cabbage. Once the potatoes are tender, then your *cocido* is ready. Adjust the seasoning with salt and black pepper as necessary.

Strain off most of the stock and place it in a separate pot. Bring the stock to the boil, add the *fideos* or pasta and cook until tender. Serve the soup as a starter (appetizer).

Chop the beef, the pig's trotter (foot), the *chorizo* and *morcilla* into serving pieces and arrange them on a platter with the chicken. Pile the chickpeas and vegetables on another dish and serve.

Previous page: Bacalao con Garbanzos y Espinacas, page 108
Opposite: Arroz Negro, page 99

My great friend Cheche hates to spend a moment longer in the kitchen than she needs to. These lentils make a real "hungry but hectic" dish that takes just moments to put together. Lentils are great winter comfort food: it's well worth preparing a huge pot of these at the weekend for friends, family or just you to pick at. This recipe uses a stock (bouillon) cube and a jar of tomato *passata* (bottled strained tomatoes), but of course you can upgrade and use homemade stock and fresh tomatoes if you have sufficient time.

You should use the brown lentils such as the tiny *lenteja Pardina* or the bigger *lenteja de Armuña* for this dish; steer away from split red lentils as they will disintegrate into a soup.

Variations

* You could add *morcilla*, black pudding (blood sausage), in slices at the same time as the lentils.
** Other vegetables such as carrots, turnips and celery could be added with the onion, then potatoes added halfway through the cooking time.
*** This is a fabulous topping for tiny toastie canapés, garnish with a slice of cherry tomato and a whole flat-leaf parsley leaf.
**** I love to serve this as an accompaniment to simple roast chicken with maybe a dollop of garlicky natural (plain) yogurt.

Lentejas Estofadas

Cheche's Quick Lentils

Serves 4

4 tbsp olive oil
2 onions, diced
4 garlic cloves, crushed
200 g/7 oz soft cooking *chorizo*, hot or sweet the choice is yours, diced
450 g/1 lb brown lentils
2 bay leaves
400 g/14 oz canned tomato *passata* (bottled strained tomatoes) or *tomate frito*
1 tbsp organic bouillon powder or 1 stock (bouillon) cube
Salt and freshly ground black pepper
Drizzle of extra virgin olive oil

Heat the olive oil in a large, heavy-based saucepan or casserole. Add the onions and fry gently until soft. Add the garlic and *chorizo* and continue to cook until the pan is brick red with the rendered fat.

Add the lentils and stir to cover them in the delicious juices.

Next add the bay leaves, tomato *passata* (bottled strained tomatoes), stock and water. Bring to the boil and simmer until the lentils are soft and cooked through. You may need to add a little water to the pan occasionally to keep the lentils covered.

The idea is to finish up with something that can be spooned rather than poured.

Black rice is a popular dish along the Catalan coast and recipes vary greatly. In Sitges this dramatic dish is served jet-black, stained with the ink from the squid or cuttlefish. Further north on the Costa Brava many would claim that an authentic *arroz negro* contains no ink at all; there the dark colour of the dish comes from the lengthy caramelization of the onions. I will leave it up to you, but I just love the striking appearance and the salty flavour of the ink.

Cuttlefish will provide you with more ink but I prefer the texture of squid, and they are more readily available too. Just remind your fish supplier to save the ink sacs if he is preparing them for you. Cleaned squid and no ink sacs? Never fear, small sachets (envelopes) of ink can be purchased in many fish suppliers' and delicatessens.

Tip

* This is a diva dish if ever there was one, served with lashings of garlicky *allioli* and perhaps a green salad to follow, a glorious one-pot lunch.

Arroz Negro

Black Squid Rice

Serves 6 as a main course

900 g/2 lb fresh squid, cleaned and prepared, setting the ink sacs aside or using 1–2 sachets (envelopes) of squid ink
150 ml/5 fl oz/²⁄₃ cup white wine
8 tbsp olive oil
2 onions, diced
2 red (bell) peppers, sliced
3 garlic cloves, crushed
4 fresh tomatoes, peeled and de-seeded or 200 g/7 oz canned tomatoes
Juice of 1 lemon
2 tbsp chopped fresh flat-leaf parsley

400 g/14 oz/1³⁄₄ cups Spanish paella or other round-grain rice
750 ml/1¹⁄₄ pints/3 cups fish or vegetable stock
Salt
300 g/10 oz fresh *almejas finas*, carpet clams or any other mollusc (mollusk) that takes your fancy, thoroughly cleaned, optional

To serve
1 lemon, cut into wedges
1 x recipe *allioli*, to serve (see page 132)

Place the ink sacs in a small bowl with the wine, then break open the sacs with a knife and stir them around a little to colour the wine. I often use a sachet (envelope) as well to intensify the colour and flavour.

Heat the olive oil in a wide sauté dish or paella pan. Cut the squid into bite-sized pieces, add to the pan and fry over a really high heat until just cooked and opaque. Remove the squid and reserve until required. Add the onion and (bell) peppers to the pan and fry until they are deliciously soft and golden. Be patient, here lies the secret to a really delicious result.

Next add the garlic, tomatoes, lemon juice and most of the parsley and leave to bubble for 5 minutes before adding the rice. Stir in the rice, smothering it in the oily juices. Add the fish stock and bring to the boil.

Strain the wine and ink through a sieve (strainer) on to the rice. Taste the stock for seasoning and add some salt if necessary. You may find that the ink is salty enough. Return the squid to the pan and stir into the rice. I like to leave some wonderful purple tentacles poking out, like little flowers. Simmer, uncovered, for about 20 minutes, or until all the liquid has been absorbed. Remove the pan from the heat and leave the rice to rest for 5 minutes.

Meanwhile, you can steam the clams if using. Just place them in a saucepan and add a few tablespoons of water. Cover with a tight-fitting lid and cook over a high heat. Give the pan a couple of shakes and the clams will open and be ready to use within moments.

Serve the rice topped with clams, if using, the lemon wedges, remaining parsley and with *allioli* on the side.

A dish that has become synonymous with Spain, a national favourite, born in the province of Valencia but cooked at family gatherings and celebrations as far north as the Pyrenees. Piles of mushy, yellow rice found in tourist haunts on the Costas have tarnished the great name of *paella*, but eat the real thing and you will realize what all the fuss is about.

This recipe is based upon the *Paella Parellada*, a Barcelona speciality packed with a myriad of flavours. The true *parellada* contains no bones or shells but I prefer to leave my chicken on the bone and oh, it does look so much more dramatic with black mussel shells and dazzling pink prawns (shrimp), so I have taken the liberty to leave these in too.

This may look arduous and long-winded, but don't forget this is one-pot cooking and just fabulous for entertaining.

Tip

* You will require a really large frying pan (skillet), sauté pan or, better still, a paella pan for this recipe. My pan measures 35 cm/14 inches across and is just right for 6 hungry diners.

Paella

Serves 6

3 tbsp olive oil
6 chicken thighs, skin on
6 pork sausages, coarser country-style ones are best
250 g/9 oz pork loin, cut into thin ribbons
225 g/½ lb squid, cleaned and cut into bite-sized pieces
225 g/½ lb monkfish (angler fish) or any other firm white fish, skinned, boned and cut into pieces
6 large raw king prawns (jumbo shrimp)
2 medium onions, diced
2 garlic cloves, crushed

4 red (bell) peppers, grilled (broiled), skinned and cut into strips
4 ripe tomatoes, peeled and diced
300 g/10 oz/1⅓ cups Spanish *paella* or other round-grain rice
100 g/4 oz/1 cup peas, frozen will do
750 ml/1¼ pints/3 cups chicken stock
Large pinch of saffron strands
Small bunch of fresh flat-leaf parsley, finely chopped
20 live mussels, cleaned and steamed until opened
Salt
1 lemon, cut into 6 wedges, to serve

Heat the olive oil in a large pan. Add the chicken pieces and begin to brown. As soon as they are golden turn them over and add the sausages and pork . When everything looks browned and appetizing remove from the pan and reserve until required.

Add the squid to the pan and fry briefly. It will be a matter of seconds until it turns opaque. Remove from the pan and reserve separately from the chicken. Add the fish to the pan and brown slightly before adding to the squid. Lastly add the prawns (shrimp) to the pan and fry until they turn that delicious pink, then reserve with the fish and squid. Now that's all the preparation done.

Add the onion to all the delicious oils left in the pan and fry until softened. You may need to add a little more oil. Next add the garlic and fry for a minute, then add half the (bell) peppers and the tomato. Add the rice, chicken and meat to the pan and stir around for a minute.

Crush the saffron in a mortar with a pestle with a little salt and pepper and add it to the pan together with the peas and parsley. Pour on the carefully measured stock, too much and the rice will be stodgy.

Bring the pan to the boil before reducing the heat to a simmer and adding the reserved squid, fish and prawns (shrimp).

Cook until the stock has all been absorbed, about 20 minutes. Arrange the mussels and the remaining (bell) peppers on top and reserve, covered with a cloth or newspaper for 10 minutes before serving. This allows the rice grains to separate.

Serve the *paella* at the table with lemon wedges. A couple of bowls for shells and chicken bones are also a good idea.

7 Fish and Shellfish

Galicia is famed throughout Spain for its gloriously fresh seafood. I shall never forget a couple on the Costa de la Muerte, who gorged upon a huge platter without as much as a word between them. It was compulsive viewing as they eyed the plate like a chessboard. It was all down to strategy; one large, time-consuming choice, such as a lobster claw could result in the loss of half a dozen tender prawns (shrimp).

I can think of no better way to celebrate a special occasion than to dive into a huge platter of shellfish with lashings of *allioli*. All sense of formality and stuffy etiquette is forcibly abandoned with all the cracking, gnawing and sucking that has to go on.

Now, there are two ways with a *mariscada*: many restaurants will serve the seafood hot off the *plancha,* or griddle, while others will boil or steam the shellfish and serve it cold. I adore both. But, where home cooking is concerned the latter is certainly easier and has the added advantage that everything can be pre-prepared.

Tips

* Large napkins, finger bowls and shellfish crackers are an absolute must. (I have even managed with nutcrackers in the past).
** Do remember that shellfish really can't hang around for long at room temperature. Chill anything that you are not serving at once. In France shellfish platters are often served on crushed ice, a very good idea on a hot day.
*** If you prefer the easy life, or you're short of time, then you can ask your fish supplier to prepare all the crustaceans for you. That leaves you with a few shells to steam and some *allioli* to make – a breeze.

Mariscada

Shellfish Platter

Serves 4

2 x 450 g/1 lb lobsters
2 x 675 g/1½ lb brown crabs
8 x langoustines/Dublin bay prawns (lobsterettes)
16 x raw prawns (shrimp)
250 g/9 oz live mussels
250 g/9 oz fresh clams, such as carpet shell, Venus or 8 razor clams
2 lemons cut into wedges
1 x recipe *Allioli* (see page 132)

For the lobster, place the lobsters in the freezer for 2 hours, rendering them unconscious. Next boil them in your largest saucepan with plenty of salty water (about 4–5 tablespoons of salt for 3 litres/6 pints/12¾ cups of water. It should be as salty as seawater). Once the water has reached the boil, cook each lobster for about 5 minutes, then an extra 10 minutes for every 450 g/1 lb.

Leave the lobster to cool, pull off the claws, then cut it in half using a large knife, lengthways through the head and tail.

Remove the stomach sac from behind the mouth and the thread-like intestine that runs down the tail. If not serving straightaway, place the bodies and claws in the refrigerator.

For the crab, first you will need to kill the crab. It's more humane and will also stop it losing its claws. Skewer the crab, right through to the shell, with a strong instrument such as a screwdriver between the eyes and also underneath the small triangular flap or "apron" on its underside. Next cook in a large saucepan of boiling salted water (see lobster method above) for about 15 minutes for every 450 g/1 lb.

Allow the crab to cool, then pull off the legs and claws. Next lay the crab on its back and remove the pale undershell. Remove and discard the stomach sac from behind the eyes at the top of the shell. Pull off the feathery grey gills and throw them out too. Cut the crab in half from front to back. Chill until ready to serve.

For the langoustines and the prawns (shrimp), boil a large saucepan of well-salted water and drop in the langoustine and prawns (shrimp). Once the water has returned to the boil cook for a further 1 minute. Drain then cool the shellfish under cold running water. Chill until ready to serve.

For the mussels and the clams, place the clams in fresh water for about 15 minutes to let them spit any sand they may contain. Wash and scrub the clams and the mussels, keeping them separate. Check that the shells are all firmly closed and remove the beards from the mussels. Next add a slosh of white wine to a large saucepan and when it's very hot, add the mussels. Cover with a lid and cook until they have all

* You could use any combination of the shellfish above, or even just serve a huge plate of prawns (shrimp). Oysters, scallops, cockles, winkles and whelks could be added too, if you can buy them.
** You could even crown the dish with a few of the legendary goose-necked barnacles, *percebes* (see page 36). These are dropped into boiling water and removed as soon as the water returns to the boil.

Gone are the days when the rivers of Asturias teamed with wild salmon and trout, nevertheless hopeful anglers are a still a common sight in the spring and early summer months. Nowadays fishing is strictly controlled and it is much more likely that you will be preparing this recipe with farmed fish, although do at least try to make sure that it is organic. The salty ham and acidic cider contrast beautifully with the salmon's oily flesh.

Tip

* This dish would tend to be served alone in Spain but some new potatoes and fresh spinach would make a tasty and balanced accompaniment.

opened. Remove from the heat and leave them to cool. Discard any mussels that remain closed. Repeat with the clams. Chill the mussels and clams in the refrigerator until ready to use.

Set out the shellfish on a large platter with plenty of thick lemon wedges. Serve with a couple of bowls of *allioli* or mayonnaise if you prefer it – homemade of course (see page 134) – or maybe with a bowl of each to keep everyone happy.

Salmón a la Ribereña

Asturian Salmon

Serves 4

4 pieces of salmon fillet, about 200 g/7 oz each, skinned
Plain (all-purpose) flour, for dusting
Salt
15 g/½ oz/1 tbsp butter
2 tbsp olive oil
175 g/6 oz *jamón serrano*, cut into thin strips
Pinch of sweet unsmoked paprika
150 ml/5 fl oz/⅔ cup dry (hard) cider
150 ml/5 fl oz/⅔ cup fish stock

Begin by seasoning the fish and dredging with a little flour. Heat the butter and olive oil in a wide pan, large enough to fit your fish. Add the fish to the pan and fry for a few minutes on each side, until golden and cooked to your liking, I prefer mine a little underdone. Next remove the fish with a slotted spoon and place on a warmed serving dish.

Add the ham to the pan and stir to render any fat. Do not cook for too long otherwise it will become very tough. Add the paprika, cider and fish stock and allow to reduce a little before pouring over the salmon to serve.

The most fabulous combination of Mediterranean seafood and a rich sauce of peppers and nuts. *Romesco* is an institution in the province of Tarragona, in southern Catalonia. The dish stirs up memories of late summer lunches after a morning on the beach; tables under shady awnings, sunglasses and sarongs, chilled rosé wine and a plate of gloriously sweet, fresh fish.

You could really push the boat out and add lobster, scampi, clams and squid too. It's really a case of using the freshest fish and shellfish available on the day.

Variations

* If you choose to add a lobster, you will need to add the raw meat, cut into bite-sized pieces together with the prawns (shrimp). The head and small legs can be used with the fish bones to make a fabulous stock.
** The scampi, squid and clams may be added along with the mussels and prawns (shrimp).

Romesco de Peix

Seafood Stew with Potatoes, Garlic and Nuts

Serves 4

600 ml/1 pint/2½ cups fish stock
450 g/1 lb potatoes, peeled and sliced
4 tbsp plain (all-purpose) flour seasoned with a little salt
900 g/2 lb assorted firm fleshed fish, such as monkfish (angler fish), scorpion fish, halibut, rock fish or bass, boned, skinned and cut into small pieces
2 tbsp olive oil
4 tbsp *Romesco* Sauce (see page 135)
8 raw prawns (shrimp)
12 live mussels, cleaned and prepared
1 fresh flat-leaf parsley sprig
50 ml/2 fl oz/¼ cup dry white wine
Salt
Juice of ½ lemon, or to taste
1 tbsp fresh flat-leaf parsley, finely chopped
Crusty bread, to serve

Preheat the oven to 190°C/375°F/Gas Mark 5.

Boil the potatoes in the fish stock until they are just cooked. Meanwhile, place the seasoned flour on a large plate, add the fish pieces and toss until coated.

Next heat the olive oil in a large terracotta *cazuela* or ovenproof casserole, big enough to hold the whole stew. Add the fish and fry until just browned. Remove the fish and set aside.

Next add the *Romesco* Sauce to the pan and fry for 1–2 minutes, then add the wine. Bring to the boil before adding the potatoes and fish stock. Stir to combine all the flavours. If the potatoes begin to break up a little, don't worry this will just thicken the sauce beautifully.

Add the fish, the raw shellfish and a little salt to taste.

Bake in the oven for about 15 minutes. Once the mussels have opened and the prawns (shrimp) have turned pink you are ready to serve.

Sprinkle with the lemon juice and parsley. Make sure you have some good bread to mop up the juices.

The combination of ham and trout is a classic dish, known as *Truchas a la Navarra*. Like so many traditional recipes there are numerous variations: some insist that a whole trout be stuffed with cured ham while others wrap the fish up in a ham blanket.

I particularly like this more elegant take on the dish; with bone-free fish, crisp ham and succulent red cabbage, from the Restaurante Fátima. The restaurant was a total surprise: I quite literally stumbled upon it while sheltering in a doorway during a torrential rainstorm, in the city of Valladolid. I spent the rest of the day happily cocooned in the dining room savouring Fátima's glorious food.

Tip
* You could boil 50 ml/2 fl oz/¼ cup of red wine with 2 tablespoons of sugar until a syrup forms. This can be drizzled on the plates as a delicious garnish.

Trucha con Lombarda Braseada y Jamón Crujiente

Trout with Crisp Jamón and Braised Red Cabbage

Serves 4

2 tbsp olive oil
100 g/4 oz unsmoked lardons or diced bacon
1 onion, finely diced
2 garlic cloves, crushed
½ red cabbage, finely shredded
½ tsp sweet paprika
100 ml/3½ fl oz/generous ⅓ cup white wine
Salt and freshly ground black pepper
4 slices of *jamón serrano,* or *Ibérico* if you're feeling extravagant
Oil, for oiling
4 x 175 g/6 oz trout fillets
1 tbsp pork fat or olive oil

Preheat the oven to 160°C/325°F/Gas Mark 3.

Begin by heating the olive oil in a large saucepan. Add the bacon and fry until any fat has rendered.

Next add the onion and continue cooking until it is soft and translucent.

Stir in the garlic and red cabbage and, once the garlic smells fabulous, add the paprika.

Stir for a moment or two, then pour over the wine and increase the heat to boil off the alcohol.

Next pour over just enough water to cover the cabbage and cook for about 20 minutes until tender and most of the juices have evaporated. Season with salt and pepper to taste.

Meanwhile, place the *jamón* on a lightly oiled tray and bake in the oven for about 10 minutes, or until it crisps once cooled.

Next cook the trout. Fátima fries her fish in a pan with thin slices of *Ibérico* pork fat while I prefer to place mine under the grill (broiler) brushed with a little oil, it's up to you. Just make sure that you don't overcook the fish; the flesh should remain really succulent and juicy.

Serve a spoonful of braised cabbage alongside the trout topped with a slice of crispy *jamón*.

This recipe was inspired by a trip to the legendary Arzak restaurant in San Sebastián. Juan Mari Arzak, one of the founding fathers of the *Nueva Cocina*, and his daughter Elena are a dynamic team, constantly inventing breathtaking combinations of local Basque ingredients and exotic new flavours.

The original recipe involved all sorts of intricacies such as lightly smoking the tuna, grinding up toasted tuna skin and inserting melon balls into hollowed shallots, and I can assure you that the result was pure perfection. I am assuming that few of you have a small army in your kitchen or two days to prepare the recipe so here is my very simplified adaptation, it might not quite earn you three Michelin stars but it will certainly impress your friends. The combination of sweet, refreshing melon and oily fish such as tuna or anchovies is truly inspired.

Tips
* Cornichons, or tiny gherkins (dill pickles), do seem to vary enormously in quality and flavour; the variety I buy from my deli are extremely flavoursome but you may have to add a touch of vinegar if the vinaigrette does not have a really fresh and zesty flavour.
** When searing fish it should be at room temperature otherwise the centre will remain cold if you are leaving it deliciously rare.

Bonito a la Plancha con Cebolletas Caramelizadas y Melón

Seared Tuna with Caramelized Onions and Melon

Serves 4

1 tbsp olive oil, plus extra for cooking
16 button onions or shallots, peeled but left whole
½ sweet melon, cut into 16 balls or dice
2 tbsp cider vinegar
4 x 175 g/6 oz tuna steaks, at room temperature
Pinch of salt
Pinch of ground ginger

For the vinaigrette
1 tbsp chopped fresh flat-leaf parsley
10 cornichons or tiny gherkins (dill pickles)
3 tbsp extra virgin olive oil

For the red pepper oil
1 tbsp red peppercorns
2 tbsp extra virgin olive oil.

Preheat the oven to 180°C/350°F/Gas Mark 4.

Toss the onions or shallots in the 1 tablespoon of olive oil and bake them in the oven for about 40 minutes until soft and golden.

Meanwhile, for the vinaigrette: just purée the parsley, cornichons and olive oil together, or chop them very finely. Add just enough water to give a sauce consistency and season with salt and pepper to taste.

Coarsely grind the red peppercorns in a mortar with a pestle and add them to the olive oil. Reserve.

Once your onions are ready, its time to heat a heavy-based frying pan (skillet) or griddle with 1 teaspoon of olive oil. Add the melon and onions, shaking them around until they brown slightly and are heated through. Add a little cider vinegar and salt and pepper to taste. Remove from the pan and reserve until required.

Brush the tuna with a little olive oil and the salt and ginger. Place the tuna in the pan and sear for a couple of minutes on each side. Serve it as rare as you dare.

Serve on individual plates; placing the tuna next to the onion and melon accompaniment. Drizzle the red pepper oil over the tuna and garnish the dish with the lush green vinaigrette.

This recipe was inspired by a trip to a very smart restaurant, the Real Balneario, set on the beach at Salinas in Asturias. It was an odd sensation; all buttoned up in an air-conditioned dining room amidst suited gentlemen and coiffed ladies, with oiled bathers lying at an arm's length on the other side of the huge glass window.

A nearby pair of excruciatingly small trunks were nearly enough to put me off my lunch, but then the red mullet arrived and I was thankfully transported to rather higher realms.

The oily white flesh of the mullet is delicious just grilled (broiled) or fried and served with zesty, fresh flavours such as this simple vinaigrette.

Tip

* This is ideal for a light and refreshing summer lunch but you could serve the fish with Mashed Potato with Black Olives (see page 85) for something more substantial.

Lomos de Salmonete con Vinagreta de Pimientos y Alcaparras

Red Mullet with a Pepper and Caper Vinaigrette

Serves 4

4 x 225 g/8 oz whole red mullet
  or red snapper, filleted
2 tbsp plain (all-purpose) flour seasoned
  with a little salt
2 tbsp olive oil

For the vinaigrette
½ red onion, finely diced

1 red and 1 green (bell) pepper,
  finely diced
2 small tomatoes, chopped
3 tbsp capers, rinsed and chopped
1 tbsp finely chopped fresh
  flat-leaf parsley
2 tbsp extra virgin olive oil
Salt and freshly ground black pepper

Begin by making the vinaigrette, giving the flavours a chance to develop a little. Just mix everything together then add a little salt and pepper to taste. You may not need any salt at all, as some capers can be very salty.

Remove any remaining pinbones and scales from the fish fillets and toss the fish in the seasoned flour.

Heat the olive oil in a large frying pan (skillet). Add the fish, a few fillets at a time, skin-side down, and fry until the skin begins to crisp. Turn the fish over and continue to cook for a further 1–2 minutes until the fish is firm and opaque.

Drain the fish on kitchen paper (paper towels) and serve with the beautiful pink skin-side up, and a pile of the crisp vinaigrette.

Sardines are midsummer fare all along the north coast of Spain. What could be better than a sardine cooked on the barbecue at the beachside bar? No cutlery required; there is something very satisfying about using fingers and gnawing at the bone, leaving a pile of skeletons worthy of Felix the cartoon cat.

These stuffed sardine fillets are a little more refined and really delicious. They would make a wonderful summer lunch.

Sardinas al Horno de Picadillo

Baked Sardines

Serves 4

1.5 kg/3 lb fresh sardines

For the stuffing
2 red onions, finely diced
2 garlic cloves, crushed
2 *piquillo* peppers (see page 23) or 2 red
  (bell) peppers, roasted and peeled
  (see page 24)

10 green olives, stoned (pitted)
  and diced
1 tsp dried oregano
2 tbsp fresh flat-leaf parsley, chopped
2 tbsp fresh breadcrumbs
Zest and juice of 1 lemon
Salt and coarsely ground black pepper
6 tbsp olive oil

Preheat the oven to 180°C/350°F/Gas Mark 4.

Begin with the sardines. Cut down the belly and remove the innards. Place the fish skin-side up, like an open book, and press down gently on its back, this will loosen the backbone. Chop through the backbone just below the head and pull out the spine bringing all the bones with it. Remove any bones you have left behind with tweezers or fingertips. You may like to leave the heads on the sardines or alternatively remove them and cut each fish into 2 fillets.

Mix together all the stuffing ingredients and season with salt and pepper to taste.

Pour 2 tablespoons of olive oil into a large, ovenproof dish to prevent the sardines from sticking.

Stuff the sardines with the herby filling, or sandwich it between the fillets, it's up to you. Drizzle the fish with the remaining olive oil and bake in the oven for 10-20 minutes (it will depend on their size), or until the sardines are just cooked and firm. Serve at once.

Foreigners are often bewildered by the rather unappetizing piles of grey salt cod sitting next to stalls heaving with gleaming fresh fish in Barcelona's Boquería market. Who would chose to eat the dried fish with so much fresh around? Well, you might just choose to eat a slice of cured ham instead of pork. It's the classic case where preservation has resulted in something terribly good in its own right.

Mercè Brunés runs a fabulous cookery school and guest house, El Folló, in the Catalan hills. She has become a great friend and it didn't take much persuading to lure her over to London's Books for Cooks store to teach a class with me. She chose to demonstrate this classic dish.

Variations

* You may like to add some toasted pine kernels (pine nuts) and sultanas (golden raisins) to the spinach.
** *Bacalao* is also served in another delicious Catalan combination with *Samfaina* (see page 89)

Bacalao con Garbanzos y Espinacas
Salt Cod with Chickpeas and Spinach

Serves 4. You will need to begin preparing your salt cod 36 hours in advance.

6 tbsp olive oil
2 onions, diced
4 tomatoes, peeled, de-seeded and diced or 200 g/7 oz canned plum tomatoes
300 g/10 oz fresh spinach, washed

300 g/10 oz/1¾ cups cooked chickpeas or 150 g/5 oz/¾ cup dried (see page 00)
700 g/1½ lb salt cod, cut into 4 pieces then soaked, boned and skinned (see page 33)

Heat 4 tablespoons of olive oil in a frying pan (skillet). Add the onions and fry, stirring occasionally, until they turn golden brown.

Next add the tomato and allow the mixture to cook down until the excess liquid has evaporated. You have just made a *sofregit*, the classic base sauce of the Catalan kitchen.

Meanwhile, place the washed spinach in a saucepan with a tight-fitting lid and cook over a low heat until it has wilted.

Drain the cooked chickpeas and return them to a clean saucepan. Add the *sofregit* and heat gently to warm them through. Next, stir in the spinach and check the seasoning, adding salt as required.

Heat the remaining 2 tablespoons of olive oil in a large, heavy-based frying pan (skillet). Add the salt cod and fry for 5–10 minutes, or until cooked through. Serve at once on a bed of the chickpeas and spinach.

Vizcaya, one of the three Basque provinces of Spain, is home to the most famous salt cod dishes of all. This is a classic with almost as many recipe variations as there are chefs but all will agree that essential to the sauce are the dried, sweet *choricero* peppers (see page 24). At a pinch you could use some sweet paprika instead, but not the smoked variety, about a half a tablespoon for each pepper will do.

In order to keep the cod really tender it is recommended to cook it slowly in oil, rather than poaching it in water. The cod is in effect already cooked as it has been cured, so care must be taken not to overcook it.

Variations

* Some chefs add a little tomato to the recipe, you could throw in 200g/7 oz chopped canned tomatoes when you add the *choricero* pepper flesh.
** You could use this sauce with any fresh white filleted fish such as hake, cod or haddock, just don't tell the Basques.

Bacalao a la Vizcaína

Vizcayan Salt Cod

Serves 4. You will need to begin preparing your salt cod 36 hours in advance.

8 dried *choricero* peppers, de-stalked and de-seeded
2 tbsp olive oil
900 g/2 lb red onions, finely diced
2 green (bell) peppers, finely diced
50 g/2 oz ham fat (*tocino de jamón*) or unsmoked bacon, diced
1 small dried red chilli (chili pepper), left whole
675 g/1½ lb salt cod, cut into 4 pieces then soaked, boned and skinned (see page 33)
3 tbsp olive oil
2 garlic cloves, peeled and left whole
Crusty bread, to serve

Begin by placing the dried *choricero* peppers in a bowl of warm water and leaving them to soak for at least 1 hour.

Heat the olive oil in a heavy-based saucepan. Add the onions, green (bell) peppers and ham fat or bacon and cook over the lowest heat possible; they really should not brown. Once the onions have softened, cover the pan but continue cooking. Good things come to those wait and the longer you wait the more delicious your sauce, but you will have to watch it and stir it occasionally to prevent it from catching.

Remove the *choricero* peppers from the bowl, reserving the soaking water, and scrape out the soft flesh from the inside of the skin. Reserve the flesh.

After an hour or two, if you can bear to wait, add the pepper flesh to the onion mixture (or your paprika if you are using it) together with the chilli (chili pepper) and enough of the reserved soaking water to cover. Continue to cook for 15 minutes then blend in a blender or better still use a *pasapurés*.

At last it's time to cook the cod! In a pan, large enough to hold all the fish, begin by infusing the oil. Just fry the garlic cloves in the olive oil until golden, then remove them. Reduce the heat, add the fish and cook for about 5–10 minutes.

Lastly bring the sauce to the boil, add the fish together with a tablespoon of their cooking oil and simmer for a couple of minutes.

Serve the *bacalao* at once with plenty of bread to mop up the fabulous juices.

The low, winter sun glinted on the Mediterranean as a chef scuttled out into the restaurant garden below and snatched some fresh herbs. The scene was set for one of the most memorable feasts I have ever eaten. The Restaurante San Pau, on the Catalan Costa Brava, is a Mecca for lovers of the local Mediterranean cuisine and Carmen Rusculleda, the chef, gives everything her own very personal creative twist.

The eight-course tasting menu was preceded by four glorious *tapas de aperitivo* and followed by a selection of exquisite *petit fours*; recipe for a sluggish afternoon or a *siesta* on the nearest park bench. Miraculously, I felt positively sprightly, all down to the fresh, light style of the food.

Carmen generously parted with this recipe, which I have simplified for the home cook. It's certainly a special occasion dish, quite fiddly and extravagant too but just wait until you taste it!

Tips
* If you really can't find Dover sole, any firm, flat white fish will be delicious prepared in this way.
** Leftover stock may be frozen ready for any number of fish dishes.
*** The pepper sauce is fabulous with a cold chicken salad. I have discovered that you can cheat using canned or bottled artichokes, and they are really very good. It will never be quite the same but it certainly cuts out a bit of hard labour. (400 g/14 oz in brine will do the trick).

Lenguado, Alcachofas y Escarola con Caldo de Ñoras

Fillet of Dover Sole with Artichokes, Curly Endive and Ñora Pepper Broth

Serves 4

4 x 350 g/12 oz Dover sole, skinned and filleted with heads and bones reserved

For the stock
½ tbsp olive oil
1 carrot, peeled and halved
1 leek, trimmed and quartered
1 onion, peeled and quartered
1 celery stick (stalk), halved
3 garlic cloves, peeled but left whole
1 tomato, quartered
50 ml/2 fl oz/¼ cup wine

Pepper sauce
1 tbsp olive oil
4 garlic cloves, sliced
pulp of 4 soaked *ñoras* peppers
4 pieces of sun blush/sun-dried tomato preserved in oil
1 small fresh chilli (chili pepper) or pinch of chilli flakes (adjust to personal taste)
250 ml/8 fl oz/1 cup water
2 handfuls of curly endive, washed and cut into bite-sized pieces
6 small or 2 large artichokes, trimmed and prepared (see page 87)
Olive oil, for frying

Preheat the oven to 190°C/375°F/Gas Mark 5.

For the fish stock, brown the fish heads and bones in the olive oil in an ovenproof pan such as a cast-iron casserole or frying pan (skillet) with a heatproof handle.

Add the carrot, leek, onion, celery, garlic and tomato. Roast in the oven for 20 minutes. Next add the wine and scrape the base of the pan with a wooden spatula. Pour over enough water to cover the bones and leave to simmer for 20 minutes.

Strain the stock into a saucepan and reduce, by boiling, until really dense and tasty.

For the pepper broth, heat the olive oil in a frying pan (skillet). Add the garlic and fry until it begins to turn golden, then add the *ñoras* pepper pulp, the sun-dried tomatoes and chilli (chili pepper), stir and add the water. Simmer gently for 10 minutes. Purée the mixture in a blender or using a hand-held blender.

Adjust the salt and chilli if necessary.

Cut the artichokes in the thinnest slices imaginable, the easiest way is using a mandolin.

Heat a little olive oil in a separate pan. Add the artichokes and fry until crisp and brown. Drain on kitchen paper (paper towels) and keep warm.

Season the fish with salt and pepper to taste and brush with a little olive oil, before placing it under a preheated hot grill until just cooked – a matter of moments, it will depend on the size of the fillets.

Meanwhile, season the curly endive with salt and pepper and toss it in a hot frying pan (skillet) with a touch of olive oil. Mix the endive and artichoke together.

Next place about 2 teaspoons of pepper sauce in the middle of 4 hot plates (No more or the delicate fish will be overpowered).

Sandwich the fillets of sole together with some of the artichoke and endive mixture. Pop the fish on the plates, top with the remaining artichoke and endive and pour a pool of the delicious fish stock on to the plates. Serve at once.

Merluza a la Gallega

Galician Hake

Hake is the most popular fish in Spain, in fact the Spaniards eat so much of the stuff that the rest of us find it hard to come by.

The local line-caught hake, *merluza de anzuelo,* is like gold dust, snapped up by restaurant chefs and gourmets at extortionate prices. The net-caught hake is more common. Just make sure that it is really fresh as some of the fish has spent a few days on the trawler before it even hits the market floor.

Any dish served "*a la Gallega*", or Gallician style, is bound to contain paprika. It does seem odd that the spice has become a regional signature since paprika is produced miles away in Extremadura and Murcia, in the south of Spain.

Variation
* You could try this dish with any firm white-fleshed fish such as cod, haddock or whiting.

Serves 4

1 onion, cut in half
1 bay leaf
675 g/1½ lb potatoes, peeled and cut into large chunks
Salt
4 large or 8 smaller hake steaks
450 g/1 lb broccoli, trimmed and broken into florets
200 g/7 oz/1¾ cups fresh or frozen peas

For the paprika dressing
8 tbsp extra virgin olive oil
2 garlic cloves, finely sliced
2 tsp sweet unsmoked paprika
1 tbsp wine vinegar

First make the paprika dressing by heating the extra virgin olive oil with the garlic until it just begins to turn golden. Remove the pan from the heat and stir in the paprika, then leave to cool. Once the oil has cooled, add the vinegar and a little salt to taste.

Next place the onion, bay leaf and potatoes in a large, wide saucepan of cold salted water and bring to the boil. Once the potatoes are cooked, add the hake and allow the water to return to the boil for a moment before removing the pan from the heat. Cover and leave to stand for about 5 minutes to cook through (this will depend on the thickness of your steaks).

Meanwhile, boil or steam the broccoli and peas until they are just cooked and still really bright green and crunchy.

Using a slotted spoon, remove the fish from the pan and carefully drain the potatoes. Next arrange the potatoes, broccoli and peas on individual serving plates, place the fish on top and drizzle with the delicious garlic and paprika dressing.

Fish and apples are not a common partnership but when I tucked into this dish in the Asturian city of Oviedo I was instantly smitten. You could add some cooked potatoes to the sauce or use a different fish altogether. I ate another delicious version made with red sea bream.

Merluza con Manzana al Aroma de Sidra

Hake with Apples and Cider

Serves 4

4 x 200 g/7 oz hake fillets, skinned (or 175 g/6 oz fillets if you are serving potatoes too)
2 tbsp plain (all-purpose) flour seasoned with a large pinch of salt
4 tbsp olive oil
1 onion, finely diced
3 garlic cloves, crushed
1 tbsp plain (all-purpose) flour
150 ml/5 fl oz/⅔ cup cider
150 ml/5 fl oz/⅔ cup fish stock
2 ripe tomatoes, peeled, de-seeded and diced or 3 tbsp canned chopped tomatoes
2 tbsp chopped fresh flat-leaf parsley
15 fresh clams (optional)
4 raw king prawns (jumbo shrimp), optional
Salt and freshly ground black pepper

To garnish
15 g/½ oz/1 tbsp unsalted (sweet) butter
1 dessert (eating) apple, sliced

Make sure your fillets are free from any bones, then toss them in the seasoned flour.

Heat the olive oil in a large sauté pan or better still a terracotta *cazuela*. Add the onion and fry until softened. Add the garlic and hake, turning the fish over after 2 minutes or once it begins to brown.

Next sprinkle the onion with a little flour and give the pan shake.

Add the cider, fish stock, tomatoes and parsley together with the clams and prawns (shrimp) if you are using them.

Reduce the heat and leave to simmer, covered, for 5–10 minutes until the fish is cooked. Season with salt and pepper to taste.

Meanwhile, melt the butter in a small frying pan (skillet). Add the apple slices and fry until they begin to caramelize.

Place the fish on individual serving plates with the shellfish. Pour over the sauce and garnish with the caramelized apple slices.

Opposite: Bonito a la Plancha con Cebolletas Caramelizadas y Melón, page 106
Following page: Pato con Peras, page 120

This recipe is an example of the pure simplicity of the traditional Basque kitchen. The hake must be wonderfully fresh for such a basic combination to really shine. Purists would have you omit the flour, allowing the sauce to thicken naturally with the oil and gelatine from the fish and some careful pan shaking in the manner of another classic Basque sauce the *pil-pil.* This is a tricky business and probably best left to the professionals, I go along with the housewives on this one and add a little flour. Clams are often thrown in with the sauce while *kokotxas,* the gelatinous morsels of flesh from the hake's throat, are a celebrated addition in smart restaurants and the men's cooking societies. You may like to add cooked asparagus tips, peas and even the odd slice of boiled egg too, in which case you have transformed the dish into *Merluza a la Koxkera.*

Merluza con Salsa Verde

Hake with Parsley and Clams

Serves 4

4 x 200 g/7 oz hake fillets, skin left on
2 tbsp plain (all-purpose) flour seasoned with a little salt
100 ml/3½ fl oz/generous ⅓ cup extra virgin olive oil
2 garlic cloves, crushed
3 shallots, very finely diced
3 tbsp fresh flat-leaf parsley, very finely chopped
4 tbsp fish stock
4 tbsp *txacolí,* or dry white wine
20 fresh clams, cleaned and steamed until open, optional

Check the fish for any bones. Spread the seasoned flour out on a plate, then add the fish and toss until the fish is coated in the flour.

In a wide pan, large enough to hold all the hake in a single layer, fry the shallots and the garlic for a moment, until you begin to smell the garlic.

Reduce the heat and add the fish, skin-side up. Sprinkle the pan with any seasoned flour you have left over from the fish and cook for about 3–4 minutes, moving the pan in a circular motion occasionally so that the fish does not stick.

Turn the fish over and continue moving the pan, helping the oil to thicken a little.

Add the wine and fish stock, giving everything a gentle shake. Cook for a further 1–2 minutes until the fish is just cooked, then sprinkle liberally with parsley. Check the seasoning, adding salt if necessary. If you are adding cooked clams do remember they can be quite salty themselves.

Serve the fish at once with the deliciously delicate sauce.

Previous page: Lomo de Ciervo o Corzo con Frutas Otoñales, page 123
Opposite: Mar i Muntanya: Pollastre amb Gambes, page 119

Sea bass has fantastically firm, white flesh and such a glorious flavour that it is a shame to mask it with complicated sauces. This Catalan recipe is simplicity itself and often used for other whole fish as well, such as the Mediterranean *dorada,* or gilt-head sea bream.

When cooking whole fish it's tricky to gauge quantities, as there is quite a bit of waste. I usually allow about 325–350 g/ 11–12 oz per person, but you obviously have to go with what's available. Two smaller sea bass would be an option too.

I worked for many years as a chef on a sailing boat and this was always an absolute favourite with crew and guests alike. I loved it too – there was just so little preparation involved.

Tip

* You could add black olives to this dish too.

Lubina al Horno

Baked Sea Bass

Serves 4

Olive oil, for brushing and drizzling
450 g/1 lb firm, waxy potatoes, peeled and sliced very thinly, preferably on a mandoline.
1 mild Spanish onion, finely sliced
3 large ripe tomatoes, sliced
3 garlic cloves, crushed
2 tbsp finely chopped fresh flat-leaf parsley
1 fresh thyme sprig
1 bay leaf
1 x 1.5 kg/3–3 ½ lb sea bass, scaled and gutted
100 ml/3 ½ fl oz/generous ⅓ cup dry white wine
1 lemon, cut into wedges

Preheat the oven to 180°C/350°F/Gas Mark 4.

Oil a large ovenproof dish, big enough to hold your fish, and cover the base with a layer of slightly overlapping potato slices.

Cover with half the onion slices, half the tomato, a pinch of the garlic and parsley, and drizzle with olive oil. Season with salt and pepper to taste.

Next make a new layer with the rest of the potato, onion and tomato slices.

Season again and sprinkle with the remaining garlic and parsley. Add the thyme and the bay leaf and drizzle with olive oil. Bake in the oven for 15 minutes.

Meanwhile, rinse the sea bass and check over for any stray scales. Make 3 diagonal slashes into the flesh, nearly through to the bone. Season the fish inside and out with salt and pepper.

Place the sea bass on top of the potatoes, pour over the wine and drizzle with olive oil. Bake for 25–35 minutes, or until the fish is just opaque and firm.

Serve at the table with lemon wedges.

8

Poultry, Meat and Game

On the last weekend before Christmas Catalan families flock to Vilafranca de Penedés for the *Fira del Gall* or poultry fair. The streets are lined with stalls selling live chickens, capons, cockerels (roosters), ducks, geese and turkeys. You choose your bird, pop off for a coffee and a spot of shopping and return a few hours later to collect it plucked, drawn and ready for the oven. The Spaniards are realists; they learn from an early age where their meat comes from.

This stuffing (dressing) is a delicious treat for Christmas or a great way to liven up a Sunday roast chicken.

Gall Dindi Farcit a la Catalana

Turkey with Fruit and Nut Stuffing

Serves 6–8

For the stuffing (dressing)
100 g/4 oz/2 cups dried stoned (pitted) prunes
50 g/2 oz/⅓ cup dried apricots
50 g/2 oz/⅓ cup sultanas (golden raisins)
3 tbsp olive oil or lard
300 g/10 oz sausage meat, *butifarra* with casing removed would be ideal
100 g/4 oz unsmoked streaky bacon, diced
50 g/2 oz/⅜ cup pine kernels (pine nuts)
200 g/7 oz cooked, peeled chestnuts
½ tsp ground cinnamon
1 fresh thyme sprig or ½ tsp dried
1 tsp dried oregano

Salt and freshly ground black pepper
200 ml/7 fl oz/scant 1 cup *vi ranci* (see page 46), sweet sherry or Italian Vin Santo

For the bird
1 x 3–4 kg/7–9 lb turkey
1 tbsp lard or butter
Salt and freshly ground black pepper
2 onions, peeled and quartered
1 leek, sliced
2 carrots, sliced
100 ml/3½ fl oz/generous ⅓ cup white wine
750 ml/1¼ pints/3 cups turkey (made from the giblets) or chicken stock

For the stuffing (dressing), soak the dried fruits in a bowl of boiling water for 2 hours until they are plumped and juicy.

Next heat the olive oil or lard in a frying pan (skillet). Crumble in the sausage meat, add the bacon and fry until the meat begins to firm and cook. Add the nuts and seasoning.

Drain the dried fruit, chop it roughly and add to the pan. Pour in the sweet wine and cook for a moment or two longer. Taste and adjust the seasoning if necessary, then leave the stuffing (dressing) to cool.

Preheat the oven to 200°C/400°F/Gas Mark 6.

Wipe and dry the turkey inside and out, then fill with the stuffing (dressing).

Smear the skin with lard or butter, then season with plenty of salt and pepper.

Place the turkey on a rack in a large roasting tin (pan) with the vegetables and wine below. (Add the vegetables and wine to the roasting tin (pan) first.) Cooking the turkey breast side down for the first hour will help to keep the meat really juicy. Cover with a large sheet of foil and roast for 30 minutes.

Reduce the oven temperature to 180°C/350°F/Gas Mark 4 and roast for a further 1½–2 hours.

Top up the roasting tin (pan) with a little stock occasionally so that the vegetables do not burn. Remove the foil for the last 30 minutes, allowing the skin to brown.

Once the bird is cooked thoroughly. (To check, insert a skewer or the tip of a sharp knife into the thickest part of the meat and if the juices run clear, then the turkey is cooked.) Leave the turkey to rest for at least 20 minutes.

Meanwhile, strain the juices from the roasting tin (pan), remove the fat with a large spoon and add any remaining stock. Season with salt and pepper to taste.

To serve, pile the stuffing (dressing) into a hot dish, place slices of turkey over the top and pour over the delicious juices.

Pollastre amb Samfaina

Chicken with Mediterranean Vegetables

Chicken has suffered the same fate in Spain as elsewhere. Tasteless, intensively reared birds have tainted its good name and now a delicious bird, once just reserved for feast days, is often thought of as a cheap, bland option. However eat a *pollo de corral,* a farm-bred chicken, and it's such a treat. I must urge you to buy fantastic, organic birds for all the recipes in this book.

Jointed chicken with the classic Catalan vegetable dish, *Samfaina,* is a very simple and popular dish. It is an ideal summer supper served with some good bread.

Serves 4

1 x 1.8 kg/4 lb organic chicken jointed into 8 pieces, or 4 chicken legs
2 tbsp olive oil
Salt and freshly ground black pepper
1 fresh thyme sprig
1 x recipe *Samfaina* (see page 89)

Preheat the oven to 180°C/350°F/Gas Mark 4.

Season the chicken pieces with plenty of salt and pepper and place them in a large terracotta *cazuela* or ovenproof casserole with the thyme sprig. Roast the chicken, skin-side up for about 45 minutes, or until thoroughly cooked. (To check, insert a skewer or the tip of a sharp knife into the thickest part of the meat and if the juices run clear, then the chicken is cooked.)

Meanwhile, make the *Samfaina.*

Remove the chicken from the pan and stir the *Samfaina* into the chicken juices. Check the seasoning and serve.

Here is a gloriously simple dish to celebrate the mushroom season. The Basques and Catalans are fanatical about their fungi and foraging for these woodland jewels is a popular weekend sport.

Tips

* You could use rehydrated dried mushrooms in this recipe too (see page 37). You will only need about 50 g/2 oz/^{1}/$_2$ cup as their flavour is so intense.
** Dried wild mushrooms make wonderful storecupboard (pantry) standbys, adding instant gamy depth and flavour to all manner of soups and casseroles. I keep a selection in my freezer at all times

Pollo con Setas

Chicken and Wild Mushrooms

Serves 4

2 tbsp olive oil
1 x 1.8 kg/4 lb organic chicken jointed into 8 pieces, or 4 chicken legs
Salt and freshly ground black pepper
1 onion, diced
3 tomatoes, peeled and diced
2 garlic cloves, crushed
450 g/1 lb assorted wild mushrooms (chanterelles, ceps, horns of plenty, morelles)
100 ml/3^1/$_2$ fl oz/generous ^{1}/$_3$ cup dry white wine
1 x recipe *Picada* Seasoning (see page 136–7)

Preheat the oven to 180°C/350°F/Gas Mark 4.

Season the chicken pieces with salt and pepper. Heat the olive oil in a large frying pan (skillet). Add the chicken pieces and fry until golden.

Place the chicken in a terracotta *cazuela* or ovenproof casserole.

Add the onions to the frying pan (skillet) and fry until lightly browned, then add the tomato. Cook until you have a paste, then add the paste to the chicken.

Add a little more olive oil to the frying pan (skillet) if necessary, then add the mushrooms and garlic and sauté for 2 minutes. Add the mushrooms to the chicken in the *cazuela* and pour over the wine.

Bake in the oven for about 45 minutes, or until thoroughly cooked. (To check, insert a skewer or the tip of a sharp knife into the thickest part of the meat and if the juices run clear, then the chicken is cooked.)

Once almost ready to serve, adjust the seasoning and stir in the *Picada*.

Serve with good bread, rice or mashed potatoes to mop up all the delicious juices.

The Catalan Costa Brava is renowned for its eclectic combinations of poultry and meat with seafood. These extraordinary dishes seem nearly as eccentric as the legendary Dalí, one of the region's most famous figures, and it is said that the local Trasmuntana wind, sweeping relentlessly down from the Pyrenees during the winter, does gradually send the locals mad. However, it turns out that the bizarre pairings of food from land and sea are not the creation of some delirious chef but the result of the constraints of the local larder. Historically chicken and pork were only eaten on feast days in the coastal settlements and even then there was barely enough to feed everyone. Thus fish was added to pad out the dish, mussels were added to stretch the rabbit a little further and, inconceivable today, lobster or prawns (shrimp) served with chicken to make the delicious poultry go round!

Make sure your chicken is the best money can buy, intensively reared plastic just won't do.

Variations

* You could, of course, cook the prawns (shrimp) ready peeled (shelled); a great shame in my eyes as I love to, somewhat unceremoniously, suck the sweet juices from the heads. Just remember to add the prawn (shrimp) shells and heads with the chicken stock and simmer for 20 minutes to extract their delicious flavour.

** Rabbit and sausage could be also added with the chicken and, if you're feeling flush, you could use pieces of fresh lobster instead of the prawns (shrimp).

Mar i Muntanya: Pollastre amb Gambes

Chicken with Prawns

Serves 4

1 medium organic chicken cut into 8 serving pieces, or 4 chicken legs
Salt and freshly ground black pepper
2 tbsp olive oil
12 large raw prawns (shrimp), heads and shells on
2 onions, diced
4 tomatoes, peeled, de-seeded and chopped or 200 g/7 oz canned chopped tomatoes
150 ml/5 fl oz/⅔ cup Spanish brandy
1 tbsp plain (all-purpose) flour
300 ml/10 fl oz/1¼ cups chicken stock
1 bay leaf
1 fresh thyme sprig
1 x recipe simple *Picada* Seasoning (see page 136–7)

Season the chicken with salt and pepper. Heat the olive oil in a pan. A terracotta *cazuela* is ideal for cooking this dish but any large, low-sided pan will do. Add the chicken pieces and fry until the skin crisps and turns golden.

Remove the chicken from the pan and reserve. Add the prawns (shrimp) to the pan and fry very briefly in the same oil. Once they are beautifully pink you can remove them and reserve until required.

Next add the onions to the pan and cook gently until they become really soft and begin to turn brown. Add the tomatoes and leave to bubble until the liquid has evaporated.

Pour on the brandy and boil off the alcohol.

Add the flour, stir and add the chicken stock, bay leaf and thyme.

Return the chicken pieces to the pan and simmer for about 20 minutes, or until the chicken is well cooked. (To check, insert a skewer or the tip of a sharp knife into the thickest part of the meat and if the juices run clear, then the chicken is cooked.)

Stir in the *picada* seasoning and taste the sauce, you may need some salt.

Add the prawns (shrimp) and simmer for a further 5 minutes before serving.

I first ate this dish at an old coaching inn, The Fonda Siques, in Besalú, a glorious medieval town in the Pyrenean foothills. It was a chilly, autumnal (fall) afternoon and the restaurant was heaving with entire families, from great-grandparents to toddlers, enjoying a long Sunday lunch. I was squashed on to the last small table by the kitchen hatch, amid the relentless bustle of waiters. I watched the spectacularly rotund ladies busying over the stoves in the kitchen while I waited and waited. I was ravenous by the time my lunch arrived but the duck was unforgettable.

Purists will use the traditional pears from around the Catalan town of Puigcerdà for this dish but I have found that any ripe pears will taste delicious. The dish is a classic with countless variations; you may decide to add some sultanas (golden raisins) together with the pine kernels (pine nuts) or even to make a sugar caramel to pour over the pears just before serving. The recipe is often used for a small goose too.

Variation
* You could substitute figs for the pears. Just soak dried figs for a couple of hours or use fresh ones. Dust with flour and fry in a little oil until browned. Add to the dish together with the pine kernels (pine nuts).

Pato con Peras

Roast Duck with Pears

Serves 4

1 x 2 kg/5 lb duck
Salt and freshly ground black pepper
300 ml/10 fl oz/1¼ cups chicken stock (or duck stock made with the giblets and necks if you are lucky enough to have some)
4 ripe pears, peeled and halved or 8 tiny whole pears
Juice of ½ lemon
2 tbsp olive oil
2 onions, finely chopped
6 garlic cloves, crushed

2 carrots, diced
1 tbsp fresh flat-leaf parsley, chopped
2 bay leaves
4 ripe tomatoes, de-seeded and chopped (I have cheated with well-drained canned tomatoes before now)
100 ml/3½ fl oz/generous ⅓ cup sherry or *vi ranci*
25 g/1 oz/⅛ cup pine kernels (pine nuts), toasted
Crusty bread or fresh green salad (salad greens), to serve

Preheat the oven to 200°C/400°F/Gas Mark 6.

Prick the duck all over, then lightly dust it with salt and place on a rack in a roasting tin (pan). Roast in the oven for 1½ hours. Place the duck breast-side down in the tin (pan) for the first 30 minutes, then turn it over to ensure a wonderfully juicy result.

Parboil the pears with a squeeze of lemon juice, for about 5 minutes and reserve until required.

Heat a little olive oil and 1 tablespoon of duck fat from the roasting tin (pan) in a terracotta *cazuela* or an ovenproof casserole. Add the onions and fry until they are beginning to caramelize and turn brown. Add the garlic, carrots, parsley and bay leaves and stir for 1–2 minutes before adding the tomatoes. Leave the pan juices to bubble away until the mixture thickens.

Once the duck has cooked, drain well and cut it into quarters, removing the backbone. Set it aside and keep warm. Skim off the fat in the roasting tin (pan), there will be plenty of it – great for roast potatoes at a later date. Next add a little sherry or *vi ranci* to the tin (pan), stir around over a low heat, then pour all these delicious juices together with the chicken or duck stock into the onion mixture. Boil for 5–10 minutes, or until reduced to a good sauce consistency.

Toast the pine kernels (pine nuts) in a dry frying pan (skillet) for about 2–3 minutes until golden. Keep shaking the pan to turn the kernels (nuts). Next add the pears, the pine kernels (pine nuts) and duck to the pan and leave to simmer for 10 minutes.

You can serve the dish alone, as the Spaniards do, with some good country bread. I love to serve this, somewhat less traditionally, with a green salad (salad greens).

Partridge is the most plentiful feathered game in Northern Spain and features on most autumnal (fall) country menus. The flesh of slightly older birds can become tough and dry if you are not careful. This recipe keeps the meat moist and the rich chocolate sauce makes a delicious and unusual accompaniment.

Nowadays we think of chocolate as a sweet flavouring, but originally in Pre-Colombian Mexico, the Mayans and Aztecs enjoyed it as a savoury drink. Today the Mexicans still enjoy their celebrated dish of turkey *mole* with its chilli (chili pepper) and chocolate sauce, and they are not alone; many Spanish game and red meat dishes are enriched with a hint of chocolate too.

Perdices con Chocolate
Partridge with Chocolate Sauce

Serves 4

4 tbsp olive oil
16 button onions or small shallots, peeled and left whole
2-4 partridges, cleaned and split in half (kitchen scissors are handy for this)
Salt and freshly ground black pepper
2 garlic cloves, crushed
1 tbsp plain (all-purpose) flour
3 tbsp white wine vinegar
100 ml/3½ fl oz/generous ⅓ cup dry white wine
2 bay leaves
1 tbsp fresh parsley, finely chopped
300 ml/10 fl oz/1¼ cups chicken stock
45 g/1¾ oz plain dark (bittersweet) chocolate, finely chopped

Heat the olive oil in a terracotta *cazuela* or large casserole. Add the onions or shallots and fry over a low heat for about 15 minutes until they begin to colour and soften.

Season the partridge halves with salt and pepper, then place them in the pan with the onions and sauté until nicely browned. Remove the partridge from the pan.

Next add the garlic and when it begins to smell wonderful, add the flour.

Stir the flour into the oil, then gradually add the vinegar and wine, stirring to avoid any lumps. Return the partridge to the pan, add the bay leaves, parsley and just enough stock to cover.

Cover the pan and leave to simmer for about 45 minutes, or until the meat is tender.

Melt the chocolate in small heatproof bowl with a little of the hot juice from the pan, then add it to the partridges. Taste and adjust the seasoning. Continue to simmer for about 10 minutes.

Serve the partridge surrounded by shallots and covered with the delicious chocolate sauce.

Rabbit is very popular in Spain – it's eaten just as regularly as chicken. Most of the meat on sale in the markets is the domestic variety but the wild, mountain rabbit is certainly the tastiest with its diet of herbs and grasses so it's worth looking out for.

I couldn't resist this dish when I spotted it on the menu of a traditional restaurant in the Galician city of Orense. The previous day, while winding along a mountain road, I'd screeched to a halt to admire a beautiful scene. There was a dovecote clothed in morning mist and the sun cast long shadows through the woods. Among the trees was a huddle of chestnut collectors; they were bent double and wore thick, rubber gloves to protect their hands while prizing the nuts from the spiked husks. They welcomed an unexpected break, so we chatted for a while and of course they wouldn't let me leave before they'd filled my pockets with chestnuts.

Conejo con Castañas

Rabbit and Chestnut Ragout

Serves 4

2 rabbits, jointed

For the marinade
2 garlic cloves, crushed
1 tbsp sweet unsmoked paprika
2 bay leaves
1 tbsp roughly chopped fresh flat-leaf parsley
100 ml/3½ fl oz/generous ⅓ cup white wine
2 tbsp olive oil

For the ragout
Salt and freshly ground black pepper
3 tbsp olive oil
1 onion, finely diced
2 garlic cloves, crushed
2 carrots, finely diced
150 g/5 oz *jamón serrano*, cured ham, diced
   (unsmoked bacon could just about be substituted)
Large pinch of saffron strands
1 tbsp plain (all-purpose) flour
100 ml/3½ fl oz/generous ⅓ cup brandy
250 ml/8 fl oz/1 cup chicken or vegetable stock
300 g/10 oz cooked and shelled chestnuts

Place the rabbit in a large bowl with all the marinade ingredients, cover and leave to marinate in the refrigerator overnight. The following day, begin by drying off the rabbit joints with some kitchen paper (paper towels) and seasoning them with salt and pepper. Reserve the marinade.

Heat the olive oil in a large terracotta *cazuela* or casserole big enough to hold all the rabbit. Add the meat and fry until it begins to brown slightly. Add the onion, carrot and *jamón* and continue cooking until everything begins to soften. Add the garlic and stir until it smells divine.

Next add the saffron and flour and give the pan a good shake before pouring in the reserved marinade, brandy and stock.

Cover the pan and simmer really gently for about 40 minutes, or until the meat is tender. Add the chestnuts and season with salt and pepper to taste. Heat through for a few minutes and serve.

Game is usually quite a hefty dinner option, especially in Spain where it's often served with rich, dark sauces. This combination of seared venison with steamed vegetables, quince, berries and nuts is pure simplicity. Having waddled in to the fabulous Restaurante Las Duelas in Haro, Rioja, after a hard day of wine tasting and *tapas* sampling, the dish seemed so refreshingly light.

The chef, Juan Nales, prepares incredibly clean, modern food in marked contrast with some of the more traditional fare such as roast lamb, beans and offal (variety meats) that the Rioja region is famous for.

Tips

* Quinces can be purchased in some supermarkets and good greengrocers (grocery stores) in the autumn (fall).
** Cooked chestnuts are available in vacuum-packs from most supermarkets.

Lomo de Ciervo o Corzo con Frutas Otoñales

Venison Fillet with Autumnal Fruits

1 quince or pear, peeled, diced and tossed in the juice of 1 lemon
3 tbsp sugar
400 g/14 oz firm, tasty potatoes such as Roseval or Pink Fir Apple, peeled or not, it's up to you
8 baby carrots, peeled and trimmed or 4 carrots, sliced
8 florets of broccoli or cauliflower
A few leaves of Savoy cabbage, finely shredded
8 cooked chestnuts, peeled and finely sliced
12 roasted hazelnuts
A handful of berries such as raspberries, blackberries or redcurrants
4 x 2.5 cm/1 inch thick venison fillet steaks, at room temperature.
1 tbsp olive oil
Salt and freshly ground black pepper

Place the quince in a small saucepan with the sugar and enough water to cover. Boil until the quince is soft and delicious, about 20 minutes. You will need only about half the quince for this recipe; the rest would be delicious with rice pudding or vanilla ice cream.

Next prepare the vegetables. Should you own one of those multi-tiered steamers, now is the time to use it. Boil or steam your vegetables with a pinch of salt, until they are cooked but nicely firm and crunchy. If you are entertaining, you may like to do this in advance, cool the vegetables in ice cold water, then toss them in a hot saucepan with 1 tablespoon of extra virgin olive oil or butter when you are ready to serve. You could even reheat them carefully in the microwave.

Brush the venison with a little olive oil and season with salt and plenty of black pepper. Heat a ridged griddle pan (stovetop grill pan) or heavy-based frying pan (skillet) until really hot. Add the venison and cook for about 3–4 minutes on each side for medium-rare. If you like your meat really rare just reduce the cooking time. Better done? Then reduce the heat after the initial blast and cook for about 5–6 minutes on each side. The meat should rest for a few minutes before you cut into it, to retain all the delicious juices so don't worry if it takes a little time to serve.

Place the venison in the middle of the individual serving plates, surrounded by the vegetables. Garnish with the chestnuts, hazelnuts, berries and half the quince pieces.

Beef is not a common sight in most Spanish butchers where younger veal is usually favoured. Yet, up in the mountainous north you will find the darker red meat, packed with flavour. In Bermeo, a Basque fishing port, they hold an annual stew or *guiso* competition, the *Sukalki*. Over a thousand people gather in the local park to cook, drink, eat and laugh before finally snaking their way in one huge, inebriated, Conga down the hill into town for a few evening drinks.

This recipe is based upon the prize-winning dish I ate with Ignacio Monasterio Bastida and his friends. The meat was so tender it just melted in the mouth while the meticulously round potatoes remained perfectly intact.

Variations

* Add a couple chopped garlic cloves to the onions at the same time as the beef and throw in a bouquet garni of thyme, marjoram and parsley tied together along with the wine.
** A Catalan version of the dish would be made without the (bell) peppers and red wine, substituting carrots, garlic and white wine instead. The stew is finished off with the chocolate *Picada* on page 136. Unusual, but delicious.

Estofado de Buey

Sukalki Beef Stew

Serves 4

2 tbsp olive oil
3 red onions, diced
1 red (bell) pepper, diced
3 tbsp plain (all-purpose) flour
900 g/2 lb chuck or stewing steak cut into large chunks about 4 cm/1½ inches square
100 ml/3½ fl oz/generous ⅓ cup red wine, such as Rioja
2 large ripe tomatoes, peeled and chopped
Flesh of 1 *choricero* pepper or 1 tbsp sweet paprika
600 ml/1 pint/2½ cups beef stock
Salt and freshly ground black pepper
450 g/1 lb firm, waxy potatoes, peeled and cut into 4 cm/1½ inch cubes or shaped into perfect spheres if you are feeling diligent

Heat the olive oil in a large saucepan that is big enough to hold the meat and potatoes and has a tight-fitting lid. Add the onion and red (bell) pepper and fry gently until really soft and sweet. This will take at least 30 minutes.

Spread the flour out on a large plate. Add the meat and toss until coated in the flour. Add the meat to the pan and fry with the onions and (bell) pepper until it begins to colour.

Add the wine, tomato, *choricero* pepper flesh or paprika and beef stock and stir well. Season with a little salt and pepper, then cover and leave to simmer over a very low heat for 1½ hours, or until the meat is quite tender. Alternatively, bake in an oven preheated to 160°C/325°F/Gas Mark 3.

Remove the meat from the pan and pass the vegetables through a *pasapurés*, (see page 21) or process in a blender or use a hand-held mixer until you have a smooth sauce. If you are taking the rustic approach, you can avoid this step altogether!

Next add the potatoes to the meat and vegetables and cook for a further 30 minutes until they are just tender. Check the seasoning and serve.

The Spanish term *ternera*, or veal, does not refer to the meat of tiny milk-fed calves (that's *ternera lechal*) but to young beef cattle of up to a year old. Good grazing land is scarce in Catalonia and so animals have always been slaughtered young, freeing up the pastureland for the next year's herd. The meat is a rosy-pink and tender.

Albert Asín, the chef at the Bar Pinotxo in Barcelona's Boquería market makes a fine *fricandó*. His kitchen is minute, just a few burners behind the bar, but he still manages to keep up with a constant demand for *tapas* and lunch dishes. You have to be quick with your order, or just eat with your eyes; every dish has a dozen names on it before he's even lit the gas.

Fricandó

Braised Veal with Wild Mushrooms

Serves 4

550 g/1¼ lb wild mushrooms, typically the *moixernó* (St George's mushroom), *cama-sec* (Fairy ring mushroom) or *camagroc* (chanterelles) or any other wild mushrooms *or* 50 g/2 oz/½ cup dried wild mushrooms (I brought some *cama-sec* back from my last trip to Barcelona)
3 tbsp plain (all-purpose) flour
Salt and freshly ground black pepper
675 g/1½ lb boneless veal topside (round) or loin, or beef in 1 cm/½ inch thick slices, cut into 10 cm/4 inch pieces
4 tbsp olive oil
1 large onion, finely diced
2 ripe tomatoes, peeled, de-seeded and chopped
2 carrots, diced
1 small bunch of fresh thyme, oregano, a bay leaf and flat-leaf parsley tied together or *farcelet* (dried herbs wrapped in bay leaves like tiny cigars available in some delis)
600 ml/1 pint/2¼ cups beef stock
200 ml/7 fl oz/scant 1 cup dry white wine
1 x recipe Simple *Picada* seasoning (see page 136–7), optional

Begin by cleaning the mushrooms with a damp cloth or soaking dried mushrooms for at least 30 minutes in just enough water to cover.

Next spread the flour out on a plate and season with plenty of salt and black pepper and dredge the pieces of veal in the flour.

Heat the olive oil in a pan. Add the veal, a few pieces at a time, and fry until it just begins to brown.

Set the meat aside, add the onion to the pan and cook until the onion has softened completely. Add the carrot and tomato and continue to cook over a low heat for about 15 minutes until the mixture is brick brown, but on no account burnt.

Add the herbs, the stock and wine to the pan, then cover and simmer for a further 15 minutes. Add the mushrooms and veal and simmer gently for a further 20 minutes, or until the meat is tender.

I love to add a *picada* too, although many chefs insist that this is not the classical dish. Well, have a taste and you make you're mind up!

Extravagant, almost instant, fabulously rich and delicious – a special occasion dish. You could serve this with a few naughty homemade chips (french fries) or with steamed green vegetables.

Make sure that your fillet is really tasty. Dark burgundy butcher's meat means flavour, leave the insipid pink stuff on the shelf.

Tip

* You could stir sautéed field (portobello) mushrooms and garlic in with the sauce – divine.

Solomillo de Buey con Salsa Cabrales

Fillet Steak with Cabrales Blue Cheese Sauce

Serves 4

4 x fillet steaks, about 3 cm/1¼ inches thick
Salt and freshly ground black pepper
2 tbsp olive oil
1 x recipe Cabrales Cheese Sauce (see page 139)

Remove the steak from the refrigerator 2 hours before cooking.

Brush the steak with olive oil and season with salt and pepper.

Heat an extremely heavy-based frying pan (skillet) or ridged griddle pan (stovetop grill pan) until very hot. Add the steak and sear for about 2 minutes on each side for rare, 3 minutes for medium and 4–5 minutes for well done.

Serve with the Cabrales Blue Cheese Sauce.

The *Sagardotegiak*, or cider houses, outside San Sebastián are bursting with revellers from January to April. It's time to taste the new-season cider. "*Gutxi eta maiz*" is the house rule, "little and often", as you catch the thin jet of cider that spurts directly from the barrel: just a couple of inches in the bottom of the glass, down it in one before it settles, and off you go again.

The highlight of the unchanging cider house menu is the vast steak, the *chuletón*. The best *chuletón* is a fantastically well-hung piece of deep red meat. Such meat, from older beef cattle, is uncommon in most of Spain and is known as *carne de buey* as opposed to *ternera* (young beef or veal). The meat is brought to the table in one piece, a fabulously juicy and daringly rare slab of meat.

Chuletón

Basque Steak with Red Peppers

Serves 4

2 x 1 kg/2 lb 4 oz T-bone or Porterhouse Steaks, sliced about 5 cm/2 inches thick.
    (The weight, but not the thickness, is up to you – this may seem wildly excessive
    but I have seen Basque trenchermen demolish such steaks single-handedly)
Salt and freshly ground black pepper
2 tbsp olive oil
Coarse grain sea salt
6 red (bell) peppers, roasted, peeled and de-seeded (see page 24)
    or a 200 g/7 oz jar of *El Bierzo* peppers

Remove the steaks from the refrigerator 2 hours before cooking, allowing the meat to reach room temperature. Preheat the oven to 140°C/275°F/Gas Mark 1.

Heat your largest and heaviest frying pan (skillet), ridged griddle pan (stovetop grill pan) or char-grill. It must be as hot as you can get it.

Season the steak with salt and pepper and brush with olive oil. Add the meat to the hot pan and char it for 2–3 minutes on each side until well browned.

Next place the meat on a rack in a roasting tin (pan) and place it in the warm oven for 10 minutes. The idea is to heat the centre of the rare meat without really cooking it.

Allow the meat to rest for 5 minutes before sprinkling over a few flakes of coarse sea salt and serving it up on a really hot platter with the delicious peppers and a drizzle of extra virgin olive oil alongside.

Cordero Asado

Roast Spring Lamb

Serves 4–6

1 x 1.5 kg/3 lb leg of spring lamb
2 tbsp lard or olive oil
Salt and freshly ground black pepper
3 garlic cloves, crushed
1 tbsp sweet unsmoked paprika
1 tbsp mixture of chopped fresh thyme, oregano, rosemary, parsley
Juice of 2 lemons
1 glass white wine
900 g/2 lb potatoes, peeled and left in large chunks

Preheat the oven to 220°C/425°F/Gas Mark 7.

Rub the lamb with the lard or olive oil, then season with the salt, pepper, garlic, paprika and herbs. Roast in the oven for 15 minutes.

Reduce the oven temperature to 180°C/350°F/Gas Mark 4.

Arrange the potatoes around the lamb, turning them in the lamb fat or juices. Sprinkle the lamb with the lemon juice, pour over the wine and return it in the oven.

Roast for a further 1 hour, (about 20 minutes per 450 g/1 lb) basting and turning the potatoes occasionally. Just add a little water if the tin (pan) looks a little dry, and do not allow the delicious juices to burn.

Once the lamb is cooked to your liking leave the meat to rest for at least 15 minutes before slicing and serving with the potatoes and perhaps a refreshing salad.

Traditional restaurants, called *asadores,* are an institution once you reach the inland regions of Aragón, Rioja and Castille. They're old-fashioned places: crammed with beams, dark oak furniture and gastronomic medals lining the walls. If you're in luck there will be a signed snap of the King and Queen too: always a good sign.

The *asadores* specialize in roasting the tiny, milk-fed lamb in wood-fired ovens and the result is deliciously lean and tender. Lamb is highly prized on the dry Spanish plains, where the animals eat a mixture of hardy, aromatic herbs giving the meat a particularly good flavour. The *cordero Pascual,* or Easter (spring) lamb is very good too and certainly easier to come by.

Tip
* If you prefer your roast lamb pink, and the Spanish don't, reduce the cooking time to about 15 minutes per 450 g/1 lb.

Family gatherings and local *fiestas* often revolve around huge makeshift barbecues. Meat is often cooked over the vine prunings, which impart a fabulous flavour. It's wonderful to eat these cutlets (chops) with your fingers, gnawing at the bone and dipping into some wickedly pungent *allioli*. On such occasions the lamb requires no extra flavouring at all but when grilled (broiled) at home the herbs do add an extra dimension.

In Spain, with the passion for the tiny, spring lamb, your chops may be minuscule and you might even need five or six each. Traditionally lamb is eaten well done but I prefer mine pink and juicy.

Variations

* Locals would be happy to tuck into the lamb without any vegetable accompaniment at all but I love to eat this with a bowl of smoky aubergine (eggplant) and red (bell) pepper *Escalivada* (see page 90)
** If you're not a great garlic lover then *Piquillo* Pepper Sauce (see page 139) would be delicious too and maybe even a little Potato Mash with Black Olives (see page 85).

Chuletas de Cordero con Allioli de Membrillo

Grilled Lamb Cutlets with Quince Allioli

Serves 4

12 trimmed lamb cutlets (chops)
2 tbsp olive oil
1 tsp finely chopped fresh herbs, such as thyme, rosemary or oregano
Salt and freshly ground black pepper
1 x recipe Quince *Allioli* (see page 133)

Preheat the grill (broiler) to its highest setting.

Brush the cutlets (chops) with the olive oil and sprinkle with herbs and seasoning.

Place the lamb under the grill (broiler) and cook for about 2–3 minutes on each side for pink flesh and a minute or two longer for well done.

Serve the lamb at once with a spoonful of sweet and garlicky Quince *Allioli*.

Opposite: Chuletas de Cordero con Allioli de Membrillo
Following page: Melocotones con Vino y Sobaos Pasiegos, page 147

This is a very traditional dish from the inland regions of Rioja, Navarre and Aragón.

Sheep have been reared on the arid plains for centuries and their wool was once a mainstay of the Spanish economy. The countryside was carved up by ancient droving ways, the *cañadas*, which allowed shepherds to pass unhindered from one side of the country to the other. Today you can walk many of the paths and when you spot a flock of dusty sheep crossing the deserted landscape it seems that time has stood still.

I adore the combination of lamb and peppers. The acidity and freshness of the vegetables cut the richness of the meat quite beautifully.

Variations

*   You could add rosemary or thyme to the lamb at the same time as the peppers for a more aromatic stew.
** A teaspoon of ground cumin, ground coriander and a cinnamon stick will provide a touch of Moorish magic.
*** You could add some green olives to the dish for the last 5 minutes of the cooking time.

Tip

*   The dish is traditionally served alone. But do try it with the Potato Mash with Olives on page 85 or with some plain white rice.

Cordero al Chilindrón

Lamb and Pepper Hotpot

Serves 4

2 tbsp olive oil
1 kg/2 lb 4 oz lamb shoulder or leg meat, trimmed and cut into bite-sized pieces
2 onions, diced
100 g/4 oz *jamón Serrano,* diced (you could substitute unsmoked bacon)
4 garlic cloves, crushed
2 green (bell) peppers, de-seeded and sliced
2 red (bell) peppers, de-seeded and sliced
2 dried *choricero* peppers, soaked and diced with their soaking water (see page 24).
    You could use *ancho* or *pasilla* chillies (chili peppers) or even 1 tbsp sweet paprika
4 ripe tomatoes, peeled and diced or 200 g/7 oz canned chopped tomatoes
100 ml/3½ fl oz/generous ⅓ cup dry white wine
Salt and freshly ground black pepper
1 tsp hot unsmoked paprika (optional)

Heat the olive oil in a large casserole or frying pan (skillet) with a tight-fitting lid. Add the lamb and cook over a medium heat until the lamb is really well browned. This is not actually sealing the meat it's just creating flavour and colour. I usually cook mine half at a time otherwise the pan becomes too crowded.

Next add the onion and *jamón* to the pan and continue to cook over a medium heat until the onions are soft and golden.

Add the garlic and stir until you really smell its delicious aroma, then add the red and green (bell) peppers. Cook for a few minutes until the (bell) peppers soften.

Add the dried *choricero* peppers, tomatoes, wine and enough of the pepper soaking water to cover the lamb.

Season with salt and pepper, and some paprika if you like a little kick, and cover the pan. Cook over a very low heat for about 1–1½ hours until the meat is really tender.

Check the seasoning and serve.

Previous page: Tarta de Santiago, page 143
Opposite: Flan de Castañas con Helado de Chocolate y Almíbar de Jenjibre, page 151

Pork and apples are a classic combination, more commonly associated with Normandy or England than Spain, but we should not forget that the region of Asturias has her own Celtic past. This is a land of bagpipers and cider drinkers. It is also one of the few regions where butter and milk play a large role in the kitchen and is often known as the dairy of Spain.

This recipe is an all-time favourite, equally good eaten hot or cold. It's great to make a day ahead and leave the pork, ready sliced, in the sauce. I adore the way the milk keeps the meat really moist and then reduces and sweetens making an ambrosial rich sauce.

In Catalonia a pork loin is stuffed with winter truffles and cooked in milk, a luxurious treat.

Tip
* This would be delicious with mashed potato or brown rice but in Spain it would be more commonly served alone.

Lomo de Cerdo con Leche y Puré de Manzana

Milk-roast Pork Loin with Apple Purée

Serves 4

1 x 1 kg/2 lb 4 oz loin of pork, skin removed, fat left on
Salt and freshly ground black pepper
3 tbsp olive oil or pork fat
4 garlic cloves, peeled but left whole
750 ml/1¼ pints/3 cups milk
½ stick cinnamon
1 bay leaf

For the pureé
2 sweet dessert (eating) apples, peeled, cored and cut into small chunks
1 fresh thyme sprig
3 tbsp water
1 tbsp butter

Heat the olive oil in a large casserole with a lid. Add the pork and brown evenly on all sides before adding the garlic. Cook the garlic until it is golden brown and smells wonderful, then add the milk, cinnamon, bay leaf and a little salt and pepper.

Bring the milk to a simmer and cook, partially covered, over a very low heat for about 1½ hours, or until the pork is cooked. The juices should run clear but the meat remain tender. Turn the pork occasionally so that it does not catch on the base of the pan.

Meanwhile, place the apples, thyme and water in a small saucepan. Cover and simmer for about 15 minutes until the apple has softened. Mash the apple and stir in the butter, then reserve until required.

Once the meat is cooked, don't worry the sauce will look a curdled mess, remove the pork and cinnamon and skim off any excess fat. The milk should have reduced by about two-thirds. If you have too much sauce, boil to reduce it down a little more; too little, add some milk.

Next blend the sauce until relatively smooth, a hand-held blender is the easiest or alternatively if you use the blender do be careful .You will need to blitz the hot liquid a little at a time or you will finish up wearing the sauce.

Slice the pork and serve with the sauce and apple purée.

9

Sauces and Seasonings

Allioli translates quite literally, from Catalan, as garlic and oil. Traditionally it contains no egg yolk at all, it is not the garlicky mayonnaise we so often encounter in restaurants, although I love that too. Authentic *allioli* is more difficult and time consuming to make and so I have included a recipe for both; one for the purists who feel like a little exercise with the mortar and pestle and another for the heathens among us who would rather use a blender or whisk.

Whichever way, the sauce is pretty pungent and those with little self-control will be left reeking of garlic, wonderfully good for the health, not so good for the love life!

If you prefer something subtle try replacing the fresh garlic with roast. Just place a whole head of garlic in a small roasting tin (pan) and place in an oven preheated to 180°C/350°F/Gas Mark 4 for about 40 minutes, or until the bulb is soft and the garlic can be squeezed like a purée from the cloves.

Tip

* If the emulsion splits do not panic. There is a traditional version of Allioli from the Costa Brava that is, just that, *allioli negat or* "swamped allioli". You have just created a wonderful addition for rice dishes and fish stews.

Allioli

The Real Thing

Serves 6–8

6 garlic cloves, peeled but left whole
½ tsp salt
250 ml/8 fl oz/1 cup olive oil (use half extra virgin olive oil and half ordinary olive oil or sunflower oil)
Wine vinegar, lemon juice or Seville (Temple) orange juice
Freshly ground black pepper (optional)

Make a paste with the garlic and salt in a large mortar with a pestle. Next, using plenty of elbow grease, gradually add the oil drop by drop, using the pestle to stir and pound the paste. Go slowly or the mixture will curdle.

Once you have used all the oil add a splash of vinegar or citrus juice and a little black pepper if you like.

Cheat's allioli

Serves 6–8

2–4 garlic cloves, peeled but left whole
½ tsp salt
2 egg yolks (at room temperature)
250 ml/8 fl oz/1 cup olive oil (use half extra virgin olive oil and half ordinary olive oil or sunflower oil)
Wine vinegar, lemon juice or Seville (Temple) orange juice
Freshly ground black pepper

Make a paste with the garlic and salt in a mortar with a pestle or just use a garlic press. Place the garlic in a bowl and mix thoroughly with the egg yolks. If you are using eggs straight from the refrigerator, beware; they have a tendency to curdle so you will need to add the first few drops of oil very slowly.

Add the oil to the yolks and garlic very slowly, whisking constantly, until you have incorporated all the oil. Splash in a little vinegar or citrus juice to taste and a pinch of black pepper.

Very lazy allioli can be processed in a blender in a matter of minutes. You will lose a little in texture and richness but it is ideal if you are feeding the five thousand and need to make a larger quantity. Just use the cheat's recipe above but add a whole egg instead of one of the yolks. You will be able to add the oil steadily with the motor running. Magic.

Almond Allioli

This version is heaven with roasted autumnal (fall) vegetables such as pumpkin and beetroot (beet) or just a simple plate of steamed greens.

Follow any of the above Allioli recipes opposite, then stir in 50 g/2 oz/⅓ cup of roughly chopped toasted almonds.

Place the almonds in a preheated oven (180°C/350°F/Gas Mark 4) for 10–15 minutes. Do set a timer; I have burned more nuts than I care to remember. Blitz the nuts quickly in a food processor, too much processing and they will turn into a greasy paste. Alternatively, just chop by hand. The idea is to have small crunchy pieces of almond in the smooth paste.

Allioli amb Codonys, Pomes o Peres

Quince, Apple or Pear Allioli

This is wonderful served with roasted meats or grilled (broiled) fish and absolutely addictive with good sourdough bread. The fruit stabilizes the mixture and so there really is no need to add any egg yolk.

Serves 6–8

2 apples, pears or quinces
2–4 garlic cloves, peeled but left whole
½ tsp salt
100 ml/3½ fl oz/generous ⅓ cup olive oil (use half extra virgin olive oil and half ordinary olive oil or sunflower oil)
Lemon juice or honey to taste

Peel and core the fruit then cut it up into rough chunks.

Place the fruit in a small saucepan, cover with water and simmer until quite tender; this will take about 15 minutes for apples and pears but 30 minutes for the quince. Drain the fruit.

Make a paste with the garlic and salt in a mortar with a pestle or even in a small blender. Next add the fruit and mash everything to a purée. Slowly drizzle in the olive oil, stirring madly as you go, until you have a wonderful wobbly paste.

The lemon juice and honey are really up to you, it depends on how sweet or tart your fruit is, too bland add a little lemon, too tart add a little honey.

One of those interminable disputes: is mayonnaise a French or Spanish invention?

Many claim that the sauce was invented in Mahón, the capital of the Spanish island of Menorca. Whatever the case *salsa mayonesa* pops up all over the place, particularly in the Basque *pincho*, or bar snack.

Home-made mayonnaise is such a treat if you can get around to making it. Your eggs are less likely to curdle if they are at room temperature. But, don't forget that once made, the mayonnaise must live in the refrigerator and will keep for about five days.

Variations

*   Add a tablespoon of smoked paprika to make a delicious accompaniment for a prawn (shrimp) or chicken salad.
** I love to add finely chopped watercress to make a peppery, speckled mayonnaise. I've never eaten this in Spain but there's plenty of watercress around, so why not?

Tip

*   You could substitute a few drops of extra virgin olive oil for the olive oil to enrich the mayonnaise, but do take care not to make the flavour too overpowering.

Salsa Mayonesa

Mayonnaise

2 egg yolks
salt
150 ml/5 fl oz/⅔ cup vegetable oil
1 tbsp wine vinegar
150 ml/5 fl oz/⅔ cup olive oil
squeeze of lemon juice to taste.

Beat the egg yolks and sugar together in a bowl.

Place the bowl on a damp cloth or tea (dish) towel to prevent it from slipping around.

Now, with a whisk in one hand and a jug (pitcher) of oil in the other, begin to drip the oil in, literally drop by drop, whisking all the time.

After a minute or two the mixture will begin to thicken and you can add the oil in a slow stream, whisking all the time.

Once you have added half the oil, then add the vinegar to loosen the mixture.

Now continue with the remaining oil until you have a rich, wobbly paste.

Season with pepper, lemon juice and more salt if you need it.

In early spring coach-loads of hungry diners descend upon the town of Valls, near Tarragona to eat *calçots;* peculiar overgrown spring onions (scallions), dipped in *Romesco* sauce. It's quite a spectacle as everyone puts on a bib and some even wear gloves, to tackle the wonderfully messy barbecued onions.

This is one of my favourite sauces of all time, another classic of the Catalan kitchen. The southern hillsides are covered in almond and hazelnut groves and the roasted nuts make a wonderfully rich thickening for the sauce.

If you can not buy *ñoras* peppers then you could use mild *ancho* chillies (chili peppers) instead. Failing that, purists please look away, a tablespoon of sweet paprika could just about be used, in which case add it to the hot oily pan after the bread.

Tip
* This sauce is fabulous with grilled (broiled) vegetables, or fish and shellfish .

Romesco

Tarragona Nut and Pepper Sauce

Serves 6–8

3 dried *ñoras* peppers, de-stalked and de-seeded
1 small dried red chilli (chili pepper), de-stalked and de-seeded
50 g/2 oz/⅓ cup almonds, blanched
50 g/2 oz/⅓ cup hazelnuts, skinned if possible
2 tomatoes
2 tbsp olive oil
5 garlic cloves, peeled but left whole
2 slices of white bread
1 tbsp chopped fresh flat-leaf parsley
2–4 tbsp extra virgin olive oil
2–4 tsp red wine vinegar
Salt

Preheat the oven to 180°C/350°F/Gas Mark 4.

Begin by soaking the *ñoras* pepper and chilli (chili pepper) in a bowl of warm water for 15 minutes.

Next spread the nuts out on a baking (cookie) sheet and roast in the oven for about 10 minutes, or until they are golden. Set a timer, I have burned more nuts than I care to remember. Should you need to skin the hazelnuts, leave them to cool, then rub them in a tea (dish) towel.

Meanwhile, place the tomatoes in a small roasting tin (pan) and roast in the oven for about 15 minutes.

Next, drain the peppers thoroughly and chop them roughly. Heat the olive oil in a small frying pan (skillet). Add the chopped peppers and fry for 1–2 minutes until crisp. Reserve and fry the garlic in the same oil until it turns pale gold.

Set the garlic aside with the peppers and fry the bread in the infused oil. Just brown the bread on each side, you will find that it soaks up all the delicious oil, which is just the idea.

Next, transfer the garlic and peppers to a large mortar and pestle or a food processor; the choice is yours, and pound or process to make a paste. Add the nuts and bread and continue working it to a thick paste.

Peel and chop the tomatoes and add these as well, mixing everything very thoroughly. Lastly, add the parsley, extra virgin olive oil, vinegar and salt to taste.

The *picada* is a ground blend of herbs, nuts, garlic, spices and bread or biscuit (cookie) that is added to a dish a few minutes before it is served. It has a triple role: seasoning, enriching and thickening a sauce. It's an absolute revelation to most cooks. A rather watery, bland dish can be transformed into something rich and delicious in a second. I love to add a *picada* in all sorts of non-Spanish stews and casseroles too.

The ingredients are traditionally pounded together in a large mortar with a pestle, a very satisfying business. You could, of course, purée everything in a small blender or food processor instead.

Variations to simple picada
You could add or alternate with any of the following:
* Nuts such as roasted hazelnuts or pine kernels (pine nuts)
** A pinch of saffron strands, ground cinnamon or nutmeg, a few toasted cumin seeds
*** A little orange or lemon zest
**** Herbs such as thyme or oregano
***** Raw chicken livers can be added; ensure the livers are cooked through before serving.

Picades

Catalan Picada Seasonings

Serves 4–6

Simple Picada

1 piece white bread
2 tbsp olive oil
3 garlic cloves, peeled but left whole
Pinch of salt
12 roasted almonds
2 tbsp chopped fresh flat-leaf parsley
Extra virgin olive oil

Heat the olive oil in a frying pan (skillet). Add the bread and fry until crisp and golden. Remove from the pan and chop the bread into small pieces.

Next pound the garlic with the salt in a large mortar with a pestle, then add the almonds and parsley. Keep grinding until you have a paste, then add the bread and just enough olive oil to bind everything together.

Once the *picada* is thoroughly mixed and really smooth it is ready to use.

Rich Chocolate Picada for Game and Red Meat Dishes

1 slice of white bread
2 tbsp olive oil
3 garlic cloves, peeled but left whole
Salt
25 g/1 oz plain dark (bittersweet) chocolate
½ tsp ground cinnamon
6 roasted almonds
6 roasted hazelnuts
2 tbsp chopped fresh flat-leaf parsley
Extra virgin olive oil
Black pepper

Prepare as for the simple *Picada* recipe above.

Olive paste can often be snapped up in good delicatessens and most Spaniards don't even get around to making their own. However, after a short stay with my friends, Marta and Ramón, who make all sorts of vegetarian pâtés and wonderful jams, I was truly inspired.

The combinations are limitless and the paste is so good on toast, with boiled eggs, with goat's cheese and as an accompaniment to grilled (broiled) fish, chicken or lamb.

If you want to keep the paste for more than a couple of days, then I recommend leaving out the garlic, which soon tastes stale.

Pasta de Aceitunas Negras

Black Olive Paste

200 g/7 oz black olives, stoned (pitted) – such as *arbequina* or *blanqueta*
2 garlic cloves
½ tsp chopped fresh rosemary
1 tbsp extra virgin arbequina olive oil
salt and pepper to taste

Pound all the ingredients together in a mortar with a pestle or whizz in a blender. Taste and season.

Pasta de Aceitunas Verdes

Green Olive Paste

½ tsp toasted cumin seeds
200 g/7 oz green olives, stoned (pitted) – such as *manzanilla*
1 garlic clove
1 tbsp chopped parsley.
grated zest of ½ an orange
salt and pepper

Grind the cumin seeds in a mortar with a pestle. Now pound or blend the rest of the ingredients until you have a paste.

I adore the olive stalls in Spanish markets, with so many varieties of olive to choose from and those lovely cloves of pickled garlic. The marinade is delicious with a mixture of firm green olives such as *manzanilla* and the juicy little brown *arbequinas*. Just avoid the firm, pitted black olives sold in cans; they have no flavour at all.

Aceitunas Aliñadas

Marinated Olives

250 g/9 oz mixed black and green olives in brine
2 bay leaves
Grated zest of 1 orange
1 garlic clove, finely diced
1 tsp cumin seeds, toasted and crushed
1 tsp dried thyme
1 tsp hot Spanish paprika (smoked or unsmoked)
2 tbsp sherry vinegar
4 tbsp extra virgin olive oil
Drain and rinse the olives.

Mix the olives with the rest of the ingredients and allow to marinade for a day or two.

The *membrillo*, or quince, Aphrodite's love apple, has been used since ancient times to make delicious preserves. Spanish markets are piled with these luscious golden fruits with their curious patches of fluffy down. Snap them up when you see them and leave them in a bowl to scent your home before you finally transform them into this glorious sweet paste.

This is a true labour of love; but so much cheaper and more satisfying than buying the *membrillo* from a deli. Just make sure you have good oven-gloves (potholders) and wear long sleeves; the hot jelly spits like volcanic lava. Alternatively do try the cheat's method over the page – it works!

Dulce de membrillo makes a fabulous accompaniment to cheese and keeps for weeks.

Dulce de Membrillo

Quince Paste

1 kg/2 lb quinces
750 g/1½ lb sugar – approximately (see method)

Wash the quinces and wipe off any suede-like down but leave the skin on. Now remove the core and cut the fruit into small rough chunks. Don't worry about the fruit discolouring; your paste will be a deep rusty brown by the time you have finished.

Place the fruit in heavy pan with about 300 ml/10 fl oz/1¼ cups water. Boil the quince until it softens, about 20 – 30 minutes and then strain off the water.

Now you need to make a purée, and by far the best piece of equipment for this is the *pasapurés* (see page 21) as you want to leave all the skin behind. You could use a potato masher or a food processor and then push the purée through a fine sieve (strainer).

Now weigh the purée and add an equal weight of sugar.

Cook really gently until the sugar has dissolved and then turn up the heat and boil until the mixture thickens. This will probably take at least an hour of fairly constant stirring, so have a relay organized. The purée will thicken up and turn deep red and the spoon will virtually stand up by itself.

Now spread the paste out in a layer about 3 cm/1 inch thick in a tin (pan), about 20 cm/6 inches square), lined with greased paper. Allow to set for about 12 hours.

I first came across this apple paste in the Basque country. I was in Idiazábal, famed for its delicious sheep's cheese, and was feeling decidedly peckish. I bought a chunk of the smoky cheese, a loaf of chewy country bread and sticky square of *dulce de manzana* from the local store and scoffed it in the street: what a combination!

The paste is smoother and slightly tarter than its better-known relative, quince paste. It's delicious with blue cheese too.

Dulce de Manzana

Apple Paste

1 kg/2 lb tasty apples, *reineta* in Spain, perhaps reinette or russet elsewhere
750 g/11/2 lb sugar – approximately (see method)

Follow the recipe for quince paste above, remembering that the apples will soften much more quickly than the quinces. Once you have your purée, the proportion of sugar is about 800 g for every kilo of apples (15 oz for every pound). Cook until the apple paste really thickens and turns a deep golden brown and continue as above.

Cheat's Method

The best news is that quince and apple paste can be made in the microwave. I was sceptical but have tried it, with success. Once you have your fruit purée mixed with the sugar, then place it in a deep bowl, with plenty of room for expansion. Cover with microwave cling film (plastic wrap). Now microwave on medium for 15 minutes and then give it a stir (take great care it could give you a nasty burn). Repeat the process two more times until the paste is really dark and thick. You may need to increase or decrease the time a little according to your microwave.

A Couple of Instant Sauces

Salsa de Cabrales

Cabrales Blue Cheese Sauce

This blue cheese sauce makes a fabulous accompaniment for beef and I sometimes like to add it to some sautéed mushrooms and garlic for a truly delicious vegetarian alternative.

The cheese is a pungent blue made with a blend of cow, sheep and goat's milk. If you can't get hold of *Cabrales* then *Valdeón*, or Picos de Europa, blue will be equally good.

Serves 4

100 g/4 oz *Cabrales* or *Valdeón* cheese
3 tbsp double cream
1 tsp dark, sweet sherry such as an *Oloroso* or *Pedro Jimenez*, port or brandy

Melt the cheese and gradually stir in the cream, over the heat, to make a smooth sauce. Add a little sherry, port or brandy to taste.

Salsa de Pimientos de Piquillo

Piquillo Pepper Sauce

Piquillo peppers are one of my favourite storecupboard (pantry) ingredients. They are sold in cans and jars, really bitter when raw but once roasted they have an incredibly intense flavour.

Peeling the peppers is quite a business, as every effort is made to keep the peppers whole for stuffing. You can use the more economical *tiras*, or strips, for this recipe since you will be blitzing it anyway.

Tip
* This is heaven with grilled (broiled) fish, chicken or steak.

Serves 4

2 tbsp extra virgin olive oil
2 cloves garlic, sliced
1 x 400 g/14 oz can *piquillo* pepper strips
salt and black pepper

Heat the olive oil with the garlic until the slices begin to gild.

Blitz the garlic and oil in a food processor or blender with the peppers. Season to taste with salt and pepper

Desserts

10

There are one hundred and one uses for yesterday's stale bread in Spain and this has to be the most delicious of all. *Torrijas* are a close relative of French Toast or "eggy bread". But here a simple breakfast dish is transformed into something altogether more luxuriously pudding-ish with the addition of wine or spices. I have given two versions of the recipe: one boozy (alcoholic), the other delicately aromatic.

The bread must be firm and chewy, that synthetic sliced "elephant's breath" (as my granny calls it) will just disintegrate. *Torrijas* are traditionally eaten on Shrove Tuesday, the culmination of Carnival indulgence, before the Lenten fast. They are best eaten hot and fresh from the pan, but can be kept warm for a few minutes in a gentle oven.

Tip

* These fritters are delicious on their own but I love to serve them with a spoonful of tart fruit such as fresh raspberries or poached plums.

Torrijas

Sugar-coated Bread Fritters

Serves 4

For boozy (alcoholic) fritters
150 ml/5 fl oz/²⁄₃ cup sweet sherry
½ stick cinnamon
2 strips orange rind, removed with a potato peeler leaving the pith behind

For aromatic fritters
150 ml/5 fl oz/²⁄₃ cup full-fat (whole) milk
½ stick cinnamon
2 strips lemon rind, removed with a potato peeler leaving the pith behind
½ vanilla pod (bean) or ½ tsp vanilla extract
3 tbsp sugar
4 thick slices of country bread, at least 3 days old
sunflower oil, for frying
1 tbsp butter
2–3 medium (large) eggs, beaten
3 tbsp granulated sugar
½ tsp ground cinnamon

Place the sherry or milk in a saucepan with the other corresponding ingredients and bring to the boil. Simmer for 2 minutes, then leave the liquid to cool and infuse.

Meanwhile, remove the crusts and cut the bread into triangles, fingers (bars) or whatever shape you fancy.

Dip the bread into the sherry or milk for 2 minutes, then arrange it in a single layer on a large flat plate or tray.

Heat about 1 cm/½ inch of sunflower oil in a frying pan (skillet) and add the butter.

Dip the bread in the beaten egg. then fry it, a few pieces at a time, until crisp and golden.

Drain the fritters on kitchen paper (paper towels), then sprinkle them with plenty of sugar and cinnamon.

Crema Catalana is found on the menu of virtually every traditional restaurant in Catalonia. Often known as *crema de Sant Josep*, it is traditionally eaten on 19 March, St Joseph's day. In times gone by, during the strict Lenten fast even eggs were off the menu, excepting this day when the glut of eggs, provided by hens oblivious to the Catholic calendar, was eaten into.

Gastronomes would probably consider it sacrilegious to use cornflour (cornstarch) to thicken the custard but then this is not the version dreamt up in the dining halls of a Cambridge University or even a copy of its French cousin *crème brûlée*. *Crema de San Josep* is said, by the Catalans of course, to pre-date the lot of them and if the Michelin-starred Santi Santa Maria uses cornflour (cornstarch) in his recipe, then I am quite happy to use it as well.

Tip

* No blowtorch, no branding iron, no grill (broiler); never fear. It is equally acceptable, though not as common, to serve the custard without a burnt sugar crust at all.

Variation

** I ate a delicious *crema* in a small mountain restaurant near Berga where the custard concealed a pile of freshly picked berries, it was delicious and seemed lighter than the traditional version. Since then I have experimented with all sorts of versions: raspberries, blackberries, blueberries, plums and even cooked rhubarb (virtually unheard of in Spain I have to admit). The options are almost limitless and the results delicious; just place a couple of tablespoons of fruit in each dish and pour over the custard.

Crema Catalana

Catalan Crème Brûlée

Serves 4

600 ml/1 pint/2½ cups full fat (whole) milk
1 tbsp cornflour (cornstarch)
Zest of ½ lemon
1 cinnamon stick
4 egg yolks
3 tbsp caster (superfine) sugar
4 tbsp caster (superfine) sugar to caramelize the top of the custard

Begin by mixing the cornflour (cornstarch) to a paste with about 3 tablespoons of the milk in a small bowl. Reserve until required.

Next, bring the rest of the milk to the boil with the cinnamon stick and lemon zest in a small saucepan. Once the milk has boiled, turn off the heat and leave the flavours to infuse.

Meanwhile, whisk the egg yolks, sugar and cornflour (cornstarch) together in a bowl. Return the milk to a medium heat, then add the whisked egg yolks to the hot milk. You really must keep stirring now, although the cornflour (cornstarch) will help to stabilize the custard and stop it curdling so easily. Once the mixture is slightly thicker and just the odd bubble pops to the top remove the pan from the heat and keep stirring for a further 1–2 minutes. Straining the custard will ensure a wonderful smooth texture as you pour it into ramekins or better still, the shallow terracotta dishes used in Catalonia. Place the custards in the refrigerator until serving time.

Just before serving sprinkle the custards with a thin layer of sugar and caramelize until the sugar forms a dark brown crust.

Nowadays there are plenty of ambitious amateurs who own a culinary blowtorch and at last here is a chance to use it. In Catalonia you can buy a branding iron especially for the purpose, a type of iron disc (disk) on a stick. It is most satisfying to place this in a gas flame until red-hot, then sear the sugar in seconds. They even sell electric versions! Failing all the gadgetry a hot grill (broiler) will do the trick, make sure the custards are well chilled and the grill (broiler) is as hot as it will go. Flash the dishes under the heat until they brown and serve.

This almond tart, emblazoned with the cross of the knights of St James, can be found in virtually every Galician tavern, restaurant, hotel or bakery. Even the tourist stores, crammed with pilgrimage mementoes, sell long-life versions that would probably be best put to use as frisbees. A fresh tart is quite another matter, some are more cake-like without the pastry (pie dough) crust, but I love this recipe with its hint of oaky sherry and moist filling.

The tart is usually served at room temperature and often enjoyed for breakfast. I like to serve it warm with a pile of sherry-plumped sultanas (golden raisins) and some creamy yogurt as a dessert.

Tarta de Santiago

Santiago Almond Tart

Serves 8

For the pastry (pie dough)	For the filling
175 g/6 oz/1¼ cups plain (all-purpose) flour, plus extra for dusting	200 g/7 oz/2 cups ground almonds
75 g/3 oz/6 tbsp unsalted (sweet) butter	100 g/4 oz/½ cup caster (superfine) sugar
50 g/2 oz/½ cup icing (confectioners') sugar	Pinch of ground cinnamon
1 medium (large) egg yolk and 1 tbsp cold water	Zest of ½ lemon
	4 medium (large) eggs
	4 tbsp sweet *Oloroso* sherry

Place the flour in a large bowl. Add the butter and rub it in with your fingertips until the mixture resembles breadcrumbs. Stir in the icing (confectioners') sugar and lastly add the egg yolk and 1 tablespoon of cold water, stirring with a knife, then pulling the mixture together with your hands.

Alternatively, make the pastry in a food processor: Process the flour, icing (confectioners') sugar and butter until evenly blended. Add the egg yolk and water and continue to blend until the ingredients come together.

Roll out the pastry (dough) on a lightly floured work surface (counter) and use to line a 24 cm/9½ inch tart tin (pan). Leave the pastry case (shell) to rest in the refrigerator for 1 hour or 15 minutes in the freezer if you are in a rush.

Preheat the oven to 200C/400°F/Gas Mark 6.

Line the pastry case (shell) with greaseproof (waxed) paper and fill with baking beans to weight it down. "Bake blind" for 15 minutes, then remove the beans, prick the base all over with a fork and return it to the oven for a further 5 minutes, or until the base looks dry and cooked through. This is important, raw pastry (dough) now will lead to a soggy base later.

Meanwhile, mix all the filling ingredients together well and once the pastry case (shell) is cooked pour in the filling mixture. Reduce the oven temperature to 160°C/325°F/Gas Mark 3 and cook the tart for about 30 minutes, or until firm and lightly browned.

Leave the tart to cool for a couple of minutes, then remove from the tin (pan) and dust with icing (confectioners') sugar. Serve either warm or leave until completely cold and then serve.

For the sultanas (golden raisins), take 100 g/4 oz/2/3 cup sultanas (golden raisins) and leave to macerate in a glass of *oloroso* or *Pedro Jiménez* sherry overnight.

This pudding is my own simplified rendition of a gloriously light dessert that I ate in the Asador Matxete, in Vitoria, the Basque capital. The place is a carnivore's paradise. Pudding needed to be light after a Desperate Dan-size T-bone steak, the *chuletón:* the speciality of the house, cooked over coals.

The mountains of northern Spain are covered in wild bilberries during the summer. I remember entire afternoons spent on hands and knees as a teenager in the Pyrenean foothills managing to gather enough for perhaps one jar of jam! You may be able to find wild bilberries for this recipe but failing that blueberries do taste delicious too.

Mus de Yogur con Arándanos y Pacharán

Yogurt Mousse with Bilberries and Pacharán

Serves 4

For the mousse

1 vanilla pod (bean)
300 ml/10 fl oz/1¼ cups double (heavy) cream
6 tbsp caster (superfine) sugar
300 ml/10 fl oz/1¼ cups natural (plain) yogurt
2–3 sheets of leaf gelatine or enough to set 400 ml/14 fl oz/1¾ cups (the yogurt and cream are already quite dense)

For the boozy (alcoholic) fruit

150 g/5 oz/1⅛ cups fresh bilberries or blueberries
100 ml/3½ fl oz/generous ⅓ cup *pacharán* (see page 44), sloe gin or, at a push, *crème de cassis*

Slice the vanilla pod (bean), which should feel soft and oily to the touch, lengthways to reveal the seeds. Place the pod (bean) in a saucepan with the cream and sugar and simmer for about 5 minutes. Next scrape the vanilla seeds from the pod (bean) into the cream and stir. (The pod [bean] itself can be dried and placed in a jar of sugar; the resulting vanilla sugar will be ideal for baking).

Meanwhile, place the sheets of leaf gelatine in a bowl and add just enough cold water to cover. Leave to soak until soft, then squeeze out the excess water. Add the gelatine to the hot vanilla cream (you may need to reheat it a little if it has been standing for a while) and stir around until it has completely dissolved.

Add the yogurt and stir until everything is thoroughly mixed in.

Pour the mixture into 6 small moulds, teacups or ramekins will do, but individual metal pudding moulds are by far the easiest for turning out the mousse. Leave the mousse to chill in the refrigerator for at least 4 hours, or until set.

While the mousse is chilling make the delicious berry accompaniment. Place the berries and alcohol in a small saucepan and leave to boil for a moment, just enough to boil off the alcohol and allow the berries to plump up. Remove from the heat and leave to cool and infuse until you are ready to serve.

When ready to serve, dip the moulds into hot water until the mousse just softens at the edges, then turn the mousse out on to serving plates and surround with the boozy (alcoholic) berries. You could of course just use a little fresh fruit instead.

Opposite: Mus de Yogur con Arándanos y Pacharán

Rice pudding is a great favourite; it has been eaten since the time of the Moors who introduced rice to Spain and is still spiced with a little cinnamon to this day. In mediaeval times the rice was cooked in almond milk but nowadays it's prepared with cow's milk instead. Asturias, the dairy of Spain, is real rice pudding country, and when I ate this for the first time with voluptuous figs, just bursting their skins, and local heather honey, I thought I had died and gone to heaven.

Variations

* The rice pudding is delicious served just as it is, without the caramel; just sprinkle with a little cinnamon and some toasted flaked (slivered) almonds.
** You could add a slosh of brandy or aniseed liquor to the rice together with the butter and sugar.

Arroz con Leche Requemado con Higos y Miel

Caramelized Rice Pudding with Honeyed Figs

Serves 4–6

1.5 litres/2½ pints/6¼ cups full-fat (whole) milk
Grated zest of ½ lemon
1 cinnamon stick
100 g/4 oz/½ cup pudding rice (short-grain rice)
25 g/1 oz/2 tbsp unsalted (sweet) butter
50 g/2 oz/generous ¼ cup caster (superfine) sugar, or to taste
25 g/1 oz/⅛ cup soft brown sugar
½ tsp ground cinnamon

To serve
4–6 ripe figs, stalks removed and cut into quarters
4–6 tsp runny honey

Begin by bringing the milk to the boil in a saucepan with the cinnamon and lemon zest. Next add the rice and reduce the heat as low as it will go; the pudding should barely simmer for at least 1 hour and preferably even 2 hours. Leave the pan uncovered allowing the milk to evaporate gradually. This is the key to the glorious flavour. You will need to stir the rice occasionally to prevent it from catching on the base of the pan.

Once the rice is soft and creamy add the butter and sugar. You may decide to add more, or less, a good excuse to taste as you go.

The rice is usually served cold, although there is nothing to stop you serving it warm. You may to choose to serve the pudding in a large bowl, individual ramekins or tiny terracotta *cazuelas*. Sprinkle the surface with brown sugar and cinnamon then caramelize with a culinary blowtorch or under an extremely hot grill (broiler).

Serve with the figs and a little honey drizzled on top.

Opposite: Arroz con Leche Requemado con Higos y Miel

Finding room for a pudding can be quite a challenge at the end of a wonderful meal and, as far as I'm concerned, there's just no question of going without. This dessert is the answer: it's the world's lightest and most delicate apple tart.

The recipe comes from the Biblioteca restaurant, just a stone's throw from the Boquería market in Barcelona's vibrant Raval quarter. The chef, Iñake Lopez, cooks like a dream using seasonal ingredients with refreshing simplicity.

Be sure to use a Golden Delicious apple, surprisingly it really does have the right texture and flavour for this recipe.

Tips

* The original recipe used clarified butter, so you can too if you're an absolute perfectionist.
** The tarts served in the restaurant are the size of dinner plates, they do look dramatic and are perfectly manageable as they're so light. However, you will probably want to cook a few at a time, so 2 to each baking (cookie) sheet is ideal unless you have an oven of professional proportions. You could even cut squares or rectangles if you are catering for bigger numbers and find they fit the oven better. Just play around but do remember the secret is to keep the pastry paper-thin.

Tarta de Manzana

Feather-light Apple Tart

Serves 4

Plain (all-purpose) flour, for dusting
150 g/5 oz puff pastry, make your own, or find a good store-bought brand made with butter
4 Golden Delicious apples
Lemon juice (optional)
40 g/1½ oz/¼ cup caster (superfine) sugar
40 g/1½ oz/¼ cup demerara (raw brown) sugar
100 g/4 oz/1 stick butter, melted
Pouring cream, to serve

Using a well-floured chopping (cutting) board and rolling pin, roll out the pastry until it is paper-thin (no more than 3 mm/⅛ inch).

Next cut out 4 rounds (circles), using an up-turned bowl as a guide, of about 20 cm/8 inches in diameter. Place between 2 sheets of greaseproof (waxed) paper and freeze.

Preheat the oven to 200°C/400°F/Gas Mark 6.

Peel the apple really carefully so that it retains its shape. Next cut it into quarters and remove the core. Slice the apple on a mandolin or with a really sharp knife to a thickness of 1.5 mm/¹⁄₃₂ inch or so it's virtually transparent. If you are not using the apple straight away brush it with a little lemon juice immediately to prevent the apples from discolouring.

Mix the sugars together in a bowl.

Take the pastry out of the freezer and lay the rounds (circles) on a piece of waxed baking paper on a baking (cookie) sheet. Fan the apple slices, slightly overlapping, to completely cover the pastry bases. Once totally covered, brush with half of the melted butter and sprinkle with half of the sugar.

Bake in the oven for about 12–15 minutes, or until golden

Remove from the oven, brush with the rest of the butter and sprinkle with the remaining sugar. Serve hot with a drop of pouring cream.

I always associate peaches with Spain: there is nothing like biting into a fresh peach while the sticky juice runs down your chin. It's rare to find a really fabulous peach in England, after all that chilling and travelling, but once cooked they seem to rise to their former glory. Lightly spiced, poached peaches make a deliciously refreshing summer dessert and they look stunning too. Their suede-pink skins leave behind the most beautiful blushed patterns on the flesh when poached in rosé wine.

Sobaos pasiegos are little square sponge cakes made in the verdant pastoral valleys of Cantabria, a true-life land of milk and honey. I distinctly remember arriving in the village of Vega de Pas and being overwhelmed by the homely waft of baking cakes. *Sobaos* are often eaten on their own or dunked in a cup of coffee, here they soak up the syrupy wine wonderfully well.

Tips

* You could sandwich two pieces of sponge together with a little whipped cream, a drop of rum and some toasted flaked (slivered) almonds.
** There is plenty of butter sponge left over, which is great served for breakfast the following day.

Melocotones con Vino y Sobaos Pasiegos
Wine-poached Peaches with Butter Sponge

Serves 4

For the peaches
4 ripe peaches (they must be fully ripe or you will have problems removing the skins)
200 ml/7 fl oz/scant 1 cup rosé wine and enough water to cover
150 g/5 oz/³⁄₄ cup sugar
1 cinnamon stick
4 fresh mint leaves

For the butter sponge
250 g/9 oz/1¹⁄₈ cups unsalted (sweet) butter, softened, plus extra for greasing
250 g/9 oz/1³⁄₄ cups plain (all-purpose) flour
1 tbsp baking powder
Pinch of salt
250 g/9 oz/1¹⁄₄ cups sugar
5 eggs
Zest of 1 lemon, grated
1 tbsp rum

Place the peaches in a saucepan with the wine, sugar, cinnamon, mint and just enough water to cover them. Bring to the boil, then reduce the heat to a simmer and leave to simmer for about 20 minutes.

Using a slotted spoon, remove the peaches from the liquid and peel off the skin very carefully, it should slip off fairly easily. Place the peeled peaches in a serving dish.

Meanwhile, boil the wine mixture until it reduces and becomes syrupy. Pour the syrup over the peaches and leave them to macerate for a few hours in the refrigerator.

Preheat the oven to 180°C/350°F/Gas Mark 4.

To make the butter sponge, you will need a 30 cm/12 inch x 25 cm/10 inch cake tin (pan), lined with greased greaseproof (waxed) paper. Strictly speaking, the *pasaos* should each have their own square paper case, but I'm happy to make a sheet of sponge cake and cut it into squares.

Sift the flour, baking powder and salt together and reserve.

Beat the butter and sugar together in a large bowl until soft and fluffy then begin to stir in the eggs a little at a time. If the mixture starts to curdle, add a handful of flour and keep on stirring.

Once all the eggs are added fold in the flour, lemon zest and rum.

Next spread the mixture carefully in the tin (pan) and cook for about 25–30 minutes until golden.

Remove the sponge from the oven and leave to cool, still attached to the paper, on a wire rack. Serve the peaches on individual plates with plenty of syrup and a small triangle of the butter sponge.

Here's the joker in the pack. Of all the recipes in the book this one has to be the least "Spanish" but it's a great reflection of the new generation of innovative chefs. The original recipe came from the Espai Sucre, a dessert restaurant in Barcelona's buzzing Borne district. It's just a Utopia for anyone with a sweet tooth. There are a few savoury dishes too, but the five-course dessert menu is a revelation.

This clean, crisp flavoured soup is filled with fabulous textures and surprises. The sprinkling of ground "spice" atop the sorbet (sherbet) turned out to be a pinch of a grated Fisherman's Friend throat lozenge. Don't be put off, it tastes incredible.

I have simplified the dish to suit the home cook, bereft of gadgetry and assistants.

Variation

* I have even served this without the Cider Sorbet (Sherbet), and found that it's delicious too.

Sopa de Litchee, Manzana y Apio

Lychee Soup with Apple and Celery

Serves 4

1 x recipe Cider Sorbet (Sherbet) [see page 150]
1 apple sliced into tiny julienne, skin left on, dipped in lemon juice
2 tbsp cucumber, really finely diced, skin left on
2 tbsp tamarind paste, dissolved in 2 tbsp hot water and strained or juice ½ lemon
1 tsp grated Fisherman's Friend (use a nutmeg grater)

For the lychee (litchi) soup
800 g/1¼ lb canned lychees (litchis), drained of syrup
100 ml/3½ fl oz/generous ⅓ cup water
Juice of ½ lemon

For the candied celery
100 ml/3½ fl oz/generous ⅓ cup water
100 g/4 oz/½ cup sugar
4 celery sticks (stalks), finely sliced

Begin by making the Cider Sorbet, (you will need to do this a day in advance if you do not have an ice cream machine).

Now, for the soup. Check the lychees (litchis) are free from stones (pits), then blend them until smooth. Add the water and adjust the flavour with the lemon juice to take the edge off the sweetness.

For the celery, dissolve the sugar in the water in a saucepan, then bring it to the boil for 5 minutes. Add the celery and simmer for 5 minutes, making sure that it does not lose its crunch.

Take 4 shallow bowls. Pile the celery, then the apple and lastly the cucumber into the middle of the bowls.

Add enough lychee (litchi) soup to just about cover the apple. Drizzle the soup with the sharp tamarind or lemon juice, then place a quenelle or scoop of Cider Sorbet (Sherbet) on the top. Finish with a sprinkle of Fisherman's Friend and prepare to amaze your friends.

A Spanish Christmas would be unthinkable without the odd bar of *turrón*, the delicious Moorish confection of almonds, honey and egg whites. There's the tooth-shattering Alicante style that resembles French *nougat* and the soft Jijona *turrón* that's more similar to Middle Eastern *halva*. I just can't get enough of the stuff. As a student I made a daily excursion to the specialist *turrón* store in Barcelona's Portal de l'Angel and came home with a waistline to show for it. I distinctly remember my father's somewhat tactless cry at the airport, "Who is this sumo wrestler?"

Turrón is widely available in specialist Spanish stores and delicatessens. This ambrosial ice cream requires no specialist equipment but do remember to move it to the refrigerator a few hours before serving. The combination of almonds and raspberries is a marriage made in heaven.

Helado de Turrón con Salsa de Frambuesas

Turrón Ice Cream with Raspberry Coulis

Serves 8–10

1 x 300 g/10 oz bar soft Jijona *turrón*
150 ml/5 fl oz/²⁄₃ cup milk
3 tbsp brandy
4 egg whites
Pinch of salt
4 tbsp caster (superfine) sugar
400 ml/14 fl oz/1³⁄₄ cups double (heavy) cream.
50 g/2 oz/½ cup flaked (slivered) almonds, to decorate

For the raspberry coulis
225 g/8 oz/1³⁄₄ cups fresh raspberries
icing (confectioners') sugar to taste

Crush the *turrón* with the milk and brandy and stir until you have a thick paste. You might like to do this in a food processor or you will have to give it a bit of elbow grease.

Whip the cream until it is thick but still just pouring, rather than spooning, consistency

Beat the egg whites with a pinch of salt in a clean dry bowl until they are really stiff. Add the sugar and beat again to give you a soft meringue.

Next fold the cream, then the meringue into the *turrón* mixture.

Line a 450 g/1 lb loaf tin (pan) with clingfilm (plastic wrap) and spoon in the *turrón* cream. Cover the tin (pan) and freeze for at least 8 hours.

Place in the refrigerator for a couple of hours before serving.

When ready to serve, make the raspberry coulis by pressing the raspberries through a sieve (strainer) and sweetening with sugar to taste.

Toast the almonds in dry frying pan (skillet) until crisp and golden.

Next, have a jug (pitcher) of boiling water at the ready and a supply of chilled dessert plates.

Turn the ice cream out on to a chopping (cutting) board. Dip your knife into the hot water and cut 2.5 cm/1 inch slices.

Serve the ice cream with the raspberry coulis and toasted flaked (slivered) almonds.

There really is no better way to end a summer lunch than a sorbet (sherbet). It is so refreshing, and you can never be too full to squeeze one in. If you're really pushing the boat out, a sorbet (sherbet) makes a wonderful palate cleanser between courses too. Sorbets (sherbets) such as this one, with plenty of alcohol, do remain softer and easier to serve.

Teja translates as tile and the curled, sweet crisps do perhaps resemble terracotta roof tiles. *Tejas* are a speciality of Tolosa in the Basque country. It's an industrial town, packed with paper mills but the old streets and squares of the centre have real charm. I tucked into a few crispy little *tejas* with my coffee at the renowned Pastelería Gorrochategui, just around the corner from the wonderfully vibrant Saturday market.

Sorbete de Sidra con Tejas de Tolosa
Cider Sorbet with Almond Crisps

Cider Sorbet

Serves 8

300 ml/10 fl oz/1¼ cups water
250 g/9 oz/1¼ cups sugar
300 ml/10 fl oz/1¼ cups cider, a sweetish one such as the Asturian El Gaitero, shaken to remove the bubbles
3 tbsp *calvados* (optional)
Juice of 1 lemon
2 egg whites

Put the water and sugar in a small saucepan and place over a low heat until the sugar dissolves. Next, boil the syrup for 3 minutes and set aside to cool.

Add the cider and *calvados* to the syrup and place in an ice cream maker or freezer.

Once the sorbet (sherbet) has begun to thicken and freeze, whisk the egg whites lightly and add them to the mixture.

If you are making this in the freezer you will need to stir up the sorbet (sherbet) with a fork a couple of times as it freezes. Then the best way to smooth the sorbet (sherbet) once it is frozen, but not rock hard, is a quick process in the food processor. Otherwise, you could, of course, call it a granita.

Almond Crisps

Makes 20

2 egg whites
75 g/3 oz/¾ cup icing (confectioners') sugar
50 g/2 oz/generous ⅜ cup plain (all-purpose) flour
50 g/2 oz/4 tbsp melted butter, cooled
25 g/1 oz/¼ cup flaked (slivered) almonds, roughly chopped

Preheat the oven to 200°C/400°F/Gas Mark 6. Line 2 baking (cookie) sheets with baking paper (baking parchment).

Mix the egg whites, sugar, flour and butter together with a whisk until you have a smooth paste. Stir in the almonds.

Place teaspoonfuls of the mixture on the prepared baking sheets with plenty of room for expansion. Flatten them, so that the centre does not remain cakey once cooked.

Place in the oven for about 5 minutes until the *tejas* are a deep gold.

Meanwhile, grease a rolling pin with a little butter.

Remove the crisps from the oven and leave to cool and firm up for a moment before skimming them off the paper with a palette knife or spatula.

Lay each *teja* over the rolling pin and press it gently to obtain the curved shape, then place on a wire rack to cool.

Keep in an airtight bag or tin until ready to use.

Serve the sorbet (sherbet) in small bowls with a couple of almond crisps and decorated with a sprig of flowering thyme.

Flan de Castañas con Helado de Chocolate y Almíbar de Jenjibre

Chestnut Pudding with Spiced Chocolate Ice Cream and Ginger Syrup

The hillsides of north-western Spain are covered with fantastically lush chestnut trees. In autumn (fall), country roads are strewn with empty chestnut husks, like carpets of golden sea urchins. Long ago the nuts were ground to make flour and were an absolute staple for the rural poor. Today chestnuts are a luxury; preserved in delicious syrup or roasted at roadside stalls in the big cities.

The combination of chestnut pudding, ginger, chocolate and allspice comes from Carlos Cidón at the Vivaldi restaurant in León. He makes the pudding with the local Bierzo chestnuts preserved in delicious syrup. I have used more accessible cooked chestnuts and sweetened them with a caramel instead.

The spiced chocolate ice cream is a home-friendly version that needs no churning but you will need to place it in the refrigerator to soften for a couple of hours before serving. You could just cheat with good quality store-bought ice cream sprinkled with a pinch of allspice.

Serves 6

For the puddings
3 tbsp sugar
3 tbsp water
200 g/7 oz cooked, shelled chestnuts (there are some delicious Spanish, organic chestnuts available in jars)
400 ml/14 fl oz/1¾ cups full fat (whole) milk
4 medium (large) eggs
100 g/4 oz/½ cup caster (superfine) sugar
1 tsp vanilla extract

For the spiced chocolate ice cream
100 g/4 oz good quality plain dark (bittersweet) chocolate, at least 70% cocoa solids
3 eggs, separated and at room temperature
2 tbsp rum
½ tsp ground allspice
150 ml/5 fl oz/⅔ cup double (heavy) cream
3 tbsp sugar

4 pieces stem (preserved) ginger in syrup, sliced into thin matchsticks (sticks)

Preheat the oven to 150°C/300°F/Gas Mark 2.

For the puddings, heat 3 tablespoons of sugar with the water in a small saucepan. Have 6 ramekins or individual metal moulds at the ready.

Once the sugar has dissolved, boil the syrup until it is brick brown and smells of caramel. Now there is no time to waste, quickly pour it into the base of the moulds before it burns.

Process the rest of the pudding ingredients together in a blender or food processor, until you have a completely smooth liquid.

Divide the chestnut mixture between the moulds and place them in a bain marie (a roasting tin [pan] filled with warm water) and cook in the oven for 45 minutes, or until they are set.

Leave the puddings to cool in the water, then place them in the refrigerator until ready to serve.

To make the ice cream, melt the chocolate carefully in a heatproof bowl set over a saucepan of simmering water.

Beat the egg yolks together in a separate bowl, then stir them into the melted chocolate while it is still warm. Stir in the rum and the allspice.

Beat the cream until it holds its shape in another bowl and fold it into the chocolate mixture.

Next whisk the egg whites in a clean, grease-free bowl until they are stiff then whisk in the sugar until a glossy meringue texture forms

Fold the meringue into the chocolate mixture. Transfer the mixture to a freezerproof container and freeze for at least 4 hours.

When you are ready to serve, loosen the sides of the chestnut puddings with a knife and turn them out on to individual plates. Decorate with a small mound of stem (preserved) ginger sticks and a spoonful of syrup and serve with a spoonful of the chocolate ice cream.

Tip

*   The chocolate ice cream could be used as a delicious mousse instead. Just spoon the mixture into ramekins and place in the refrigerator to cool. You could even hide some rum-soaked raisins in the base of each ramekin.

The first chocoholics in Europe were the Spanish. They sipped the bitter drink as they had learned from their Aztec subjects in the newly conquered Mexico of the 16th century. Hot chocolate is still a popular Spanish treat, nowadays unbelievably sweet and almost thick enough to stand your spoon in. *Pastelerías* often display tempting rows of beautiful artisan chocolates in glass cabinets next to the cakes. Chocolate is used in many savoury stews and sauces, yet strangely it has never played a leading role in the world of Spanish cakes and desserts.

I have been on the prowl for a delicious chocolate pudding recipe for years and so I was delighted to discover this melting, chocolate heaven at the Las Duelas Restaurant in Haro, in the heart of the Riojan vineyards. The chef, Juan Nales, very kindly parted with the recipe.

Melosa de Chocolate con Avellanas

Hot Chocolate Pudding with Hazelnuts

Serves 6

200 g/ 7 oz good quality dark chocolate (bittersweet chocolate)
170 g/ 6 oz/6 tbsp unsalted (sweet) butter
1 whole egg and 3 egg yolks, at room temperature
40 g/1¾ oz/3 tbsp caster (superfine) sugar
30 g/1 oz/¼ cup toasted hazelnuts, roughly chopped

Preheat the oven to 180 °C/350 °F/Gas Mark 4.

Grease 6 ramekins with butter.

Melt the chocolate with the butter. Just go gently – I melt mine in the microwave on its lowest setting or you could use a bowl placed over a pan of simmering water. If you chop everything very small, you will really speed up the process.

Whisk the eggs with the sugar until they are really white and mousse-like. You will need an electric whisk for this, or muscles like Popeye.

Now fold the chocolate into the egg mixture and spoon into the individual ramekins.

Bake in the hot oven for 10 minutes, sprinkle with the hazelnuts and a dollop of fresh cream or vanilla ice cream and serve straight away.

I have chosen to serve the puddings in the ramekins, rather than turning them out as they did in the restaurant. It's all very well for restaurant chefs to be dabbling with careful presentation at the eleventh hour but who needs that sort of stress when you're entertaining?

If you are serving ice cream do make sure you have it "balled" and ready to go by the time the puddings come out of the oven. You really do want to serve this piping hot.

The first of November is All Saint's Day, *Todos los Santos*. It's the time to gorge on chestnuts and sweet potatoes cooked on the open fire. It's also the day of the dead, when family graves are traditionally visited. All over Spain *pastelería* windows are packed with trays of macabre-looking saint's bones made out of marzipan.

The Catalans have their own speciality, *panallets*, tiny almond cakes that are eaten with a glass of sweet wine at the end of a meal. I love them with coffee too; it's worth making plenty as they keep for a few days.

These are fabulous things to make with small children – nursery classes in Catalonia are packed with sticky fingers at this time of year.

Tip

* If your hands become terribly sticky while you are rolling, just dip them in warm water between *panallets*.

Panallets

All Saint's Petit Fours

Makes about 40

For the dough
250 g/9 oz potato, left whole, skin on
250 g/9 oz/2½ cups ground almonds
250 g/9 oz/1¼ cups caster (superfine) sugar
Zest of ½ lemon
1 tsp vanilla extract
Butter, for greasing

For the pine kernel (pine nut) panallets
50 g/2 oz/⅜ cup pine kernels (pine nuts)
1 medium (large) egg

For the coffee panallets
1 tbsp brandy
2 tsp instant coffee powder, ground to a fine powder in a mortar and pestle
10 coffee beans

For the coconut panallets
1 tbsp *anís* or any aniseed-flavoured liqueur
3 tbsp desiccated (dry unsweetened shredded) coconut
2 tbsp caster (superfine) sugar

To make the dough, boil the potato in its skin in a large saucepan of boiling water until soft. Next, drain, peel and mash the potato thoroughly, or better still push it through a *pasapurés*.

Mix in the sugar, ground almonds, lemon zest and vanilla and leave to cool.

Divide the dough into 3.

Preheat the oven to 180°C/350°F/Gas Mark 4.

For pine kernel (pine nut) panallets, roll the dough into small walnut-sized balls.

Separate the egg and whip the white just enough to loosen it a little.

First dip the balls into the egg white then roll them in the pine kernels (pine nuts). Really press the pine kernels (pine nuts) into the surface.

Brush with a little egg yolk, place on a greased baking (cookie) sheet or baking paper (baking parchment) and bake in the oven for 15–20 minutes, or until golden. Try dipping in chopped hazelnuts or almonds too.

For coffee panallets, mix the brandy and coffee into the dough. Roll into balls and flatten a little. Press a coffee bean into the top.

Place on a greased baking (cookie) sheet and bake in the oven for 15 minutes. Dust with icing (confectioners') sugar.

For coconut panallets, mix the *anís* and coconut with the almond dough and roll into walnut-sized balls. Next roll the balls in the sugar, place on a greased baking (cookie) sheet and bake in the oven for 15 minutes.

Queimada
Galician Firewater

Serves 8-10

500ml *orujo (aguardiente)*, French *marc* or Italian *grappa*
4 tbsp of white sugar
peel of ½ an unwaxed lemon, in large strips

Optional (less orthodox but popular all the same)

8 coffee beans
An apple or pear, peeled, cored and cut into eighths

Pour the *orujo* into a terracotta *cazuela* or earthenware casserole and add the sugar and lemon peel.

Take a large ladle and scoop up some liquor, (the Galicians have terracotta ladles just for this purpose, but a metal one will do fine along with a thick oven glove).

Light the liquor in the ladle and, once flaming, tip this into the casserole.

Now stir and tip the burning, blue alcohol carefully from the ladle, creating dramatic shafts of light in the darkness. Beware, those flames are quite ferocious.

Allow the fire to die down a little and then cover the pot with any large lid to extinguish the flames. *Orujo* is like rocket fuel but the longer the *queimada* burns, the smoother and less alcoholic the result will be.

Now ladle the hot liquid into punch cups, coffee cups or the traditional Galician china bowls and sip the magical elixir.

"Mouchos, curuxas, sapos e bruxas…"
"Owls, magpies, toads and witches…"

Low voices murmur the ancient incantation whilst blue flames dance over a terracotta pot of the locally distilled grape spirit, *aguardiente de orujo*. Celtic ritual and sorcery lives on in the misty hills of Galicia and the *queimada* is a purifying draft, guaranteed to ward off evil spirits and put hairs on your chest too. The *queimada* is traditionally prepared out of doors in the eerie glow of a full moon but a candlelit room will set the scene too.

Featured Bars, Restaurants and the Odd Guest House

Just in case you feel like visiting any of the wonderful establishments mentioned in the book here's the rather eclectic collection from Michelin-starred restaurants to market bars.

Asador Matxete, Plaza Matxete 4, Vitoria, Basque Country
Bar Bergara, General Artetxe, 8, San Sebastián, Basque Country
Bar Ganbara, San Jeronitio 21, San Sebastián, Basque Country
Bar Pinotxo, Boquería Market, Barcelona, Catalonia
Café Iruña, Jardines de Albia, Bilbao, Basque Country
Casa de Aldea La Valleja, Guest house, Rieña, Ruenes, Asturias
El Folló Guest house and restaurant, Tagamanent, Nr Barcelona, Catalonia
Escola-Restaurante Espai Sucre, Calle Princes 53, Barcelona, Catalonia
Estrella de Plata, Plaza de Palau 9, Barcelona, Catalonia
Fonda Siqués, Besalú, Girona, Catalonia
Pasteleria Gorrochategui, Calle Arbol de Gernika, Tolosa, Basque Country
Real Balneario, Salinas Asturias
Restaurante Antigua Bodega de Don Cosme Palacio, Laguardia, Basque Country
Restaurante Arzak, Alto de Miraceuz 21, San Sebastián, Basque Country
Restaurante Asensio, Rua Do Tollo, 2, Goian, Pontevedra Galicia
Restaurante Biblioteca, Junta de Comerç, Barcelona, Catalonia
Restaurante Casa Marcelo, Rúa Hortas 1, Santiago de Compostela, Galicia
Restaurante Fátima, Pasión 3, Valladolid, Castille and León
Restaurante Izago, Tomás de Zumárraga 2, Vitoria, Basque Country
Restaurante Las Duelas, Pza Monseñor Florentino Rodríguez, Haro, Rioja
Restaurante La Escalinata, Plaza de Prim, Villafranca del Bierzo, Castille and León
Restaurante Sant Pau, Sant Pol de Mar, Nr Barcelona, Catalonia
Restaurante Toñi Vicente, Rosalia de Castro, 24, Santiago de Compostela, Galicia
Restaurante Vivaldi., Platerías 4, León
Sidrería La Galana, Plaza Mayor 10, Gijón, Asturias

Specialist Suppliers

London

Brindisa (Monday–Friday)
32, Exmouth Market,
Clerkenwell
London, EC1R 4QE
020 7713 1666

Brindisa
(Thursday–Saturday)
Borough Market
London, SE1 9AH
020 7407 1036

Garcia and Sons
248 Portobello Road
London, W11 1LL
020 7221 6119

Jeroboams W11
(for cheeses)
96 Holland Park Avenue
London, W11 3RB
020 7727 9359

Bayley & Sage
60 High Street
Wimbledon
London, SW19 5EE
020 8946 0206

Outside London

Bristol
Chandos Deli
6 Princess Victoria St
Bristol, BS8 4BP
0117 974 3275
+ Great George St in Bath

Papadeli
84 Alma Road
Bristol, BS8 2DJ
0117 973 6569

Cheshire
deFine Food and Wine
Chester Road
Sandiway, Cheshire
01606 882 101

Devon
Effings
50 Fore Street
Totnes
Devon, TQ9 5RP
01803 863 435

East Sussex
Real Eating Company
86–87 Western Road
Hove
East Sussex, BN3 1JB
01273 221 440

Kent
Williams & Brown
28a Harbour Street
Whitstable
Kent, CT5 1AH
01227 274507

Leicestershire
Stones Deli, Leicester
2-6 St Martins Walk
St Martins Square
Leicester
LE1 5OG
0116 261 4433

Norfolk
Humble Pie
Market Place
Burnham Market
Norfolk, PE31 8HE
01328 738581

Shropshire
Appleyards
85 Wyle Cop
Shrewsbury
Shropshire, SY1 1UT
01743 240 180

Teeside
Chapters Deli
27 High Street
Stokesley
Teeside, TS9 5AD
01642 714692

Warwickshire
Aubrey Alen Shop
108 Warwick Street
Royal Leamington Spa
Warwicks
CV32 4QP
01926 315464

Worcestershire
Broadway Deli
6-7 Cotswold Court
The Green
Broadway
Worcs.
WR12 7AA
01386 853040

Yorkshire
Roberts & Speight
40 Norwood
Beverley
Yorkshire
HU17 9EW
01482 870717

Scotland
Terroir
22 Thistle Street
Aberdeen, AB10 1XD
01224 623 262

Valvona & Crolla
19 Elm Row
Edinburgh, EH7 4AA
0131 556 6066

Heart Buchanan
380 Byres Road
Glasgow, G12 8AR
0141 334 7626

Wales
Ultracomida
3 Bridge Street
Aberystwyth, SY23 1PY
01970 625 400

Specialist Spanish Wine suppliers

Laymont & Shaw Ltd
The Old Chapel
Millpool
Truro
Cornwall, TR1 1EX.
01872 270 545
Do mail order and have a
great web site.
www.laymont-shaw.co.uk

Index

GALICIA

ASTURIAS

LEON

GALICIA

ENTRE DOURO E MINHO

TRAS OS MONTES

BEIRA

ESTREMADURA

S.Marta
Ferrol
Villaronte
Mondonedo
Betanzos
Villaba
Arou
Villano
Cormen
Berza
Velote
Lugo
Lara
Arzia
Santiago de Compostella
Lagonde
Padron
Sabrado
Vega
Peñalba
Robledo
Llamas
Castropol
Solas
Santa
Oviedo
Luron
Arroyo
Campo
Colcao
Mures
Aviles
Coya
Peon
Puron
Oruis
Belena
Cabezon
Nansa
S.Roque
Poles
S.Pedro
Espnosa
Alba
Valderneda
Fresno
Almanza
Leon
Montejos
Cea
Toral
Valhprodrigo
Medina
Herrera
Fnas
Amcu
Burgo
Valbases
Barg
Palmyra
Villafranca
R.Mino
Pontevedra
Arcade
Vigo
Orense
Firado
Péjevros
Terroso
Astorga
Bana
Baneza
Farton
Codesal
Poyo
Ravens
R.Tera
Penevente
Mopel
R.Esla
Zamora
Almonacid
Villanon
Aquilar
Medina
Toro
R.Duero
Cisneros
Carrion
Pina
Palencia
Valladolid
Lavarubus
Valtanos
Sotillo
R.Duero
Braga
Guimaraens
Amarante
Lamego
Salamanca
Medina del Campo
Nava
Leon
Carbonero
Segovia
Oporto
Carvabal
Horta
Lamar
Miralta
San Felices
Casdela
Carrascal
Villaria
Aldeasca
Alaxas
Pedraza
Baracas
Bemposta
Visen
Transcaro
Pinhel
Almeida
Fuentes de Onoro
Val verde
Miranda
Yacinos
Beulla
Villanueva
Espnar
Bota
Mello
Vinha
Guarda
Mariage
Avila
Coimbra
Portugal
Begis
Ceberas
Escorial
Miranda
Laurinal
Fuente
Cabeza
Gata
Abadiar
Valmajode
Illescas
MADRID
Arganda
Obtiqusa
Pedrogao
Camporia
Plasencia
Talavera
Mosquedh
Toledo
Leyria
Formosa
Alcaide
Coria
Oropesa
Thamar
Arade
Portage
Carraveral
Jaraice
Nuez
Orgas
Agalla
Ericeira
Ortiqua
Cuxbal
Campo May
Alcandra
Carbajo
Brozos
Caceres
Prasilon
Molbuller
Herrera
Villarubia
Fresmo
Nova
Villar
S.Vincente
Alicuda
Merida
Fuentabrada
Evora
Setubal
Zafra
Ilera
Xerex